GRADED ACCOUNTING QUESTIONS

for Leaving Certificate

RAY O'LOUGHLIN

GILL EDUCATION

Gill Education
Hume Avenue
Park West
Dublin 12
www.gilleducation.ie

Gill Education is an imprint of M.H. Gill & Co.

ISBN: 978 07171 4870 7

Print origination by MPS Limited

The paper used in this book comes from the wood pulp of sustainably managed forests.

10 9 8 7

Topics

Foreword

Over thirty years of teaching Leaving Certificate Accounting has left me in no doubt that students need to practise accounting questions regularly to maximise their potential. This book consists of a series of questions based on the Honours Leaving Certificate Accounting course.

Each section has a Leaving Certificate sample question with a solution as a template to assist in answering the questions that follow. Questions are presented under relevant topics and have a progressive degree of difficulty. Some are even longer and more difficult than those currently in the Leaving Certificate paper.

This book is designed to provide a comprehensive collection of questions under relevant topics loosely based on actual Leaving Certificate questions. The emphasis throughout is upon continual practise of Leaving Certificate-style questions together with a number of different and challenging variations which should provide you, the student, with excellent study material.

In addition to the actual Leaving Certificate questions this book should also provide you with a comprehensive collection of exam-style questions which will be invaluable in your preparation for the exam itself.

Arnold Palmer, the famous golfer, always attributed his success to a simple mantra that also applies to the serious accounting student, as follows:

The more I practise, the luckier I get.

Ray O'Loughlin

TOPIC

1

Final a/c's of Sole Trader

Most people get ahead during the time that others waste.

Henry Ford

1 DOLAN – SAMPLE EXAM QUESTION

The following Trial Balance was extracted from the books of **Orla Dolan** on 31/12/2007.

	€	€
Buildings (cost €580,000)	485,000	
8% Investments 1/4/2007	130,000	
Delivery vans (cost €85,000)	73,000	
6% Mortgage (incl. €50,000 increase on 1/4/2007)		150,000
Patents	52,400	
Commission	4,200	
Debtors and creditors	40,000	113,000
Purchases and sales	512,400	729,000
Stock 1/1/2007	65,600	
VAT		4,100
PRSI		3,900
Insurance (incl. suspense)	6,150	
Drawings	36,200	
Capital		485,000
Salaries and general	85,000	
Provision for bad debts		1,200
Discount net	1,900	
Rent	9,000	
Mortgage interest paid for three months	1,250	
Bank		15,900
	1,502,100	1,502,100

The following information and instructions are to be taken into account:

(i) Stock at 31/12/2007 at cost was €75,000. No record had been made in the books for goods in transit on 31/12/2007. The invoice for these goods had been received showing a recommended selling price of €6,000 which is cost plus 25%.

(ii) The suspense figure arises as a result of a discount received of €200 entered only in the creditors account, and the posting of an incorrect figure for mortgage interest to the mortgage interest account. The correct interest was entered in the bank account.

(iii) Patents, incorporating 3-months' investment interest, are to be written-off over a 5-year period starting in 2007.

(iv) Provide for depreciation on vans at 15% on cost from the date of purchase to the date of sale. Note: On 31/3/2007 a delivery van which cost €30,000 on 30/9/2004 was traded in against a new van costing €36,000. An allowance of €10,000 was made on the old van. The cheque for the net purchase of the new van was incorrectly entered in the purchases account although entered correctly in the bank account. These were the only entries made in respect of this transaction.

(v) Goods with a retail selling price of €10,000 were returned to a supplier. The selling price was cost plus 25%. The supplier issued a credit note showing a restocking charge of 10% of cost price. No entry was made in respect of the restocking charge.

(vi) Provision is to be made for mortgage interest due. 20% of the mortgage interest for the year refers to the private section of the building.

(vii) A cheque for €600 had been received in respect of a €1,000 debt previously written-off as bad. The debtor has agreed to pay the remainder within one month. No entry was made to record this transaction.

(viii) Goods withdrawn by the owner for private use during the year with a retail value of €2,000, which is cost plus 25%, were omitted from the books.

(ix) Provide for depreciation on buildings at the rate of 2% of cost. It was decided to revalue the buildings at €800,000 on 31/12/2007.

You are required to prepare:

(a) Trading Profit and Loss account for the year ending 31/12/2007.

(b) Balance Sheet on 31/12/2007.

Dolan Solution

Trading Profit and Loss Account for year ending 31/12/2007

	€	€	€
Sales			729,000
Less cost of sales			
Stock		65,600	
Purchases		490,400	
Less closing stock		(79,800)	(476,200)
Gross Profit			252,800
Less expenses			
Administration			
Patents written off	11,000		
Salaries and general	85,000		
Discount	1,700		
Rent	9,000		
Insurance	6,100		
Depreciation of buildings	11,600	124,400	
Selling and distribution			
Commission	4,200		
Disposal	8,750		
Depreciation of delivery vans	13,425	26,375	(150,775)
			102,025
Add operating income			
Bad debt recovered			1,000
Operating profit			103,025
Add investment income			7,800
Less mortgage interest			(6,600)
Net profit			104,225

Balance Sheet as at 31/12/2007

	Cost €	Depc €	Value €
Intangible Fixed Assets			
Patents			44,000
Tangible Fixed Assets			
Buildings	800,000		800,000
Delivery vehicles	91,000	14,175	76,825
Financial assets	891,000	14,175	
8% investments			130,000
			1,050,825
Current Assets			
Stock	79,800		
Debtors (40,400 less provision 1,200)	39,200		
Investment interest due	5,200	124,200	
Creditors : Amounts falling due within one year			
Creditors	118,600		
Bank	15,300		
VAT	4,100		
PRSI	3,900		
Mortgage interest due	6,750	148,650	(24,450)
Total Net Assets			1,026,375
Financed By :			
Creditors : Amounts falling due for more than one year			
6% Mortgage			150,000
Capital and Reserves			
Capital		485,000	
Add net profit		104,225	
Less drawings		(39,450)	549,775
Revaluation reserve			326,600
Total capital employed			1,026,375

Notes to Accounts

Purchases	512,400 +	4,800 –	26,000	800 –	1,600	=	**490,400**
Closing stock	75,000 +	4,800				=	**79,800**
Patents	52,400 +	2,600 –	**11,000**			=	**44,000**
Discount	1,900 –	200				=	**1,700**
Delivery vans	85,000 +	36,000 –	30,000			=	**91,000**
Insurance	6,150 –	250 +	200			=	**6,100**
Vehicle depreciation this year	1,125 +	4,050 +	8,250			=	**13,425**
Accumulated depreciation	12,000 +	13,425 –	11,250			=	**14,175**
Disposal (loss)	30,000 –	11,250 –	10,000			=	**8,750**
Investment income	2,600 +	5,200				=	**7,800**
Mortgage interest	1,250 +	250 +	**6,750** –	1,650		=	**6,600**
Buildings	580,000 +	220,000				=	**800,000**
Accumulated Depc on buildings	95,000 +	**11,600** –	106,600			=	**nil**
Revaluation reserve	220,000 +	106,600				=	**326,600**
Debtors	40,000 +	400				=	**40,400**
Creditors	113,000 +	4,800 +	800			=	**118,600**
Bank	15,900 –	600				=	**15,300**
Drawings	36,200 +	1,650 +	1,600			=	**39,450**

2 ARNOLD

The following accounts were extracted from the books of **A. Arnold** on 31/12/2012.

	€	€
8% Investments 1/5/2012	270,000	
Delivery vans (cost €225,000)	127,500	
Patents (incorporating 4-months' investment interest)	97,800	
Buildings (cost €975,000)	915,000	
Debtors and creditors	131,550	98,250
Purchases and sales	840,750	1,344,000
Stock 1/1/2012	85,200	
VAT		16,500
PRSI		6,750
Insurance (incl. suspense)	15,900	
Drawings	82,200	
Capital		704,400
Advertising	6,900	
Salaries and general	243,600	
Provision for bad debts		5,250
Discount net		9,900
Rent		13,500
6% Mortgage (incl. increase of €180,000 on 1/4/2012)		600,000
Mortgage interest paid for 3 months	6,750	
Bank		24,600
	2,823,150	2,823,150

The following information and instructions are to be taken into account:

(i) Stock at 31/12/2012 at cost was €101,250. This figure includes damaged stock costing €12,900 now worth €6,150.

(ii) The suspense figure arises as a result of discount allowed. €1,200 is entered only in the discount account, and the posting of an incorrect figure for mortgage interest to the mortgage interest account. The correct interest was entered in the bank account.

(iii) Patents, incorporating 4-months' investment interest are to be written-off over a 5-year period starting in 2012.

(iv) Provide for depreciation on vans at 20% on cost from the date of purchase to the date of sale. Note: On 30/4/2012 a delivery van which cost €90,000 on 30/6/2008 was traded in against a new van costing €90,000. An allowance of €30,000 was made on the old van. The cheque for the net purchase of the new van was incorrectly entered in the purchases account although entered correctly in the bank account. These were the only entries made in respect of this transaction.

(v) Provision is to be made for mortgage interest due.

(vi) The provision for bad debts is to be adjusted to 5% of debtors.

(vii) A new warehouse was purchased during the year for €180,000 plus VAT at 12.5%. The amount paid to the vendor was entered in the buildings account. No entry was made in the VAT account.

(viii) Provide for depreciation on buildings at the rate of 2% of cost. It was decided to revalue the buildings at €1,425,000 on 31/12/2012.

You are required to prepare:

(a) Trading Profit and Loss account for the year ending 31/12/2012.

(b) Balance Sheet on 31/12/2012.

3 BRENNAN

The following Trial Balance was extracted from the books of **B. Brennan** on 31/12/2012.

	€	€
8% Investments 1/4/2012	120,000	
Delivery vans at cost	112,000	
Accumulated depreciation on vehicles 1/1/2012		48,000
Patents (incorporating 4-months' investment interest)	56,800	
Buildings at cost	420,000	
Accumulated depreciation on buildings 1/1/2012		40,000
Debtors and creditors	32,200	35,400
Purchases and sales	525,000	721,000
Stock 1/1/2012	26,900	
VAT		3,200
PRSI		2,500
Insurance (incl. suspense)	11,400	
Drawings	22,100	
Capital		370,000
Advertising	12,800	
Salaries and general	54,200	
Provision for bad debts		1,400
Discount net		5,200
Commission		12,000
6% Mortgage (incl. increase of €30,000 on 1/6/2012)		120,000
Mortgage interest paid for 4 months	2,200	
Bank		36,900
	1,395,600	1,395,600

The following information and instructions are to be taken into account:

(i) Stock at 31/12/2012 at cost was €29,800. This figure includes damaged stock costing €3,700 now worth €1,400.

(ii) The suspense figure arises as a result of discount received of €200 entered only in the creditors account, and the posting of an incorrect figure for mortgage interest to the mortgage interest account. The correct interest was entered in the bank account.

(iii) Patents, incorporating 4-months' investment interest are to be written-off over a 5-year period starting in 2012.

(iv) Provide for depreciation on vans at 20% on cost from the date of purchase to the date of sale. Note: On 31/5/2012 a delivery van which cost €33,000 on 1/1/2006 was traded in against a new van costing €39,000. An allowance of €2,400 was made on the old van. The cheque for the net purchase of the new van was incorrectly entered in the purchases account although entered correctly in the bank account. These were the only entries made in respect of this transaction.

(v) Provision is to be made for mortgage interest due.

(vi) The provision for bad debts is to be adjusted to 4% of debtors.

(vii) A new warehouse was purchased during the year for €120,000 plus VAT at 12.5%. The amount paid to the vendor was entered in the buildings account. No entry was made in the VAT account.

(viii) Provide for depreciation on buildings at the rate of 2% of cost. It was decided to revalue the buildings at €510,000 on 31/12/2012.

You are required to prepare:

(a) Trading Profit and Loss account for the year ending 31/12/2012.

(b) Balance Sheet on 31/12/2012.

(c) Why do **sole traders** prepare **final** accounts?

4 CULLEN

The following Trial Balance was extracted from the books of **C. Cullen** on 31/12/2012.

	€	€
4.5% Investments 1/5/2012	200,000	
Delivery vans at cost	180,000	
Accumulated depreciation on vans 1/1		60,000
Patents (incorporating 4-months' investment interest)	77,000	
Buildings at cost	590,000	
Accumulated depreciation on buildings 1/1		70,000
Debtors and creditors	50,400	86,400
Purchases and sales	649,680	988,000
Stock 1/1/2012	56,400	
VAT		12,400
PRSI		6,400
Insurance (incl. suspense)	18,820	
Drawings	30,100	
Capital		380,000
Commission		4,800
Salaries and general	82,600	
Provision for bad debts		2,000
Discount net		3,200
Rent		8,400
6% Mortgage (incl. increase of €80,000 4% mortgage on 1/4/2012)		280,000
Mortgage interest paid for 3 months	3,500	
Bank		36,900
	1,938,500	1,938,500

The following information and instructions are to be taken into account:

(i) Stock at 31/12/2012 at cost was €67,400. This figure includes damaged stock costing €8,200 now worth €3,900.

(ii) The suspense figure arises as a result of an incorrect figure for mortgage interest in the mortgage interest account and discount allowed of €400 entered only in the discount account. The correct interest was entered in the bank account.

(iii) Patents, incorporating 4-months' investment interest, are to be written-off over a 5-year period starting in 2010.

(iv) A new warehouse was purchased on 1/7/2012 for €80,000 plus VAT at 12.5%. The amount paid to the vendor was entered in the buildings account, no entry made in the VAT a/c.

(v) Provide for depreciation on vans at 15% on cost from the date of purchase to the date of sale. Note: On 31/5/2012 a delivery van which cost €36,000 on 31/3/2008 was traded in against a new van costing €60,000. An allowance of €12,000 was made on the old van. The cheque for the net purchase of the new van was incorrectly entered in the purchases account although entered correctly in the bank account. These were the only entries made in respect of this transaction.

(vi) Provide for depreciation on buildings at 2% of cost per annum. It was decided to revalue buildings at €760,000 on 31/12/2012.

(vii) Provision is to be made for mortgage interest due. 10% of the mortgage interest for the year refers to the private section of the building.

(viii) A cheque for €400 had been received on 31/12 in respect of a debt of €900 previously written-off as bad. The debtor has guaranteed to pay the remainder within one month. No entry was made in the books to record this transaction. The provision for bad debts to be adjusted to 5% of debtors.

You are required to prepare:

(a) Trading Profit and Loss account for the year ending 31/12/2012.

(b) Balance Sheet on 31/12/2012.

(c) Explain what is meant by **'patents'** and why it is customary to write them off over a number of years.

5 DARCY

The following Trial Balance was extracted from the books of **Des Darcy** on 31/12/2012.

	€	€
Buildings (cost €656,250)	485,000	
12% Investments 1/6/2012	150,000	
Delivery vans (cost €90,000)	55,000	
9% Mortgage (incl. €40,000 increase on 1/4/2012)		200,000
Patents (incl. 4-months' investment interest)	50,500	
Debtors and creditors	45,400	64,400
Purchases and sales	495,000	774,000
Advertising	20,000	
Salaries and general	96,100	
Provision for bad debts		2,200
Discount net		2,700
Stock 1/1/2012	47,600	
VAT		6,700
PRSI		1,800
Insurance (incl. suspense)	7,200	
Rent		8,800
Mortgage interest paid for 3 months	4,500	
Drawings	29,200	
Capital		350,000
Bank		74,900
	1,485,500	1,485,500

The following information and instructions are to be taken into account:

(i) Stock at 31/12/2012 at cost was €46,900, which includes damaged stock €3,900, now worth €2,400.

(ii) No record had been made in the books for goods in transit on 31/12/2012. The invoice for these goods had been received showing the recommended retail selling price of €12,500 which is cost plus 25%.

(iii) During the year a store worth €20,000, which housed goods for resale valued at cost price €15,000, was destroyed by fire. A new store was built by the firm's own workers. The cost of their labour €15,000 had been treated as a business expense and the materials costing €32,000 were taken from the firm's stocks. The insurance company has agreed to pay full compensation for the loss due to the fire. No record had been made in the books in respect of the old or new store.

(iv) The suspense figure arises as a result of an incorrect figure for mortgage interest in the mortgage interest account and discount received of €400 entered only in the creditors account. The correct interest was entered in the bank account.

(v) Patents, incorporating 4-months' investment interest are to be written-off over 5-years starting in 2012.

(vi) Provide for depreciation on vans at 15% on cost from the date of purchase to the date of sale. Note: On 31/3/2012 a delivery van which cost €16,000 on 31/5/2008 was traded in against a new van costing €20,000. An allowance of €7,000 was made on the old van. The cheque for the net purchase of the new van was incorrectly entered in the purchases account, although entered correctly in bank account. These were the only entries made in respect of this transaction.

(vii) Provision be made for mortgage interest due. 25% of mortgage interest for the year is for private use.

(viii) Goods withdrawn by the owner for the year for private use were not recorded and amounted to €5,000 selling price, which is cost plus 25%.

(ix) Provide for depreciation on buildings at 2% of cost. It was decided to revalue the buildings at €1.2m.

(x) Provision for bad debts adjusted to 4% of debtors.

You are required to prepare:

(a) Trading Profit and Loss account for the year ending 31/12/2012.

(b) Balance Sheet on 31/12/2012.

(c) What is a **suspense** account and why is it created?

6 EGAN

The following Trial Balance was extracted from the books of **Edward Egan** on 31/12/2012.

	€	€
6% Investments 1/6/2012	160,000	
Delivery Vans	130,000	
Accumulated depreciation on vehicles 1/1		69,500
Patents (incorporating 3-months' investment interest)	60,600	
Buildings	900,000	
Accumulated depreciation on buildings		45,000
Debtors and creditors	76,500	85,500
Purchases and sales	650,000	980,000
Stock 1/1/2012	65,700	
VAT		4,300
PRSI		2,500
Insurance	13,800	
Drawings	36,000	
Capital		735,000
Advertising	14,000	
Salaries and general (incl. suspense)	192,500	
Provision for bad debts		3,900
Discount net		3,600
Royalties received		12,000
5% Mortgage (incl. increase of €100,000 on 1/4/2012)		300,000
Mortgage interest paid for 3 months	3,000	
Bank		60,800
	2,302,100	2,302,100

The following information and instructions are to be taken into account:

(i) Stock at 31/12/2012 at cost was €72,500. No record had been made in the books for goods in transit on 31/12/2012. The invoice for these goods had been received showing a recommended selling price of €7,000 which is cost plus 25%.

(ii) The suspense figure arises as a result of discount received of €700 entered only in the creditors account, and an incorrect figure for mortgage interest to the mortgage interest account. The bank a/c is correct.

(iii) Patents, incorporating 3-months' investment interest are to be written-off over a 5-year period starting in 2012.

(iv) Provide for depreciation on vans at 15% on cost from the date of purchase to the date of sale. Note: On 30/4/2012 a delivery van which cost €35,000 on 31/10/09 was traded in against a new van costing €41,000. An allowance of €15,000 was made on the old van. The cheque for the net purchase of the new van was incorrectly entered in the purchases account although entered correctly in the bank account. These were the only entries made in respect of this transaction.

(v) Goods with a retail selling price of €20,000 were returned to a supplier. The selling price was cost plus 25%. The supplier issued a credit note showing a restocking charge of 10% of cost price. No entry was made in respect of the restocking charge.

(vi) Provision be made for mortgage interest due. 20% of the mortgage interest for the year is for private use.

(vii) A cheque for €500 had been received in respect of a €1,200 debt previously written-off as bad. The debtor has agreed to pay the remainder within one month. No entry was made to record this transaction. Also the provision for bad debts is to be adjusted to 3% of doubtful debts.

(viii) Goods withdrawn by the owner for private use during the year with a retail value of €2,000, which is cost plus 25%, were omitted from the books.

(ix) A new warehouse was purchased during the year for €200,000 plus VAT at 12.5%. The amount paid to the vendor was entered in the buildings account. No entry was made in the VAT account.

(x) Depreciate buildings at 2% of cost. Buildings are to be revalued at €1.2m on 31/12/2012.

You are required to prepare:

(a) Trading Profit and Loss account for the year ending 31/12/2012.

(b) Balance Sheet on 31/12/2012.

(c) Calculate the period of credit to debtors and assess the result.

7 FARRELL

The following Trial Balance was extracted from the books of **Frank Farrell** on 31/12/2012.

	€	€
Buildings (cost €290,000)	242,500	
8% Investments 1/4/2012	65,000	
Delivery vans at cost	42,500	
Accumulated depreciation on vans 1/1/		6,000
6% Mortgage (incl. €25,000 increase on 1/4/2012)		75,000
Patents	26,200	
Advertising	2,100	
Debtors and creditors	20,000	56,500
Purchases and sales	256,200	364,500
Stock 1/1/2012	32,800	
VAT		2,050
PRSI		1,950
Insurance (incl. suspense)	3,075	
Drawings	18,100	
Capital		242,500
General administration expenses	42,500	
Provision for bad debts		600
Discount net	950	
Directors' fees	4,500	
Mortgage interest paid for 3 months	625	
Bank		7,950
	757,050	757,050

The following information and instructions are to be taken into account:

(i) Stock at 31/12/2012 at cost was €37,500. No record had been made in the books for goods in transit on 31/12/2012. The invoice for these goods had been received showing a recommended selling price of €3,000 which is cost plus 25%.

(ii) The suspense figure arises as a result of discount received with €100 entered only in the creditors account, and the posting of an incorrect figure for mortgage interest to the mortgage interest account. The correct interest was entered in the bank account.

(iii) Patents, incorporating 3-months' investment interest are to be written-off over a 5-year period starting in 2012.

(iv) Provide for depreciation on vans at 15% on cost from the date of purchase to the date of sale. Note: On 30/3/2012 a delivery van which cost €15,000 on 30/9/09 was traded in against a new van costing €18,000. An allowance of €5,000 was made on the old van. The cheque for the net purchase of the new van was incorrectly entered in the purchases account although entered correctly in the bank account. These were the only entries made in respect of this transaction.

(v) Goods with a retail selling price of €5,000 were returned to a supplier. The selling price was cost plus 25%. The supplier issued a credit note showing a restocking charge of 10% of cost price. No entry was made in respect of the restocking charge.

(vi) Provision is to be made for mortgage interest due. 20% of the mortgage interest for the year refers to the private section of the building.

(vii) A cheque for €300 had been received in respect of a €500 debt previously written-off as bad. The debtor has agreed to pay the remainder within 3 months. No entry was made to record this transaction.

(viii) Goods withdrawn by the owner for private use during the year with a retail value of €2,000, which is cost plus 25%, were omitted from the books.

(ix) Provide for depreciation on buildings at the rate of 2% of cost. It was decided to revalue the buildings at €400,000 on 31/12/2012.

You are required to prepare:

(a) Trading Profit and Loss account for the year ending 31/12/2012.

(b) Balance Sheet on 31/12/2012.

8 GRENNAN

The following Trial Balance was extracted from the books of **Gerry Grennan** on 31/12/2012.

	€	€
Buildings (cost €696,000)	582,000	
8% Investments 1/4/2012	156,000	
Delivery vans at cost (€102,000)	87,600	
6% Mortgage (incl. €60,000 increase on 1/4/2012)		180,000
Patents	62,880	
Advertising	5,040	
Debtors and creditors	48,000	135,600
Purchases and sales	614,880	874,800
Stock at 1/1/2012	78,720	
VAT		9,600
Insurance (incl. suspense)	7,380	
Drawings	43,440	
Capital		582,000
General administration expenses	102,000	
Provision for bad debts		1,440
Discount net	2,280	
Rent	10,800	
Mortgage interest paid for 3 months	1,500	
Bank		19,080
	1,802,520	1,802,520

The following information and instructions are to be taken into account:

(i) Stock at 31/12/2012 at cost was €90,000. No record had been made in the books for goods in transit on 31/12/2012. The invoice for these goods had been received showing a recommended selling price of €7,200 which is cost plus 25%.

(ii) The suspense figure arises as a result of discount received of €240 entered only in the creditors account, and the posting of an incorrect figure for mortgage interest to the mortgage interest account. The correct interest was entered in the bank account.

(iii) Patents, incorporating 3-months' investment interest are to be written-off over a 5-year period starting in 2012.

(iv) Goods stolen during the year amounted to €5,000 retail price which is cost plus 25% and they were insured. The compensation claim will not be paid until January 2013 less a 10% excess of the insured value.

(v) Provide for depreciation on vans at 15% on cost from the date of purchase to the date of sale. Note: On 1/4/2012 a delivery van which cost €36,000 on 1/10/09 was traded in against a new van costing €43,200. An allowance of €12,000 was made on the old van. The cheque for the net purchase of the new van was incorrectly entered in the purchases account although entered correctly in the bank account. These were the only entries made in respect of this transaction.

(vi) Goods with a retail selling price of €12,000 were returned to a supplier. The selling price was cost plus 25%. The supplier issued a credit note showing a restocking charge of 10% of cost price. No entry is made in respect of the restocking charge.

(vii) The advertising payment is toward a 24-month campaign which began on 1/10/2012.

(viii) Provision is to be made for mortgage interest due. 20% of the mortgage interest for the year refers to the private section of the building.

(ix) A cheque for €720 had been received in respect of a €1,200 debt previously written-off as bad. The debtor has agreed to pay the remainder within two months. No entry was made to record this transaction.

(x) Goods withdrawn by the owner for private use during the year with a retail value of €2,400, which is cost plus 25%, were omitted from the books.

(xi) Provide for depreciation on buildings at the rate of 2% of cost. It was decided to revalue the buildings at €960,000 on 31/12/2012.

You are required to prepare:

(a) Trading Profit and Loss account for the year ending 31/12/2012.

(b) Balance Sheet on 31/12/2012.

TOPIC

2

Final a/c's of Company

My grandfather once told me that there were two kinds of people: those who do the work and those who take the credit. He told me to try to be in the first group; there was much less competition.

Indira Gandhi

1 Carey – Sample Exam Question

Carey Ltd has an authorised share capital of 690,000 Ordinary shares of €1 each and 300,000 Preference shares of €1 each. The following Trial Balance was extracted on 31/12/2003.

	€	€
Land and buildings at cost	780,000	
Accumulated depreciation on buildings		39,000
6% Investments 1/5/2003	180,000	
Delivery vans at cost	172,000	
Accumulated depreciation		78,000
Patents (incl. 2-months' investment income)	58,200	
Debtors and creditors	73,900	81,000
Purchases and sales	620,000	990,000
Stock 1/1/2003	76,600	
VAT		16,500
Bank		5,500
Directors' fees	80,000	
Interim dividend for first 6 months	40,000	
Salaries and general expenses	176,000	
Provision for bad debts		3,600
Profit and Loss balance on 1/1/2003		67,600
Issued capital		
550,000 ordinary shares @ €1 each		550,000
200,000 7% preference shares		200,000
9% debentures (incl. €80,000 increase on 31/3/2003)		230,000
Debenture interest paid	4,500	
	2,261,200	2,261,200

The following information and instructions are to be taken into account:

(i) Stock at 31/12/2003 at cost was €85,000. This figure includes damaged stock costing €8,000 and now worth 60% of cost.

(ii) Patents, incorporating 2-months' investment interest are to be written-off over a 5-year period starting in 2003.

(iii) Provide for depreciation on vans at 20% on cost from the date of purchase to the date of sale. Note: On 31/9/2003 a delivery van which cost €60,000 on 1/6/2001 was traded in against a new van costing €84,000. An allowance of €22,000 was given on the old van. The cheque for the net purchase of the new van was incorrectly entered in the purchases account although entered correctly in the bank account. These were the only entries made in respect of this transaction.

(iv) The figure for the bank in the Trial Balance has been taken from the firm's bank account. However, a bank statement on 31/12/2003 has arrived showing a credit balance of €4,040. A comparison of the bank account and bank statement has revealed the following discrepancies:
1. Investment income of €2,700 had been paid direct to the firm's bank account.
2. A credit transfer of €750 had been paid direct to the firm's bank account on behalf of a bankrupt debtor. This represents a first and final payment of 30c in the €.
3. A cheque issued for €6,000 to a creditor had not been presented for payment.
4. A cheque for €780 issued to a supplier had been entered as €870 in the books.

(v) Provide for depreciation on buildings at the rate of 2% of cost.(Land at cost was €130,000.) At the end of 2003 it was decided to revalue the buildings at €880,000.

(vi) The directors recommend that:
1. Preference dividend due be paid.
2. A final ordinary dividend be provided bringing the total dividend to 9c per share.
3. Provision be made for both Investment income and Debenture interest due.
4. Provision for bad debts be adjusted to 4%.

You are required to prepare:

(a) Trading Profit and Loss account for the year ending 31/12/2003.

(b) Balance Sheet on 31/12/2003.

Sample Solution Carey 2004

Trading Profit and Loss Account for year ending 31/12/2003

	€	€	€
Sales			990,000
Less cost of sales			
Stock		76,600	
Purchases		558,000	
Less closing stock		(81,800)	552,800
Gross profit			437,200
Less expenses			
Administration			
Patents written off	12,000		
Salaries and general	176,000		
Directors' fees	80,000		
Depreciation of buildings	13,000	281,000	
Selling and distribution			
Bad debts	1,750		
Depreciation of delivery Vans	35,600		
Loss on disposal of van	10,000	47,350	(328,350)
			108,850
Add operating income			
Over-provision for bad debts			744
Operating profit			109,594
Add investment income			7,200
Less debenture interest			(18,900)
Net profit			97,894
Less appropriation			
Preference dividends		14,000	
Ordinary dividends		49,500	(63,500)
Retained profit			34,394
Profit and Loss balance 1/1/2003			67,600
Profit and Loss balance 31/12/2003			101,994

Balance Sheet as at 31/12/2003

	Cost	Depc	Value
Intangible Fixed Assets	€	€	€
Patents			48,000
Tangible Fixed			
Buildings	880,000		880,000
Delivery vehicles	196,000	85,600	110,400
Financial Assets			
8% investments			180,000
			1,218,400

Current Assets			
Stock	81,800		
Debtors (71,400 less Provision 2,856)	68,544		
Investment interest due	2,700	153,044	
Creditors: Amounts falling due within one year			
Creditors	81,090		
Bank	1,960		
VAT	16,500		
Ordinary dividend due	16,500		
Preference dividend due	7,000		
Debenture interest due	14,400	(137,450)	15,594
Total net assets			1,233,994
Financed by:			
Creditors : Amounts falling due for more than one year			
8% debenture			230,000
Capital and Reserves	Authorised	Issued	
Ordinary share capital at €1 each	690,000	550,000	
6% preference share capital	300,000	200,000	
	990,000	750,000	
Profit and Loss balance 31/12/2003		101,994	
Revaluation reserve		152,000	
			1,003,994
Total capital employed			1,233,994

Notes to Accounts

Purchases	620,000 –	62,000			=	**558,000**
Closing stock	85,000 –	3,200			=	**81,800**
Patents	58,200 +	1,800 –	**12,000**		=	**48,000**
Provision for bad debts	3,600 –	2,856			=	**744**
Delivery vans	172,000 +	84,000 –	60,000		=	**196,000**
Depreciation of vans this year	4,200 +	9,000 +	22,400		=	**35,600**
Accumulated depreciation of vans	78,000 +	35,600 –	28,000		=	**85,600**
Disposal of vehicles (loss)	60,000 –	22,000 –	28,000		=	**10,000**
Investment income	1,800 +	2,700 +	2,700		=	**7,200**
Debenture interest	4,500 +	14,400			=	**18,900**
Buildings	780,000 +	100,000			=	**880,000**
Accumulated depreciation on buildings	39,000 +	**13,000** –	52,000		=	**Nil**
Revaluation reserve	100,000 +	52,000			=	**152,000**
Debtors	73,900 –	750 –	1,750		=	**71,400**
Creditors	81,000 +	90			=	**81,090**
Bank o/d	5,500 –	2,700 –	750 –	90	=	**1,960**
Preference dividend	7,000 +	**7,000**				**14,000**
Ordinary dividend	33,000 +	**16,500**				**49,500**
Debenture interest	4,500 +	14,400			=	**18,900**

2 ABACUS

Abacus Plc has an authorised share capital of 500,000 Ordinary shares of €1 each and 280,000 6% Preference shares of €1 each. The following balances were extracted from the books on 31/12/2012.

	€	€
Land and buildings (cost €520,000)	475,000	
Motor vehicles	135,000	
Accumulated depreciation 1/1/2012		28,500
9% Investments 1/5/2012	120,000	
Patents (incl. 3-months' investment interest)	38,300	
Stock 1/1/2012	42,500	
VAT		18,200
Bank		16,200
Administration expenses	28,200	
Selling expenses	14,100	
Debtors and creditors	38,000	41,800
Purchases and sales	624,300	824,000
Dividend paid	20,900	
Salaries and general	95,000	
Provision for bad debts		3,200
Profit and Loss balance on 1/1/2012		1,800
Issued capital – 370,000 Ordinary shares @ €1 each		370,000
– 180,000 8% Preference shares		180,000
8% debentures (incl. €60,000 increase on 1/6/2012)		150,000
Debenture interest paid for 4 months	2,400	
	1,633,700	1,633,700

The following information and instructions are to be taken into account:

(i) Stock at 31/12/2012 at cost was €36,400. This figure includes damaged stock costing €3,100 and now worth €1,400.

(ii) Patents, incorporating 3-months' investment interest are to be written-off over a 4-year period starting in 2012.

(iii) Provide for depreciation on vans at 20% on cost from the date of purchase to the date of sale. Note: On 30/4/2012 a delivery van which cost €24,000 on 30/9/2009 was traded in against a new van costing €33,000. An allowance of €9,500 was made on the old van. The cheque for the net purchase of the new van was incorrectly entered in the purchases account although it was entered correctly in the bank account. These were the only entries made in respect of this transaction.

(iv) The figure for the bank in the Trial Balance has been taken from the firm's bank account. However, a bank statement on 31/12/2012 has arrived showing an overdraft figure of €5,930. A comparison of the bank account and bank statement has revealed the following discrepancies:

1. Investment income of €2,500 had been paid direct to the firms bank account.
2. A direct debit of €480 for electricity had not been recorded in the books.
3. A cheque issued for €4,200 to a creditor had not been presented for payment.
4. A cheque for €720 issued to a supplier had been entered as €270 in the books.

(v) Provision is to be made for both investment income and debenture interest due.

(vi) Provision for bad debts to be adjusted to 5% of debtors.

(vii) Provide for depreciation on buildings at the rate of 2% of cost. It was decided to revalue the buildings at €800,000 at the end of 2012.

(viii) The directors are proposing that €10,000 be transferred from profit to a General Reserve account.

You are required to prepare:

(a) Trading Profit and Loss account for the year ending 31/12/2012.

(b) Balance Sheet on 31/12/2012.

3 BLIARY

Bliary Ltd has an authorised share capital of 550,00 ordinary shares of €1 each and 240,000 7% Preference shares of €2 each. The following balance was extracted from the books on 31/12/2012.

	€	€
Land and buildings at cost	420,000	
Motor vehicles (cost €162,000)	96,000	
9% Investments 1/1/2012	150,000	
Goodwill (incl. 4-months' investment income)	12,500	
Insurance	15,000	
Debtors and creditors	31,000	41,000
Advertising (incl. suspense)	6,800	
Purchases and sales	587,000	896,000
Stock 1/1/2012	38,000	
Discount (net)		3,000
Bank		16,800
Directors' fees	20,000	
Dividends paid	32,000	
Salaries and general expenses	130,000	
Provision for bad debts		1,600
Profit and Loss balance on 1/1/2012		22,700
Issued capital – 280,000 Ordinary shares @ €1 each		280,000
– 100,000 8% Preference shares		100,000
8% debentures (incl. €60,000 increase on 31/3/2012)		180,000
Debenture interest paid for 3 months	2,800	
	1,541,100	1,541,100

The following information and instructions are to be taken into account:

(i) Stock at 31/12/2012 at cost was €40,000. This figure includes damaged stock costing €4,500 now worth 40% of cost.

(ii) Goodwill, incorporating 4-months' investment interest are to be written-off over a 2-year period starting in 2012.

(iii) The suspense figure arises as a result of the incorrect figure for debenture interest (correct figure entered in bank account) and discount allowed of €200 entered only in the discount account.

(iv) Provide for depreciation on vans at 20% on cost from the date of purchase to the date of sale. Note: On 31/5/2012 a delivery van which cost €20,000 on 1/3/2010 was traded in against a new van costing €32,000. An allowance of €14,000 was made on the old van. The cheque for the net purchase of the new van was incorrectly entered in the purchases account although entered correctly in the bank account. These were the only entries made in respect of this transaction.

(v) The figure for the bank in the Trial Balance has been taken from the firm's bank account. However, a bank statement on 31/12/2012 has arrived showing an overdraft of €8,740. A comparison of the bank account and bank statement has revealed the following discrepancies:
1. Investment income of €6,750 had been paid direct to the firm's bank account.
2. A cheque for €100 had been lodged directly to the firm's bank account on behalf of a bankrupt debtor. This represents a first and final payment of 20c in the euro.
3. A cheque issued for €1,300 for rent had not been presented for payment.
4. A cheque for €540 issued to a supplier had been entered as €450 in the books.

(vi) The directors recommend that:
1. Provision be made for both income and debenture interest due.
2. Provision for bad debts be adjusted to 6% of debtors.

You are required to prepare:

(a) Trading Profit and Loss account for the year ending 31/12/2012.

(b) Balance Sheet on 31/12/2012.

(c) Are there any occasions when the Trial Balance is in balance, even though errors have occurred?

4 CAPRI

Capri Plc has an authorised share capital of 450,000 Ordinary shares of €1 each and 250,000 6% Preference shares of €1 each. The following Trial Balance was extracted on 31/12/2012.

	€	€
Land and buildings at cost	500,000	
Accumulated depreciation on buildings		30,000
Motor vehicles at cost	160,000	
Accumulated depreciation on vehicles		70,000
6% investments 1/5/2012	200,000	
Patents (incl. 4-months' investment income)	44,000	
Debtors and creditors	36,000	43,000
Purchases and sales	590,000	880,000
Stock 1/1/2012	40,000	
VAT		11,000
Bank		26,800
Directors' fees	30,000	
Dividends paid	20,000	
Salaries and general expenses	114,000	
Provision for bad debts		2,200
Profit and Loss balance on 1/1/2012		24,000
Issued capital – 300,000 Ordinary shares @ €1 each		300,000
– 150,000 8% Preference shares		150,000
8% debentures (incl. €50,000 increase on 31/3/2012)		200,000
Debenture interest paid for 3 months	3,000	
	1,737,000	1,737,000

The following information and instructions are to be taken into account:

(i) Stock at 31/12/2012 at cost was €48,000, which includes damaged stock €8,000 now worth 60% of cost.

(ii) Patents, incorporating 4-months' investment interest are to be written-off over 4-years starting in 2012.

(iii) Provide for depreciation on vans at 20% on cost from the date of purchase to the date of sale. Note: On 31/5/2012 a delivery van which cost €42,000 on 1/6/2010 was traded in against a new van costing €48,000. An allowance of €18,000 was made on the old van. The cheque for the net purchase of the new van was incorrectly entered in the purchases account although entered correctly in the bank account. These were the only entries made in respect of this transaction.

(iv) The figure for the bank in the Trial Balance has been taken from the firm's bank account. However, a bank statement on 31/12/2012 has arrived showing an overdraft of €24,430. A comparison of the bank account and the bank statement has revealed the following discrepancies:
1. Investment income of €2,000 had been paid direct to the firm's bank account.
2. A direct debit of €600 for electricity had not been recorded in the books.
3. A cheque issued for €1,090 to a creditor had not been presented for payment.
4. A cheque for €850 issued to a supplier had been entered as €580 in the books.
5. A credit transfer of €150 had been paid direct to the firm's bank account on behalf of a bankrupt debtor. This represents a first and final payment of 10c in the €.

(v) Provision is to be made for both investment income and debenture interest due.

(vi) Provision for bad debts to be adjusted to 6% of debtors.

(vii) Provide for depreciation on buildings at the rate of 2% of cost. At the end of the year it was decided to revalue the buildings to €750,000. Of this revalued figure €100,000 represented land.

(viii) The directors are proposing that a Debenture Redemption Reserve be established and provision be set aside to accumulate sufficient funds annually to repay the full sum within 5 years.

You are required to prepare:

(a) Trading Profit and Loss account for the year ending 31/12/2012.

(b) Balance Sheet on 31/12/2012.

(c) Explain what is meant by the **accruals concept** in accounting.

5 DUNCAN

Duncan Ltd has an authorised share capital of 580,000 ordinary shares of €1 each and 250,000 Preference shares of €1 each. The following Trial Balance was extracted on 31/12/2010.

	€	€
Land and buildings (cost €480,000)	444,000	
Motor vehicles	150,000	
Accumulated depreciation on vehicles 1/1		54,000
6% Investments 1/4/2012	200,000	
Patents (incl. 3-months' investment income)	63,000	
Debtors and creditors	46,000	38,100
Purchases and sales	545,000	814,000
Stock 1/1/2012	32,200	
VAT	25,100	
Bank		6,800
Directors' fees	34,400	
Interim dividend for first 6 months	22,400	
Salaries and general expenses	148,200	
Provision for bad debts		1,600
Profit and Loss balance on 1/1/2012	1,800	
Issued Capital – 420,000 Ordinary Shares @ €1 each		420,000
– 220,000 8% Preference Shares		220,000
8% Debentures (incl. €40,000 increase on 31/3/2012)		160,000
Debenture interest paid for 3 months	2,400	
	1,714,500	1,714,500

The following information and instructions are to be taken into account:

(i) Stock at 31/12/2012 at cost was €38,200 which includes damaged stock €8,200 now worth €5,640.

(ii) Patents, incorporating 3-months' investment interest are to be written-off over a 10-year period.

(iii) During the year a store worth €20,000 with goods valued €15,000 was destroyed by fire. A new store was built using Duncan's own materials €42,000 and labour €18,000. No record was made in the books of old or new store. Insurance Co. has agreed to pay full compensation for loss due to fire.

(iv) Provide for depreciation on vans at 20% on cost from the date of purchase to the date of sale. Note: On 31/3/2012 a delivery van which cost €48,000 on 1/9/2010 was traded in against a new van costing €54,000. An allowance of €31,000 was given on the old van. The cheque for the net purchase of the new van was incorrectly entered in the purchases account although entered correctly in the bank account. These were the only entries made in respect of this transaction.

(v) The figure for the bank in the Trial Balance has been taken from the firm's bank account. However, a bank statement on 31/12/2012 has arrived showing an overdraft of €2,070. A comparison of the bank account and the bank statement has revealed the following discrepancies:
   1. Investment income of €2,000 had been paid direct to the firm's bank account.
   2. A credit transfer of €600 had been paid direct to the firm's bank account on behalf of a bankrupt debtor. This represents a first and final payment of 30c in the €.
   3. A cheque issued for €1,860 to a creditor had not been presented for payment.
   4. A cheque for €1,250 issued to a supplier had been entered as €1,520 in the books.

(vi) Provide for depreciation on buildings at the rate of 2% of cost. (Land at cost was €80,000.) At the end of 2012 it was decided to revalue the buildings at €660,000.

(vii) The directors recommend that:
   1. Preference dividend due be paid and a final ordinary dividend be provided bringing total to 7%.
   2. Provision is to be made for investment income and debenture interest due.
   3. Provision for bad debts to be adjusted to 5% of debtors.

You are required to prepare:

(a) Trading Profit and Loss account for the year ending 31/12/2012.

(b) Balance Sheet on 31/12/2012.

(c) What are the main objectives of **financial accounting**?

6 ECHO

Echo Ltd has an authorised share capital of 966,000 Ordinary shares of €1 each and 420,000 7% Preference shares of €2 each. The following figures were extracted from the books on 31/12/2012.

	€	€
Land and buildings at cost	1,092,000	
Accumulated depreciation on buildings		54,600
6% investments 1/5/2012	252,000	
Delivery vans at cost	240,800	
Accumulated depreciation		109,200
Patents (incl. 3-months' investment income)	81,480	
Debtors and creditors	103,460	113,400
Purchases and sales	868,000	1,386,000
Stock at 1/1/2012	107,240	
VAT		23,100
Bank		7,700
Directors' fees	112,000	
Dividends paid	56,000	
Salaries and general expenses	246,400	
Provision for bad debts		5,040
Profit and Loss balance on 1/1/2012		94,640
Issued capital – 770,000 Ordinary shares @ €1 each		770,000
– 140,000 7% Preference shares		280,000
9% Debentures (incl. €112,000 increase on 31/3/2012)		322,000
Debenture interest paid for 3 months	6,300	
	3,165,680	3,165,680

The following information and instructions are to be taken into account:

(i) Stock on 31/12/2012 at cost €119,000, which includes damaged stock €11,200 now worth 60% of cost.

(ii) Patents, incorporating 3-months' investment interest are to be written-off over 5-years starting in 2012.

(iii) Provide for depreciation on vans at 20% on cost from the date of purchase to the date of sale. Note: On 31/9/2012 a delivery van which cost €84,000 on 1/6/2010 was traded in against a new van costing €117,600. An allowance of €30,800 was given on the old van. The cheque for the net purchase of the new van was incorrectly entered in the purchases account although it was entered correctly in the bank account. These were the only entries made in respect of this transaction.

(iv) The figure for the bank in the Trial Balance has been taken from the firm's bank account. However, a bank statement on 31/12/2012 has arrived showing a credit balance of €5,256. A comparison of the bank account and the bank statement has revealed the following discrepancies:
1. Investment income of €3,780 had been paid direct to the firm's bank account.
2. A credit transfer of €1,050 had been paid direct to the firm's bank account on behalf of a bankrupt debtor. This represents a first and final payment of 30c in the €.
3. A cheque issued for €8,000 to a creditor had not been presented for payment.
4. A cheque for €1,092 issued to a supplier had been entered as €1,218 in the books.

(v) Provide for depreciation on buildings at the rate of 2% of cost. (Land at cost was €182,000.) At the end of 2012 it was decided to revalue the buildings at €1,232,000.

(vi) The directors recommend that:
1. Provision be made for both investment income and debenture interest due.
2. Provision for bad debts be adjusted to 4%.
3. €32,900 be allocated from profit to a **staff pension fund**.

You are required to prepare:

(a) Trading Profit and Loss account for the year ending 31/12/2012.

(b) Balance Sheet on 31/12/2012.

(c) Explain with an example the difference between **capital** and **current** expenditure.

7 FESTINA

Festina Ltd has an authorised share capital of €980,000 shares divided into 580,000 Ordinary @ €1 each and 400,000 7% Preference at €1 each. The following Trial Balance was extracted on 31/12/2012.

	€	€
Land and buildings (cost €700,000)	628,200	
Motor vehicles (cost €208,500)	141,700	
5% investments 1/6/2012	180,000	
Patents (incl. 3-months' investment income)	57,750	
Debtors and creditors	65,000	87,500
Purchases and sales	651,000	967,000
Stock 1/1/2012	47,500	
VAT	3,990	
Bank		8,100
Directors' fees	12,600	
Dividends paid	24,000	
Salaries and general expenses	187,800	
Provision for bad debts		1,100
Profit and Loss balance on 1/1/2012	45,000	
Issued capital – 480,000 Ordinary Shares @ €1 each		480,000
– 300,000 5% Preference shares at €1 each		300,000
7.5% Debentures (incl. €80,000 increase on 1/4/2012)		212,000
Debenture interest paid for 3 months	2,475	
Discount net		215
Audit fees	8,900	
	2,055,915	2,055,915

The following information and instructions are to be taken into account:

(i) Stock at 31/12/2012 at cost was €66,000, which includes damaged stock €8,000 now worth 60% of cost.

(ii) Patents, incorporating 3-months' investment interest are to be written-off over 5-years starting in 2012.

(iii) Goods with a retail selling price of €10,000 were returned to a supplier. The selling price was cost plus 25%. The supplier issued a credit note showing a restocking charge of 10% of cost price. No entry was made in respect of the restocking charge.

(iv) A bad debt of €700 written-off during 2011 is now recoverable in full. A further bad debt of €300 included in debtors is to be written-off and the provision for bad debts to be adjusted equal to 5% of doubtful debts.

(v) Provide for depreciation on vans at 20% on cost from the date of purchase to the date of sale. Note: On 31/5/2012 a delivery van which cost €22,500 on 1/9/2006 was traded in against a new van costing €36,000. An allowance of €5,625 was given on the old van. The only entry made regarding this transaction was the cheque for the new vehicle entered in Purchases.

(vi) The firm's banks a/c figure from the Trial Balance differed from the overdraft figure of €840 as per bank statement due to the following:
1. Investment income of €1,500 had been paid direct to the firm's bank account.
2. A credit transfer of €800 had been paid direct to the firm's bank account on behalf of a bankrupt debtor. This represents a first and final payment of 40c in the €.
3. A cheque was issued for €5,000 to a creditor that had not been presented for payment.
4. A cheque for €640 issued to a supplier had been entered as €600 in the books.

(vii) Provide for depreciation on buildings at the rate of 2% of cost. (Land at cost was €180,000.) At the end of 2012 it was decided to revalue the buildings at €970,000.

(viii) The directors recommend that provision be made for investment income and debenture interest due.

You are required to prepare:

(a) Trading Profit and Loss account for the year ending 31/12/2012.

(b) Balance Sheet on 31/12/2012.

(c) Would you, as a bank manager, recommend that a €100,000 loan at 10% annual interest be given to Festina for expansion? Support your answer with 3 relevant points.

8 CONOLO

Conolo Plc has an authorised share capital of 500,000 Ordinary shares of €1 each and 300,000 5% Preference shares of €1 each. The following Trial Balance was extracted on 31/12/2012.

	€	€
Land and buildings (cost €420,000)	388,000	
Motor vehicles (cost €220,000)	175,000	
5% investments 1/4/2012	180,000	
Patents (incl. 4-months' investment income)	47,000	
Debtors and creditors	60,000	62,500
Purchases and sales	634,000	933,000
Advertising	12,600	
Discount net		950
Stock 1/1/2012	83,600	
VAT	1,110	
Bank		18,700
Audit fees	2,890	
Dividends paid	12,600	
Salaries and general expenses	102,400	
Provision for bad debts		1,750
Profit and Loss balance on 1/1/2012	45,200	
Issued capital – 400,000 Ordinary shares @ €1 each		400,000
– 150,000 5% Preference shares		150,000
9% Debentures (incl. €60,000 increase on 1/4/2012)		180,000
Debenture interest paid for 3 months	2,500	
	1,746,900	1,746,900

The following information and instructions are to be taken into account:

(i) Stock at 31/12/2012 at cost was €63,600, which includes damaged stock €5,000 now worth €2,800.

(ii) Patents, incorporating 4-months' investment interest are to be written-off over 5 years starting in 2012.

(iii) No record has been made in the books for purchases of goods on credit in transit on 31/12/2012. The invoice for these goods had been received showing a retail price of €12,500 or cost plus 25%.

(iv) During the year a store costing €20,000 with goods valued €5,600 was destroyed by fire. A new store was built using Conolo's own materials €38,000 and own labour €22,000. No record was made in the books of the old or new store. The Insurance Co. agreed to pay compensation in full for any loss due to the fire.

(v) A bad debt of €700 written-off during 2011 is now recoverable in full. A further bad debt of €300 included in debtors is to be written-off and the provision for bad debts to be adjusted equal to 5% of doubtful debts.

(vi) Conolo's bank a/c figure taken from the Trial Balance differed from the bank's record as per the bank statement due to the following:

1. Investment income of €3,000 had been paid direct to the firm's bank account.
2. A direct debit of €850 for electricity had not been recorded in the books.
3. A cheque issued for €1,800 to a director had not been presented for payment.

(vii) Provide for depreciation on vans at 20% on cost from the date of purchase to the date of sale. Note: On 1/6/2012 a delivery van which cost €16,000 on 1/4/2007 was traded in against a new van costing €30,000. An allowance of €4,800 was made on the old van. There were **no entries** made regarding the old or new vehicles.

(viii) Provide for depreciation on buildings at the rate of 2% of cost. (Land at cost was €120,000.) At the end of the year it was decided to revalue Land and buildings to €600,000.

(ix) The directors are proposing that provision be made for Investment income and Debenture interest due.

You are required to prepare:

(a) Trading Profit and Loss account for the year ending 31/12/2012.

(b) Balance Sheet on 31/12/2012.

(c) Explain what is meant by the term **solvency** and how it can be measured.

9 PRUDENCE

Prudence Plc has an authorised capital of €1,300,000 divided into 900,000 Ordinary shares of €1 each and 400,000 6% Preference shares of €1 each. The following Trial Balance was extracted on 31/12/2012.

	€	€
Land and buildings (cost €650,000)	602,000	
Motor vehicles at cost	280,000	
Accumulated depreciation on vehicles		40,000
4% investments 1/4/2012	300,000	
Patents (incl. 4-months' investment interest)	36,000	
Advertising (incl. suspense)	32,000	
Debtors and creditors	48,600	51,200
Purchases and sales	644,100	895,950
Stock 1/1/2012	83,400	
VAT	1,300	
Bank		21,900
Directors' fees	6,800	
Discount net		450
Dividends paid	19,500	
Salaries and general	120,200	
Provision for bad debts		2,800
Profit and Loss balance on 1/1/2012		14,400
Issued capital – 700,000 Ordinary shares @ €1 each		700,000
– 250,000 6% Preference shares		250,000
8% Debentures (incl. €50,000 increase on 1/4/2012)		200,000
Debenture interest paid for 3 months	2,800	
	2,176,700	2,176,700

The following information and instructions are to be taken into account:

(i) Stock at 31/12/2012 at cost was €68,600. This figure includes damaged stock costing €8,000 and now worth €3,700. No record had been made in the books for goods in transit on 31/12/2012. The invoice for these goods had been received showing a recommended retail price of €25,000, i.e. cost plus 25%.

(ii) Patents, incorporating 4-months' investment interest, are to be written-off over a 5-year period starting in 2012.

(iii) Provide for depreciation on vans at 20% on cost from the date of purchase to the date of sale. Note: On 1/7/2012 a delivery van which cost €20,000 on 30/6/2009 was traded in against a new van costing €35,000. An allowance of €9,000 was made on the old van. The cheque paid for the new van was incorrectly entered in Purchases. This was the only entry in the books.

(iv) The suspense figure includes discount received of €1,000 and was entered only in the suppliers account.

(v) Prudence Plc bank figure in the Trial Balance differs from the Bank Statement figure of €15,600 due to:
1. Investment income of €5,000 had been paid direct to the firm's bank account.
2. A direct debit of €1,250 for electricity had not been recorded in the books.
3. A cheque issued for €2,500 to a creditor had not been presented for payment.
4. A cheque for €940 issued to a supplier had been entered as €490 in the books.
5. A credit transfer of €500 had been paid direct to the firm's bank account on behalf of a bankrupt debtor. This represents a first and final payment of 20c in the €.

(vi) Provision is to be made for debenture interest due, also the provision for bad debts to be adjusted to 5% of debtors.

(vii) Provide for depreciation on buildings at the rate of 2% of cost. At the end of the year it was decided to revalue the buildings to €900,000. Of this revalued figure €200,000 represented land on 1/1/2012.

(viii) The Directors have decided that a Debenture Redemption Reserve be established and provision be set aside to accumulate funds annually to pay the full sum within 10 years.

You are required to prepare:

(a) Trading Profit and Loss account for the year ending 31/12/2012.

(b) Balance Sheet on 31/12/2012.

10 MORGAN

Departmental Final

Morgan Plc has an authorised capital of 750,000 Ordinary shares of €1 each and 350,000 6% Preference shares of €1 each. It operates two departments: Grocery and Hardware. The following Trial Balance was extracted on 31/12/2012

	€	€
Grocery Department		
Sales		780,000
Purchases	348,000	
Carriage inwards	6,150	
Opening stock 1/1/2012	62,400	
Hardware Department		
Sales		390,000
Purchases	186,600	
Carriage inwards	3,600	
Opening stock 1/1/2012	31,350	
300,000 Ordinary shares		300,000
150,000 6% Preference shares		150,000
Profit and Loss account balance 1/1/2012		7,620
Debtors and creditors	58,200	99,600
8% Debentures		330,000
Land and buildings at cost	570,000	
Acc. depreciation		60,000
Fixtures and fittings	420,000	
Acc. depreciation		120,000
Goodwill	255,000	
Directors' fees	49,500	
Debenture interest	8,250	
Insurance	25,200	
Provision for bad debts		1,830
Advertising	30,000	
Advertising 1/1/2012		6,000
Light and heat	27,900	
Wages and general expenses	130,500	
Cleaning	27,000	
Interim dividends for 3 months	18,750	
Bank		13,350
	2,258,400	2,258,400

You are given the following information:

(i) Closing stock on 31/12/2012: Grocery €73,200, Hardware €31,500. Included in Grocery is stock which was purchased in a liquidation sale for €3,600 but is actually worth €9,000 on the open market.

(ii) No record has been made for grocery in transit purchased on 31/12/2012. RRP of these goods €15,750 which is cost plus 25%.

(iii) Insurance includes an annual premium of €10,800 for the year ending 31 March of next year i.e. 2013.

(iv) Advertising was paid on 30/8/2012 and will run until 1 May of next year i.e. 2013.

(v) Depreciation to be charged on buildings at 2% on cost (land was €120,000), fixtures and fittings at 15% of book value.

(vi) Buildings are to be revalued at €750,000.

(vii) The floor space of the store is divided as Grocery 60% and Hardware 40%.

(viii) Expenses are to be allocated to each department using sales or floor space – whatever is appropriate.

(ix) A comparison of the bank statement showing a figure of €9,570 and the cash book of €13,350, has revealed the following discrepancies:
1. A cheque for €630 to a supplier was recorded as €360.
2. Cheques for €3,750 were not presented for payment.
3. A credit transfer of €300 was paid directly to the firm's bank account on behalf of a bankrupt debtor. This represents 25% of the original debt.

(x) The directors recommend the following:
1. Provision be made for debenture interest due.
2. Provision for bad debts adjusted to 4% of debtors.
3. Preference dividend due be paid.
4. A final ordinary dividend be paid bringing the total up to 15%.

You are required to:

(a) Prepare Trading Profit and Loss account for each department as well as the entire firm for year ended 31/12/2012.

(b) Balance Sheet as at 31/12/2012.

(c) A report for management on the advisability of closing down any loss-making department.

11 GAMBERT

Gambert Plc has an authorised share capital of 1 million Ordinary shares of €1 each and 500,000 5% Preference shares of €1 each.
The following balances were extracted from the books on 31/12/2012.

	€	€
Land and buildings at cost	902,000	
Motor vehicles at cost	280,000	
Accumulated depreciation on vehicles		90,000
9% Investments 1/1/2012	320,000	
Patents (incl. 3-months' investment income)	24,800	
Debtors and creditors	100,400	86,600
Purchases and sales	1,320,000	1,760,000
Stock 1/1/2012	75,200	
Discount net		10,800
Bank		44,000
Directors' fees	48,000	
Dividends paid	48,000	
Advertising (including suspense)	14,800	
Rent	19,600	
Salaries and general expenses	199,600	
Provision for bad debts		3,200
Profit and Loss balance on 1/1/2012	17,200	
Issued capital		
800,000 Ordinary shares at €1 each		800,000
400,000 5% Preference shares		400,000
8% Debentures		180,000
Debenture interest paid for 4 months	5,000	
	3,374,600	3,374,600

The following information and instructions are to be taken into account:

(i) Stock at 31/12/2012 was €85,000 at cost and included stock which cost €8,000 but is now worth 60% of cost.

(ii) No record has been made in the books for stock purchased on credit which was in transit on 31/12/2012. (Retail price of goods is €15,000 which is cost plus 25%.)

(iii) Goods costing €6,200 at 25% mark-up and sent to a customer during Dec. 2012 on a sale or return basis was treated as credit sales.

(iv) During 2012 a fire destroyed a store costing €20,000 and stock to the value of €5,600. Gambert Ltd built an extension to the factory. The work was carried out by the firm's own employees. The cost of their labour was €22,000 and is included in wages and salaries. The materials costing €38,000 were taken from the firm's stocks of raw materials. The insurance company agreed to pay the full cost of the fire damage. No entry was made in respect of the fire or the extension.

(v) Goods with a retail selling price of €10,000 were returned to a supplier. The selling price was cost plus 25%. The supplier charged a restocking charge of 10% of cost price but no entry was made of the restocking charge.

(vi) Patents incorporating 3-months' investment income are to be written-off over a 5-year period.

(vii) Provide for depreciation on delivery vans at 12.5% on cost from date of purchase to the date of sale. On 31/3/12 a van which cost €24,000 (purchased on 30/6/06) was traded in against a new van costing €56,000. An allowance of €10,000 was given for the old van and a cheque for the net payment of the new van was entered incorrectly in the purchases figure. This was the only entry made.

(viii) A suspense figure arises as a result of the incorrect figure for debenture interest in the debenture interest account only, and the discount received of €700 is only entered in the creditors account.

(ix) The bank statement showed an overdraft of €40,060 and a comparison has revealed the following:

1. A cheque for €400 paid to a creditor has not been presented for payment.
2. Another cheque for €670 issued to a supplier had been entered as €760.
3. Investment income of €2,700 had been paid by credit transfer directly to the firm's bank account.
4. Another credit transfer of €750 had been paid into the firm's bank account on behalf of a bankrupt debtor. This represents a final payment of 30c in the euro.

(x) A new warehouse was purchased during the year for €180,000 plus VAT at 12.5%. The amount paid to the vendor was entered in the buildings account. No entry was made in the VAT account.

(xi) Buildings are to be depreciated at 2% of cost p.a. (Land is valued at €130,000.) At the end of 2005 the firm revalued land and buildings at €1,000,000.

(xii) A bad debt of €700 that was written-off during 2010 is now recoverable in full. A further bad debt of €300 included in debtors is to be written-off and the provision for bad debts to be adjusted to 4% of debtors.

(xiii) The directors recommend that:

1. Provision be made for investment income and debenture interest due.

You are required to prepare:

(a) Trading Profit and Loss account for the year ended 31/12/2012.

(b) Balance Sheet as at 31/12/2012.

TOPIC 3

Manufacturing Final a/c's

Genius without education is like silver in the mine.
Benjamin Franklin

1 Blenheim – Sample Exam Question 2009

Blenheim Ltd is a manufacturing firm and has an authorised capital of 500,00 Ordinary shares of €1 each and 300,000 Preference shares of €1 each.

	€	€
Factory buildings (cost €525,000)	480,000	
Plant and machinery (cost €280,000)	150,000	
Discount net		3,000
Profit and Loss balance 1/1/2008		75,400
Stocks on hand 1/1/2008		
Finished goods	84,500	
Raw materials	45,000	
Work in progress	21,250	
Sales		1,085,000
Patents	60,000	
Carriage of raw materials	6,300	
Hire of special equipment	10,000	
Purchases of raw materials	480,250	
Dividends paid	40,000	
Sale of scrap material		4,500
Debtors and creditors	64,500	55,600
Bank		10,300
Direct factory wages	252,460	
Selling expenses	105,165	
9% debentures (incl. €60,000 issued on 1/4/2008)		90,000
Issued share capital		
Ordinary shares		350,000
6% Preference shares		200,000
General factory overheads	60,200	
VAT		8,400
Debenture interest paid for first 3 months	175	
Administration expenses (incl. suspense)	22,400	
	1,882,200	1,882,200

The following information is to be taken into account:

(i) Stocks on hand 31/12/08

Raw materials	€49,000
Work in progress	€26,450
Finished goods	€90,000

The figure for finished goods includes items which cost €5,000 to produce but now have a sales value of €3,000.

(ii) Included in the figure for sale of scrap materials is €800 received from the sale of an old machine on 1/9/2008. This machine cost €9,000 on 1/4/2005. The cheque had been entered in the bank account. This was the only entry in the books.

(iii) A bad debt of €500 should be written-off and a provision for bad debts should be provided at 5% of debtors.

(iv) The suspense figure arises as a result of discount allowed with €200 entered only in the discount account, including the posting of an incorrect figure for the debenture interest paid to the debenture interest account. The correct interest was entered in the bank account.

(v) It was discovered that goods, which cost the firm €6,500 to produce, were sent to a customer on a sale or return basis. These goods were charged in error to the customer at cost plus 20%.

(vi) During 2008, Blenheim Ltd built an extension to the warehouse. The work was carried out by the company's own employees. The cost of their labour was €17,000 and is included in the factory wages. The materials costing €33,000 were taken from the stocks. No entry had been made in respect of the extension.

(vii) Patents are being written-off over 6 years which commenced in 2006.

(viii) Depreciation is to be provided on fixed assets as follows:

1. Plant and machinery – 20% of cost per annum.
2. Buildings – 2% of cost per annum for a full year.
3. Land and buildings – are to be revalued at year end at €600,000.

(ix) The directors are proposing that:

1. Provision should be made for debenture interest due.
2. Corporation tax of €8,000 be provided for.

You are required to:

(a) Prepare Manufacturing, Trading and Profit and Loss accounts for the year ended 31/12/08.

(b) Prepare a Balance Sheet at 31/12/2008.

Sample Solution Blenheim

Manufacturing account of Blenheim Ltd for year ended 31/12/2008

Direct materials			
Opening stock of raw materials	45,000		
Purchases of raw materials	447,250		
Carriage on raw materials	6,300		
Less closing stock of raw materials	(49,000)		
Cost of raw materials consumed		449,550	
Direct costs			
Direct factory wages	235,460		
Hire of special equipment	10,000	245,460	
Prime cost		695,010	
Factory overheads			
General factory overheads	60,200		
Patents written off	15,000		
Depreciation – Factory buildings	11,500		
– Plant and machinery	55,400		
Loss on sale of machine	2,050	144,150	
Factory cost		839,160	
Work in progress 1/1/2008		21,250	
Less work in progress 31/12/2008		(26,450)	
		833,960	
Less sale of scrap material		(3,700)	
Cost of manufacture		830,260	
Trading Profit and Loss account for year ending 31/12/2008			
Sales			1,077,200
Less cost of sales			
Opening stock of finished goods		84,500	
Cost of manufacture		830,260	
Less closing stock of finished goods		(94,500)	(820,260)
Gross profit			256,940
Less administration expenses			
Administration expenses		22,100	
Selling and distribution			
Selling expenses	105,165		
Bad debt	500		
Provision for bad debt	2,800	108,465	(130,565)
			126,375
Discount net			3,000
Operating profit			129,375
Less debenture interest			(6,750)
Net profit before taxation			122,625
Less taxation			(8,000)
Profit after tax			114,625
Less dividends			(40,000)
Retained profit			74,625
Profit and loss 1/1/2008			75,400
Profit and loss 31/12/2008			150,025

Balance Sheet as at 31/12/2008

Intangible fixed	**Cost**	**Depc**	**Value**
Patents			45,000
Tangible fixed			
Factory buildings	600,000		600,000
Plant and machinery	271,000	179,250	91,750
	871,000	179,250	736,750
Current assets			
Stocks – Raw materials	49,000		
Work in progress	26,450		
Finished goods	94,500	169,950	
Debtors	56,000		
Less provision for bad debts	(2,800)	53,200	
		223,150	
Creditors falling due within one year			
Creditors	55,600		
Bank	10,300		
VAT	8,400		
Debenture interest due	6,075		
Tax due	8,000	(88,375)	
Net current assets			134,775
Total net assets			871,525
Financed by :			
Creditors falling due for more than one year			
9% debentures			90,000
Capital and reserves	Authorised	Issued	
Ordinary shares of €1 each	500,000	350,000	
6% Preference shares of €1 each	300,000	200,000	
	800,000	550,000	
Revaluation reserve		81,500	
Profit and Loss 31/12/2008		150,025	781,525
Total capital employed			871,525

Notes to Accounts

Sales	1,085,000 –	7,800			=	**1,077,200**
Purchases	480,250 –	33,000			=	**447,250**
Direct factory wages	252,460 –	17,000			=	**235,460**
Accumulated depreciation buildings	45,000 +	11,500			=	**56,500**
Accumulated depreciation plant and machinery	130,000 +	**55,400** –		6,150	=	**179,250**
Disposal loss	9,000 –	6,150 –		800	=	**2,050**
Plant and machinery	280,000 –	9,000			=	**271,000**
Sale of scrap	4,500 –	800			=	**3,700**
Closing stock of finished goods	90,000 –	2,000 +		6,500	=	**94,500**
Administration	22,400 –	300			=	**22,100**
Patents	60,000 –	**15,000**			=	**45,000**
Bad debt						**500**
Provision for bad debt						**2,800**
Debenture interest	175 +	500 +		**6,075**	=	**6,750**
Debtors	64,500 –	200 –	500 –	7,800	=	**56,000**
Buildings	525,000 +	50,000 +		25,000	=	**600,000**
Revaluation reserve	25,000 +	56,500			=	**81,500**

2 ASTEROID

Asteroid Plc has authorised share capital of 850,000 Ordinary shares of €1 each and 400,000 4% Preference shares of 50c each. The following Trial Balance is on 31/12/2012

	€	€
Factory land and buildings at cost	740,000	
Accumulated depreciation on 1/1/2012		54,000
Plant and machinery	330,000	
Accumulated depreciation on 1/1/2012		55,000
Profit and Loss balance 1/1/2012		32,500
Sales		936,600
Sale of scrap materials		5,400
Direct factory wages	132,000	
Bank		11,200
Debtors and creditors	42,300	49,800
Purchases of raw materials	453,900	
Selling and distribution expenses	36,400	
Administration expenses	42,900	
General factory overheads (incorporating suspense)	52,600	
Stocks on hand 1/1/2012 – Finished goods	32,800	
– Raw materials	41,500	
– Work in progress	24,200	
8% Debenture (including €150,000 issued on 1/4/2012)		240,000
Dividends paid	18,000	
Issued share capital – Ordinary shares		300,000
– 4% Preference shares		250,000
PRSI		12,100
	1,946,600	1,946,600

The following information is to be taken into account:

(i) Stocks on hand 31/12/12
Raw materials €40,400 Work in progress €29,900 Finished goods €36,100

(ii) Included in the figure for sales is €3,000 received from the sale of old machinery. This machinery had cost €18,000 on 31/10/2007 and was sold on 01/03/12. The cheque received had been entered in the bank account. These were the only entries in the books.

(iii) No record had been made in the books for raw materials costing €12,000, which were in transit on 31/12/2012. The invoice for these goods has been received.

(iv) The suspense figure arises as a result of discount allowed of €900 entered only in the discount account.

(v) It was discovered that goods, which cost the firm €6,200 to produce, were sent to a customer on a sale or return basis. These goods were charged in error to the customer on a sale or return basis. These goods were charged at cost plus 25%.

(vi) During 2012, Asteroid Plc built an extension to the warehouse. The work was carried out by the company's own employees. The cost of their labour €40,000 is included in the factory wages. The materials costing €25,000 were taken from the stocks. No entries made in respect of this extension.

(vii) Bad debts of €700 are to be written-off and a provision for bad debts of 5% of debtors to be provided for.

(viii) Depreciation is to be provided on fixed assets as follows:
1. Plant and machinery – 20% of cost per annum, from date of purchase to date of sale.
2. Buildings – 2% of cost per annum for a full year. (Land at cost on 01/01/12 was €90,000.)
3. At the end of 2012, the company revalued the land and buildings at €950,000.

(ix) The directors are proposing that:
1. Provision should be made for debenture interest due.
2. Provision should be made for corporation tax of €32,000.

You are required to:

(a) Prepare Manufacturing, Trading and Profit and Loss accounts for the year ended 31/12/12.

(b) Prepare a Balance Sheet at 31/12/2012.

3 BETAMAX

Betamax Ltd is a manufacturing firm that has an authorised capital of 750,000 Ordinary Shares of €1 each and 400,000 Preference shares of €1 each. Trial Balance was extracted on 31/12/2012.

	€	€
Factory buildings (cost €787,500)	720,000	
Plant and machinery (cost €420,000)	225,000	
Discount net		4,500
Profit and Loss balance 1/1/2012		113,100
Stocks on hand 1/1/2012 – Finished goods	126,750	
– Raw materials	67,500	
– Work in progress	31,875	
Sales		1,627,500
Patents	90,000	
Carriage on raw materials	9,450	
Hire of special equipment	15,000	
Purchases of raw materials	720,375	
Dividends paid	60,000	
Sale of scrap material		6,750
Debtors and creditors	96,750	83,400
Bank		15,450
Direct factory wages	378,690	
Selling expenses	157,748	
9% Debentures (incl. €90,000 issued on 1/4/2012)		135,000
Issued share capital – Ordinary shares		525,000
– 6% Preference shares		300,000
General factory overheads	90,300	
VAT		12,600
Debenture interest paid for first 3 months	262	
Administration expenses (incl. suspense)	33,600	
	2,823,300	2,823,300

The following information is to be taken into account:

(i) Stocks on hand 31/12/12.
Raw materials €73,500 Work in progress €39,675 Finished goods €135,000
The figure for finished goods includes items which cost €7,500 to produce but now worth €4,500.

(ii) Included in the figure for the sale of scrap materials is €1,200 received from the sale of an old machine on 1/9/2012. This machine cost €13,500 on 1/4/2009. The cheque had been entered in the bank account. This was the only entry in the books.

(iii) A bad debt of €750 to be written-off and a provision for bad debts be provided at 5% of debtors.

(iv) The suspense figure arises as a result of discount allowed of €300 entered only in the discount account and of the posting of an incorrect figure for the debenture interest paid to the debenture interest account. The correct interest was entered in the bank account.

(v) It was discovered that goods, which cost the firm €9,750 to produce, were sent to a customer on a sale or return basis. These goods were charged in error to the customer at cost plus 20%.

(vi) During 2012 Betamax Ltd built an extension to the warehouse. The work was carried out by the company's own employees. The cost of their labour was €25,500 and is included in the factory wages. The materials costing €49,500 were taken from the stocks. No entries made in respect of this extension.

(vii) Patents are being written-off over 4 years which commenced in 2012.

(viii) Depreciation is to be provided on fixed assets as follows:
1. Plant and machinery at 20% of cost per annum and buildings at 2% of cost per annum for a full year.
2. Land and buildings are to be revalued at year end at €900,000.

(ix) The directors are proposing that a provision should be made for debenture interest due and corporation tax of €12,000 be provided for.

You are required to:

(a) Prepare Manufacturing, Trading Profit and Loss accounts for the year ended 31/12/12.

(b) Prepare a Balance Sheet at 31/12/2012.

(c) What is the difference between **direct costs** and **indirect costs**?

4 CELESTIAL

Celestial Plc is a manufacturing firm and has an authorised capital of 700,000 Ordinary shares of €1 each and 300,000 6% Preference shares of €1 each. The following Trial Balance was supplied on 31/12/2012.

	€	€
Factory land and buildings at cost	680,000	
Accumulated depreciation 1/1/2012		56,000
Plant and machinery	290,000	
Accumulated depreciation 1/1/2012		75,000
Direct factory wages	185,700	
Bank		12,600
Debtors and creditors	48,000	25,400
Purchases of raw materials	520,500	
Selling and distribution expenses	38,600	
Profit and Loss balance 1/1/2012		38,800
Sales		945,500
Sale of scrap materials		6,100
Administration expenses	27,400	
General factory overheads (incl. suspense)	75,000	
Accruals		13,600
Stocks on hand 1/1/12 – Finished goods	38,100	
– Raw materials	34,000	
– Work in progress	22,500	
8% Debenture (incl. €45,000 issued on 30/04/2012)		105,000
Dividends paid	38,200	
Issued share capital – Ordinary shares		500,000
– 6% Preference shares		220,000
	1,998,000	1,998,000

The following information is to be taken into account:

(i) Stocks on hand 31/12/2012.
Finished goods €36,300 Raw materials €39,200 Work in progress €23,400

(ii) Included in the figure for sales is €600 received from the sale of old machinery. This machinery had cost €16,000 on 01/09/2008 and was sold on 01/03/2012. The cheque received had been entered in the bank account. This was the only entry in the books.

(iii) No record had been made in the books for raw materials costing €4,800, which were in transit on 31/12/2012. The invoice for these goods had been received.

(iv) The suspense figure arises as a result of discount allowed of €900 entered only in the discount account.

(v) It was discovered that goods, which cost the firm €3,800 to produce, were sent to a customer on a sale or return basis. These goods were charged in error at cost plus 25% to the customer on a sale or return basis.

(vi) During 2012, Celestial Plc built an extension to the warehouse. The work was carried out by the company's own employees. The cost of their labour €18,000 was included in the factory wages. The materials costing €15,000 were taken from the stocks. No entries made in respect of this extension.

(vii) Depreciation is to be provided on fixed assets as follows:
1. Plant and machinery at 15% of cost per annum.
2. Buildings at 2% of cost per annum for a full year. (Land at cost on 01/01/2012 was €60,000.)
3. At the end of 2012, the company revalued the land and buildings at €820,000.

(viii) The directors are proposing that a provision should be made for debenture interest due and corporation tax of €15,000 be provided for.

(ix) Goods are to be transferred to the trading account at current market value €850,000.

You are required to:

(a) Prepare Manufacturing, Trading and Profit and Loss accounts for the year ended 31/12/2012.

(b) Prepare a Balance Sheet at 31/12/2012.

(c) On 1/1/2012 there were 240 units in production. During the year work commenced on 6,550 units and 410 were still in production on 31/12/2012. Work had halted on 170 units which were sold as scrap. Calculate the unit cost of production.

5 DUCATO

Ducato Ltd is a manufacturing firm that has an authorised capital of 350,00 Ordinary shares of €1 each and 150,000 5% Preference shares of €1 each. Trial Balance extracted on 31/12/2012.

	€	€
Factory buildings	300,000	
Accumulated depreciation on 1/1/2012		45,000
Plant and machinery	140,000	
Accumulated depreciation on 1/1/2012		52,500
Discount net		1,200
Profit and Loss balance 1/1/2012		19,000
Supervisor's wages	18,600	
Stocks on hand 1/1/2012 – Finished goods	26,000	
– Raw materials	27,000	
– Work in progress	15,500	
Sales		442,900
Patents (cost €45,000)	30,000	
Carriage on raw materials	1,000	
Hire of special equipment	3,000	
Purchases of raw materials	179,500	
Dividends paid for 6 months	11,200	
Sale of scrap material		4,300
Debtors and creditors	31,500	41,000
Bank		13,800
Direct factory wages	69,000	
Selling expenses	25,700	
7% Debentures (incl. €20,000 issued on 1/4/2012)		65,000
Issued share capital – Ordinary shares		165,000
– 5% Preference shares		75,000
VAT		4,500
Administration expenses	27,900	
Provision for bad debts		1,800
General factory expenses (incl. suspense)	25,100	
	931,000	931,000

The following information is to be taken into account:

(i) Stocks on hand 31/12/2012.
Raw materials €31,500 Work in progress €16,000 Finished goods €28,000

(ii) Included in the figure for sales are goods on sale or return with a cost price of €4,000 plus 20% mark-up.

(iii) No record had been made in the books for raw materials costing €6,000, which were in transit on 31/12/2012. The invoice for these goods has been received.

(iv) The suspense figure arises as a result of discount allowed of €600 entered only in the debtors account.

(v) During 2012 a fire destroyed a store costing €10,000 and stock €2,800. Ducato Ltd built an extension to the warehouse. The work was carried out by the company's own employees. The cost of their labour was €11,000 and is included in the factory wages. The materials costing €19,000 were taken from the stocks. The insurance company agreed to pay compensation for the agreed value of the buildings and goods less the agreed excess on the policy of €500. No entry had been made in respect of the fire, extension or compensation.

(vi) Patents are being written-off over 6 years.

(vii) Goods are to be transferred from the factory at current market value of €400,000.

(viii) Depreciation is to be provided on fixed assets as follows:
1. Plant and Machinery – 20% of cost per annum, from date of purchase to date of sale.
2. Buildings at 2% of cost per annum for a full year. (Land at cost on 01/01/12 was €60,000.)
3. Depreciation on buildings to be allocated with 75% to factory, 25% to office.

(ix) A bad debt of €500 which was written-off is now known to be recoverable in full. A further bad debt of €200 included in debtors is to be written-off and the provision for bad debts to be made equal to 4% of debtors.

(x) The directors are proposing that:
1. The preference dividend due be paid.
2. The total ordinary dividend for the year should be 12c per share.
3. Provision should be made for debenture interest due.

You are required to:

(a) Prepare Manufacturing, Trading and Profit and Loss accounts for the year ended 31/12/12.

(b) Prepare a Balance Sheet at 31/12/2012.

(c) Assuming Ducato produced 1,140 units, had 240 units left over from last year, allocated 150 to scrap materials, and had a further 89 unfinished at year end. Calculate the cost per unit of the finished product.

6 SHERIDAN

Sheridan Ltd is a manufacturing firm that has an authorised capital of 700,00 Ordinary shares of €1 each and 300,000 5% Preference shares of €1 each. Trial Balance was extracted on 31/12/2012.

	€	€
Factory buildings (cost €600,000)	510,000	
Plant and machinery (cost €280,000)	175,000	
Discount net		2,400
Profit and Loss balance 1/1/2012		38,000
Supervisors' wages	37,200	
Stocks on hand 1/1/2012 – Finished goods	52,000	
– Raw materials	54,000	
– Work in progress	31,000	
Sales		885,800
Goodwill (cost €90,000)	60,000	
Carriage on raw materials	2,000	
Hire of special equipment	6,000	
Purchases of raw materials	359,000	
Dividends paid	22,400	
Sale of scrap material		8,600
Debtors and creditors	63,000	82,000
Bank		27,600
Direct factory wages	138,000	
Selling expenses	51,400	
7% Debentures (incl. €40,000 issued on 1/4/2012)		130,000
Issued share capital – Ordinary shares		330,000
– 6% Preference shares		150,000
VAT		9,000
Administration expenses	55,800	
Provision for bad debts		3,600
General factory expenses (incl. suspense)	50,200	
	1,667,000	1,667,000

The following information is to be taken into account:

(i) Stocks on hand 31/12/2012

Raw Materials	€63,000
Work in Progress	€32,000
Finished Goods	€56,000

(ii) No record had been made in the books for raw materials costing €15,000, which were in transit on 31/12/2012. The invoices for these goods have been received.

(iii) The suspense figure arises as a result of discount allowed of €600 entered only in the discount account.

(iv) It was discovered that goods, which cost the firm €8,000 to produce, were sent to a customer on a sale or return basis. These goods were charged in error to the customer as a credit sale. These goods were charged at cost plus 20%.

(v) During 2012 a fire destroyed a store costing €20,000 and raw materials worth €5,600. Sheridan Ltd built an extension to the warehouse. The work was carried out by the company's own employees. The cost of their labour was €22,000 and is included in the factory wages. The materials costing €38,000 were taken from the stocks. The Insurance company agreed to pay compensation in full. No entry had been made in respect of the fire, extension or compensation.

(vi) Goodwill is being written-off over 6 years.

(vii) Goods are to be transferred from the factory at current market value of €750,000.

(viii) Depreciation is to be provided on fixed assets as follows:
1. Plant and machinery at 20% of cost per annum.
2. Buildings at 2% of cost per annum for a full year.
3. Land and buildings are to be revalued at year end at €820,000.
4. Depreciation on buildings and general expenses to be allocated with 75% to factory and 25% to office.

(ix) A bad debt of €700 which was written-off is now known to be recoverable in full. A further bad debt of €300 included in debtors is to be written-off and the provision for bad debts is to be made equal to 4% of doubtful debts.

(x) The directors are proposing that:
1. Provision should be made for debenture interest due.

You are required to:

(a) Prepare Manufacturing, Trading and Profit and Loss accounts for the year ended 31/12/2012.

(b) Prepare a Balance Sheet at 31/12/2012.

(c) Why are manufacturing accounts prepared?

7 FLOTILLA

Flotilla Plc is a manufacturing firm that has an authorised capital of 400,00 Ordinary shares of €1 each and 200,000 9% Preference shares of €1 each. Trial Balance was extracted on 31/12/2012.

	€	€
Buildings (cost €400,000)	370,000	
Plant and machinery (cost €180,000)	120,000	
Office equipment (cost €40,000)	20,000	
Discount (incl. suspense)		2,100
Insurance	11,400	
Factory heat and power	24,000	
Bad debts	4,500	
Profit and Loss balance 1/1/2012		6,900
Supervisors' wages	39,000	
Stocks on hand 1/1/2012		
Finished goods	45,000	
Raw materials	40,000	
Work in progress	37,000	
Sales		856,000
Goodwill (incl. 4-months' investment income)	45,000	
Carriage on raw materials	12,000	
Hire of special equipment	22,000	
Purchases of raw materials	275,000	
Dividends paid	16,500	
Sale of scrap material		13,000
Advertising	34,000	
6% Investments	150,000	
Debtors and creditors	48,000	84,000
Bank		41,000
Direct factory wages	105,000	
Selling expenses	86,000	
9% Debentures (incl. €60,000 issued on 1/7/2012)		160,000
Issued share capital – Ordinary shares		300,000
– 9% Preference shares		100,000
VAT		18,000
Debenture interest 6 months	4,600	
Office salaries	72,000	
	1,581,000	1,581,000

The following information is to be taken into account:

(i) Stocks on hand 31/12/2012

Raw Materials	€42,000
Work in Progress	€38,600
Finished Goods	€37,000

(ii) Goodwill, incorporating investment income, is to be written-off over the next 5 years starting 2012.

(iii) No record had been made in the books for raw materials costing €10,000 plus VAT at 25%, which were in transit on 31/12/2012. The invoices for these goods have been received.

(iv) The suspense figure arises as a result of an incorrect figure for debenture interest paid, although the correct figure was entered in the bank account, and bad debts of €600 were only entered in the debtors account.

(v) Goods are to be transferred from the factory at the current market value of €571,000.

(vi) Insurance is to be allocated two-thirds to the factory and one-third to the office.

(vii) The figure for the bank did not agree with the bank's record showing an overdraft of €37,100. A comparison with the cash book revealed the following:

1. A cheque amounting to €1,200 for insurance has not been presented for payment.
2. A credit transfer for €2,400 representing one year's rent received appears on the bank statement in advance starting on 1/9/2012.
3. A cheque for €500 paid to a creditor was entered as €800 in the firm's books.

(viii) Depreciation is to be provided on fixed assets as follows:

1. Plant and machinery at 20% of book value.
2. Office equipment at 20% on cost.
3. Buildings at 1.5% on cost per annum for a full year.
4. Depreciation on buildings to be allocated with two-thirds to the factory and one-third to the office.

(ix) A bad debt of €700 that was written-off is now known to be recoverable in full. A further bad debt of €300 included in debtors is to be written-off and the provision for bad debts to be made equal to 4% of debtors.

(x) The directors are proposing that:

1. Provision should be made for debenture interest due.

You are required to:

(a) Prepare Manufacturing, Trading and Profit and Loss accounts for the year ended 31/12/12.

(b) Prepare a Balance Sheet at 31/12/2012.

(c) Calculate the cost per unit if 640 units were produced. Identify 3 ways this cost per unit can be reduced.

TOPIC 4

Debtors and Creditors Control a/c's

The creditor has a better memory than the debtor.

James Howell

1 O'SHEA – SAMPLE EXAM QUESTION 2008

The Creditors Ledger Control account of K O'Shea showed the following balances: €17,550 Cr. and €630 Dr. on 31/12/2007. These figures did not agree with the Schedule (list) of Creditors Balances extracted on the same date.

An examination of the books revealed the following:

(i) K O'Shea had received an invoice from a supplier for €510. This had been entered in the appropriate day-book as €570. However, when posting from this book to the ledger, no entry had been made in the personal account.

(ii) A credit note was received from a supplier for €120. The only entry made in the books was €102 credited to a creditor's account.

(iii) A creditor had charged K O'Shea interest of €76 on an overdue account. The only entry made in the books for this interest had been €67 credited to the creditor's account. After a complaint by K O'Shea this charge had been reduced to €50 but this reduction had not been reflected in the books.

(iv) Cash purchases by K O'Shea of €140 had been debited to a supplier's account.

(v) K O'Shea had returned goods worth €110 to a supplier and entered this correctly in the books. However, a credit note arrived showing a deduction of 10% as a restocking charge. The total amount of this credit note was debited to the creditor's account and €90 was entered on the incorrect side of the nominal ledger.

(vi) Discount disallowed by a supplier of €32 had been treated as discount received in the books.

You are required to:

(a) Prepare the Adjusted Creditors Ledger Control account.

(b) Prepare the Adjusted Schedule of Creditors showing the original balance.

(c) Outline the advantages of Control accounts to a firm.

Sample Solution O'Shea

Adjusted Creditors Control a/c

Balance b/d	630	Balance c/d	17,550
Invoice	60	Interest	50
Credit note	120	Discount disallowed	64
Credit note	79	Balance c/d	630
Balance c/d	17,405		
	18,294		18,294
Balance b/d	630	Balance b/d	17,405

Schedule of Creditors Accounts Balances

Balance as per list of creditors			16,190
Add	Invoice	510	
	Discount disallowed	64	
	Cash purchases	140	
	Restocking charge	110	824
Deduct	Credit note	222	
	Interest	17	(239)
Balance as per adjusted control a/c			16,775

Advantages of Control Accounts

1. They act as a check on the accuracy of the ledgers by comparing the balance of the Control account with the total as per the schedule.
2. Errors can be found more easily using Control accounts.
3. They are useful when a firm needs to find credit sales or purchases from incomplete records.
4. They allow amounts owed by **debtors** and owed to **creditors** to be found quickly by simply balancing the Control accounts.

2 CONLON

The Creditors Ledger Control account of Christy Conlon showed the following balances: €17,320 Cr. and €410 Dr. on 31/12/2012. These figures did not agree with the Schedule (list) of Creditors Balances extracted on the same date.

An examination of the books revealed the following:

(i) Conlon had received an invoice from a supplier for €610. This had been entered in the appropriate day-book as €670. However, when posting from this book to the ledger, no entry had been made in the personal account.

(ii) A credit note was received from a supplier for €125. The only entry made in the books was €152 credited to a creditor's account.

(iii) A creditor had charged Conlon interest of €86 on an overdue account. The only entry made in the books for this interest had been €68 credited to the creditor's account. After a complaint by Conlon this charge had been reduced to €50 but this reduction had not been reflected in the books.

(iv) Cash purchases by Conlon of €150 had been debited to a supplier's account.

(v) Conlon had returned goods worth €120 to a supplier and entered this correctly in the books. However, a credit note arrived showing a deduction of 10% as a restocking charge. The total amount of this credit note was debited to the creditor's account but €100 was entered on the credit side of the Returns account.

(vi) A discount of €42 disallowed by a supplier had been treated as discount received in the books.

(vii) Bills payable to value €700 had been omitted from the books.

You are required to:

(a) Prepare the Adjusted Creditors Ledger Control account.

(b) Prepare the Adjusted Schedule of Creditors showing the original balance.

(c) Explain:

1. Contra item.
2. How the **opening balance** of €410 above could have arisen.

3 CLARKE

The Creditors Ledger Control account of Conrad Clarke showed the following balances: €36,530 Cr. and €664 Dr. on 31/12/2012. These figures did not agree with the Schedule (list) of Creditors Balances extracted on the same date. An examination of the books revealed the following:

(i) Conrad Clarke had received an invoice from a supplier for €770. This had been entered in the appropriate day-book as €707. However, when posting from this book to the ledger, no entry had been made in the personal account.

(ii) A credit note was received from a supplier for €133. The only entry made in the books was €33 debited to a **debtors** account.

(iii) A creditor had charged Conrad Clarke interest of €45 on an overdue account. The only entry made in the books for this interest had been €54 debited to the creditor's account. After a complaint by Clarke this charge had been reduced to €15 but this reduction had not been reflected in the books.

(iv) Cash purchases of €480 by Clarke had been debited to a supplier's account.

(v) Clarke had returned goods worth €300 to a supplier and entered this correctly in the books. However, a credit note arrived showing a deduction of 10% as a restocking charge. The total amount of this credit note was credited to the creditor's account. In relation to the credit note no other entry was made.

(vi) Discount disallowed by a supplier of €36 had been omitted from the books.

You are required to:

(a) Prepare the Adjusted Creditors Ledger Control account.

(b) Prepare the Adjusted Schedule of Creditors showing the original balance.

(c) 1. Explain what is meant by **accounting concept**.

2. Name 2 fundamental accounting concepts.
3. Illustrate an accounting concept.

4 CARROLL

The Creditors Ledger Control account of Carroll showed the following balances: €52,245 Cr. and €800 Dr. on 31/12/2012. These figures did not agree with the Schedule (list) of Creditors Balances extracted on the same date. An examination of the books revealed the following:

(i) A creditor had charged Carroll interest of €46 on an overdue account. The only entry made in the books for this interest had been €64 debited to the creditor's account. After a complaint by Carroll this charge had been reduced to €25 but this reduction had not been reflected in the books.

(ii) Carroll had returned goods worth €420 to a supplier and entered this correctly in the books. However, a credit note arrived showing a deduction of 10% as a restocking charge. The total amount of this credit note was credited to the creditor's account. In relation to the credit note no other entry was made.

(iii) Carroll had received an invoice from a supplier for €720. This had been entered in the appropriate day-book as €702. However, when posting from this book to the ledger, no entry had been made in the personal account.

(iv) A credit note was received from a supplier for €126. The only entry made in the books was €621 credited to a creditor's account.

(v) A payment of €230 to a creditor had been entered twice in both the cash book and the Creditors Ledger.

(vi) Discount disallowed by a supplier of €100 had been treated as discount received in the books.

You are required to:

(a) Prepare the Adjusted Creditors Ledger Control account.

(b) Prepare the Adjusted Schedule of Creditors showing the original balance.

(c) Outline the advantages of **control accounts** to a firm.

(d) What other forms of verification can be used to check different figures?

5 DUNLEAVY

The Debtors Ledger Control account of Dunleavy showed the following balances: €15,530 Dr. and €580 Cr. on 31/12/2012. These figures did not agree with the Schedule (list) of Debtors Balances extracted on the same date. An examination of the books revealed the following:

(i) Discount of €50 to a customer was disallowed and had been treated as a discount allowed in the discount account and personal account.

(ii) Interest, amounting to €53, charged to a customer's overdue account had been entered as €35 in the interest account. Following a complaint from the customer, this charge was reduced to €40 but this reduction had not been entered in the books.

(iii) An invoice for €650 that was sent to a customer had been entered in the appropriate day-book as €560, but no entry had been made in the personal account.

(iv) A customer's account had been credited with cash sales of €420.

(v) Bills payable of €600 had been entered on the debit side of a customer's account.

(vi) A credit note was sent to a customer for €120. The only entry made in the books was €10 debited to the debtor's account.

(vii) A credit note for €240 was sent to a customer and entered correctly in the books. However, the accounts clerk forgot to deduct a 10% restocking charge. A new credit note was sent immediately but the only entry made in the books in respect of this credit note was €264 debited to the debtor's account.

You are required to prepare the:

(a) Adjusted Debtors Ledger Control account.

(b) Adjusted Schedule (list) of Debtors showing the original balance.

(c) Explain the difference between:

1. Bad debts.
2. Provision for bad debts.

6 DALY

On 31/12/2012 the Debtors Control account of Daly showed the following balances: €12,300 and €400. These figures did not agree with the Schedule (list) of Debtors Balances drawn up on the same date. An examination of the books revealed the following:

(i) An invoice sent to Daly showing goods at €800 less **trade discount** of 40% had been omitted from the books.
(ii) Interest amounting to €44 charged to a debtor had been entered in the personal account as €40. Following a complaint, this has been reduced to €24 but had not been entered in the books.
(iii) A credit note sent to Divilly for €90 had been entered as €900 in the day-book and recorded in the Debtors Ledger as €9.
(iv) A contra item of €120 had been transferred to the incorrect side of Daly's account in the Debtors Ledger and also appeared on the debit side of the control account.
(v) Cash sales of €600 had been debited to Daly (a debtor).
(vi) Bills receivable for €500 had been omitted from the books.
(vii) Debtors returned goods worth €500 and this transaction was entered correctly in the books. However, no record was taken of 10% restocking charge. The new credit was sent but the only entry made was €450 debited to the debtors account.

You are required to prepare:

(a) Adjusted Debtors Ledger Control account.
(b) Adjusted List of Debtors showing the original balance.
(c) What are the dangers associated with having a high **debtors** figure?
(d) Show journal entries for (i) and (ii) above.

7 DOOLEY

The Debtors Ledger Control account of S Dooley showed the balances: €63,100 Dr. and €1,600 Cr. on 31/12/2012. The figures did not agree with the Schedule (list) of Debtors Balances extracted on the same date. Dooley immediately entered the difference in a suspense account. An examination of the books revealed the following:

(i) A customer's account had been debited with bills receivable of €200 although no entry was made in the Control account.
(ii) Discount disallowed to a customer of €140 had been treated as discount allowed in the discount account, but credited as €34 in the personal account.
(iii) A credit note for €180, inclusive of a €30 restocking charge, was sent to a customer. To account for this an entry of €120 was made in the returns book, while €130 was debited to the personal account. After a complaint by the customer the restocking charge was cancelled.
(iv) Interest, amounting to €300, had been charged to a customer's overdue account, but credited as €100 in the personal account. Following a complaint by the customer this charge was reduced by €60 but this reduction had not been entered in the books.
(v) A cheque of €940 received from a debtor in full settlement of a debt of €1,000 was dishonoured. The only entry relating to the dishonouring was €140 credited to the Control account and credited to the customer's account.
(vi) Dooley sent an invoice to a customer for €2,000, less 25% trade discount. This had been entered in the sales book as €1,400. However, no entry was made in the personal account.
(vii) €240 was received from a debtor previously written-off. This represents 15% of the original bad debt that the debtor has undertaken to pay towards the remainder of the previous debt. No entries were made in the accounts.

You are required to show the following:

(a) The Adjusted Debtors Ledger Control account.
(b) The Adjusted Schedule of Debtors showing the original balance.
(c) Why it is vital to implement strict credit control on debtors.

8 CURLEY

The Creditors Ledger Control account of Curley showed the following balances: €6,100 Cr. and €25 Dr. 31/12/2012. These figures did not agree with the Schedule (list) of Creditors Balances extracted on the same date. An examination of the books revealed the following:

(i) Interest amounting to €40 was charged by a supplier on Curley's' overdue account, and was entered as €34 in the interest account. Following a protest by Curley this charge was reduced to €25. The reduction had not been entered in the books.

(ii) A €30 discount disallowed by a creditor was debited twice in the personal account. No entry was made in the discount account.

(iii) A credit note was received from a supplier for €325. A figure for €352 was entered in the purchases account but no entry was made in the personal account.

(iv) No entries were made for a contra item of €300.

(v) A credit note for €105 was received from a supplier and entered in the books. This credit note contained a restocking charge of €11. To account for the restocking charge the accounts clerk credited the creditor's account with €21. This was the only entry in respect of the restocking charge.

(vi) Bills payable of €155 had been credited as €55 to a supplier's account, while only €75 was debited in the Control account.

(vii) A cheque for €500, previously sent to a supplier in full settlement of a debt of €550, was dishonoured. The only entries regarding the dishonoured cheque were €50 credited to the supplier's account and €500 debited in the bank account.

You are required to show the following:

(a) The Adjusted Creditors Ledger Control account.

(b) The Adjusted Schedule of Creditors showing the original balance.

(c) Show the journal entries for (vii).

(d) Explain what is meant by **leaning on the trade**.

TOPIC

5

Asset Disposal and Revaluation

The greatest power is often simple patience.

E. Joseph Cossman

1 ACE – SAMPLE EXAM QUESTION

Ace Haulage prepares its final accounts to 31 December each year. The company's policy is to depreciate its vehicles at the rate of 15% of cost per annum calculated from the date of purchase to the date of disposal and to accumulate this depreciation in a provision for the Depreciation account.

On 1/1/2010 Ace Haulage owned the following vehicles:
No. 1 purchased on 1/1/2006 for €70,000.
No. 2 purchased on 1/8/2007 for €80,000.
No. 3 purchased on 1/4/2008 for €88,000.

On 1/5/2010 Vehicle No. 2 was damaged in an accident and traded in against a new vehicle costing €90,000. The company received compensation to the value of €30,000 and the cheque paid for the new vehicle was €75,000. On 1/7/2011 Vehicle No. 1 was traded in for €24,000 against a new vehicle costing €95,000. Vehicle No. 1 had a refrigeration unit fitted on 1/1/2008 which cost €20,000. This unit was depreciated at the rate of 30% of cost for the first two years and thereafter at the rate of 15% of cost per annum.

You are required to show (with workings) for each of the two years 2010 and 2011:
(a) The Vehicles account.
(b) The Vehicle Disposal account.
(c) The provision for the Depreciation account.
(d) What factors are taken into account in arriving at the annual depreciation charge?

Solution

Depreciation Table

Vehicle No.	Cost	Annual Depc	Account Depc	2010	2011	Disposal
1	70,000	10,500	42,000	10,500	5,250	
Refrigeration Unit	20,000		12,000	3,000	1,500	**74,250**
2	80,000	12,000	29,000	4,000		**33,000**
3	88,000	13,200	23,100	13,200	13,200	
4	90,000	13,500		9,000	13,500	
5	95,000	14,250			7,125	
			106,100	**39,700**	**40,575**	

(a)

Vehicles Account

1/1/2010	Balance b/d	258,000	1/5/2010	Disposal	80,000
1/5/2010	Purchases	90,000	31/12/2010	Balance c/d	268,000
		348,000			348,000
1/1/2011	Balance b/d	268,000	1/7/2011	Disposal	90,000
1/7/2011	Purchases	95,000	31/12/2011	Balance c/d	273,000
		363,000			363,000
1/1/2012	Balance b/d	273,000			

(b)

Vehicle Disposal Account

1/5/2010	Cost	80,000	1/5/2010	Depreciation	**33,000**
				Compensation	30,000
				Trade in	15,000
				Loss	2,000
		80,000			80,000
1/7/2011	Cost	90,000	1/7/2011	Depreciation	**74,250**
	Profit	8,250		Trade in	24,000
		98,250			98,250

(c)

Provision for Depreciation Account

1/5/2010	Disposal	**33,000**	1/1/2010	Balance b/d	106,100
31/12/2010	Balance c/d	112,800	31/12/2010	P & L	**39,700**
		145,800			145,800
1/7/2011	Disposal	**74,250**	1/1/2011	Balance	112,800
31/12/2011	Balance c/d	79,125	31/12/2011	P & L	**40,575**
		153,375			153,375
			1/1/2022	Balance c/d	79,125

2 SPEEDO

Speedo Cabs prepares its final accounts to 31 December each year. The company's policy is to depreciate its vehicles at the rate of 15% of **cost** per annum calculated from the date of purchase to the date of disposal and to accumulate this depreciation in a provision for the Depreciation account.

On 1/1/2013 Speedo Cabs owned the following vehicles:
No. 1 purchased on 1/1/2009 for €30,000.
No. 2 purchased on 31/3/2010 for €36,000.
No. 3 purchased on 1/9/2011 for €40,000.

On 1/4/2013 Vehicle No. 3 was involved in a crash and was traded in against a new vehicle costing €48,000. The company received compensation to the value of €12,000 and the cheque paid for the new vehicle was €28,000.

On 1/9/2014 Vehicle No.1 was traded in for €5,000 against a new vehicle costing €52,000. Vehicle No. 1 had a permanent video and entertainment unit fitted on 1/1/2011 costing €12,000. This unit was depreciated at the rate of 30% of cost in year one and two and thereafter at the rate of 15% of cost per annum.

You are required to show, with workings, for each of the two years 2013 and 2014:

(a) The Vehicles account.
(b) The Vehicle Disposal account.
(c) The Provision for Depreciation account.
(d) What is meant by **depreciation**?
(e) Why does a company charge depreciation when calculating profit?

3 FAST AND FURIOUS

Fast and Furious Transport prepares its final accounts to 31 December each year. The company's policy is to depreciate its vehicles at the rate of 20% of **cost** per annum calculated from the date of purchase to the date of disposal and to accumulate this depreciation in a provision for the Depreciation account.

On 1/1/2012 Fast and Furious Transport owned the following vehicles:
No. 1 purchased on 1/7/2009 for €60,000.
No. 2 purchased on 1/4/2010 for €48,000.
No. 3 purchased on 1/9/2010 for €72,000.

On 1/7/2012 Vehicle No. 1 was traded in against a new vehicle costing €80,000. The company received a trade-in allowance to the value of €20,000. Vehicle No. 1 had a refrigeration unit fitted on 1/1/2010 costing €6,000. This unit was depreciated at the rate of 40% of cost in year one and thereafter at the rate of 20% of cost per annum.

On 1/10/2013 Vehicle No. 3 was withdrawn from service following an accident and traded in against a new vehicle costing €90,000. The company received €19,000 compensation from the insurers.

You are required to show, with workings, for each of the two years 2012 and 2013:

(a) The Vehicles account.
(b) The Vehicle Disposal account.
(c) The provision for the Depreciation account.
(d) Explain the difference between the straight-line method and the diminishing balance of depreciation.

4 VELOCITY

Velocity Vehicles prepares its final accounts to 31 December each year. The company's policy is to depreciate its vehicles at the rate of 20% of **book value** per annum calculated from the date of purchase to the date of disposal and to accumulate this depreciation in a provision for the Depreciation account.

On 1/1/2012 Velocity Vehicles owned the following vehicles:
No. 1 purchased on 1/1/2007 for €32,000.
No. 2 purchased on 1/1/2008 for €38,000.
No. 3 purchased on 1/1/2009 for €44,000.

On 1/8/2010 Vehicle No. 1 was traded in against a new vehicle costing €46,000. A trade-in allowance of €16,000 was received. Vehicle No. 1 had a tachograph fitted on 1/1/2008 for €6,000.

On 1/5/2011 Vehicle No. 3 was involved in a crash and traded in against a new vehicle costing €52,000. The company received compensation to the value of €18,000 and the cheque paid for the new vehicle was €46,000.

You are required to show, with workings, for each of the two years 2010 and 2011:

(a) The Vehicles account.
(b) The Vehicle Disposal account.
(c) The provision for Depreciation account.
(d) The relevant entries in the Profit and Loss account and the Balance Sheet for the year ending 31/12/2013.

5 A TO Z TRANSPORT

A to Z Transport prepares its final accounts to 31 December each year. The company's policy is to depreciate its vehicles at the rate of 20% of **book value** per annum calculated from the date of purchase to the date of disposal and to accumulate this depreciation in a provision for the Depreciation account.

On 1/1/2009 A to Z Transport owned the following vehicles:
No. 1 purchased on 1/1/2005 for €50,000.
No. 2 purchased on 1/1/2006 for €55,000.
No. 3 purchased on 1/1/2007 for €60,000.

On 1/8/2009 Vehicle No. 1 was traded in for €17,000 against a new vehicle costing €65,000. Vehicle No. 1 had a sleeping and self-contained compartment fitted on 1/1/2007 for €5,500.

On 1/5/2010 Vehicle No. 3 was withdrawn from service due to a crash and it was traded in against a new vehicle costing €68,000. The company received vehicle insurance compensation to the value of €10,000 and the cheque paid for the new vehicle was €42,000.

You are required to show, with workings, for each of the two years 2009 and 2010:

(a) The Vehicles account.
(b) The Vehicle Disposal account.
(c) The provision for Depreciation account.
(d) Show the relevant entries in the Profit and Loss account and the Balance Sheet for the year ending 31/12/2010.

6 AUTO ACCELERATOR

Auto Accelerator Ltd prepares its final accounts to 31 December each year. The company's policy is to depreciate its vehicles at the rate of 20% of **book value** per annum, to be calculated from the date of purchase to the date of disposal and to accumulate this depreciation in a provision for the Depreciation account.

On 1/1/2012 Auto Accelerator owned the following vehicles:
A purchased on 1/1/2008 for €75,000.
B purchased on 1/7/2009 for €51,000.
C purchased on 1/1/2010 for €66,000.

On 1/7/2012 Vehicle A was traded in against a new vehicle costing €81,000. A trade-in allowance of €33,000 was received. Vehicle A had an overnight sleeping unit fitted on 1/1/2010 for €15,000 and it was depreciated at the rate of 32% in year one and thereafter at 20% of book value.

On 1/4/2013 Vehicle C was in an accident and traded in against a new vehicle costing €87,000. The company received compensation to the value of €20,550 and the cheque paid for the new vehicle was €69,000.

You are required to show, with workings, for each of the two years 2012 and 2013:

(a) The Vehicles account.
(b) The Vehicle Disposal account.
(c) The provision for the Depreciation account.
(d) Show the relevant entries in the Profit and Loss account and the Balance Sheet for the year ending 31/12/2013.

7 LYONS – SAMPLE EXAM QUESTION

On 1/1/2004 Lyons Ltd owned freehold buildings which cost €290,000 and adjacent land which cost €210,000. The company depreciates its buildings at the rate of 2% per annum straight-line method. It is the company's policy to apply a full year's depreciation in the year of acquisition and no depreciation in the year of sale. The property had been purchased on 1/1/2000 and depreciation had been charged against profits in each of the four years. (Land is not depreciated.)

The following details were taken from the firm's books:

1/1/2004 Revalued land and buildings at €600,000. Of this revalued amount, €240,000 was attributable to land.

1/1/2005 Sold land for €280,000 which cost €210,000 but was since revalued on 1/1/2004.

1/1/2006 Purchased buildings for €400,000. During the year 2006, €150,000 was paid to a building contractor for an extension to the newly purchased buildings. The company's own employees also worked on this extension and they were paid wages amounting to €50,000 by Lyons for this work.

1/1/2007 Revalued the buildings owned at €1,056,000 (a 10% increase in respect of each building).

1/1/2008 Sold the buildings owned on 1/1/2004 for €420,000. The remaining buildings were revalued at €750,000.

You are required to:

(a) Prepare the relevant ledger accounts in respect of the above transactions for each of the years ended 31/12/2004 to 31/12/2008. (Bank account and Profit and Loss account not required.)
(b) Show the relevant extract from the Balance Sheet as at 31/12/2008.

Solution

Land and Buildings

1/1/2004	Balance b/d	500,000			
1/1/2004	Revaluation Reserve	100,000	31/12/2004	Balance c/d	600,000
		600,000			600,000
1/1/2005	Balance b/d	600,000	1/1/2005	Disposal	240,000
			31/12/2005	Balance c/d	360,000
		600,000			600,000
1/1/2006	Balance b/d	360,000			
	Bank	400,000			
	Bank	150,000			
	Wages	50,000	31/12/2006	Balance c/d	960,000
		960,000			960,000
1/1/2007	Balance b/d	960,000			
1/1/2007	Revaluation Res.	96,000	31/12/2007	Balance c/d	1,056,000
		1,056,000			1,056,000
1/1/2008	Balance b/d	1,056,000	1/1/2008	Disposal	396,000
	Revaluation Res.	90,000	31/12/2008	Balance c/d	750,000
		1,146,000			1,146,000
1/1/2009	Balance b/d	750,000			

Provision for Depreciation Account

1/1/2004	Revaluation Res.	23,200	1/1/2004	Balance b/d	23,200
31/12/2004	Balance c/d	7,200	31/12/2004	P & L	7,200
		30,400			30,400
31/12/2005	Balance c/d	14,400	1/1/2005	Balance b/d	7,200
			31/12/2005	P & L	7,200
		14,400			14,400
31/12/2006	Balance c/d	33,600	1/1/2006	Balance b/d	14,400
			31/12/2006	P & L	19,200
		33,600			33,600
1/1/2007	Revaluation Reserve	33,600	1/1/2007	Balance b/d	33,600
31/12/2007	Balance c/d	21,120	31/12/2007	P & L	21,120
		54,720			54,720
1/1/2008	Disposal	7,920	1/1/2008	Balance b/d	21,120
	Revaluation Res.	13,200	31/12/2008	P & L	15,000
31/12/2008	Balance c/d	15,000			
		36,120			36,120
			1/1/2009	Balance b/d	15,000

Disposal of Land

1/1/2005	Land	240,000	1/1/2005	Bank	280,000
31/12/2005	P & L	40,000			
		280,000			280,000

Disposal of Buildings

1/1/2008	Buildings	396,000	1/1/2008	Bank	420,000
	P & L	31,920		Depreciation	7,920
		427,920			427,920

Revaluation Reserve

1/1/2005	Revenue Res.	30,000	1/1/2004	Land & Blgs.	100,000
1/1/2008	Revenue Res.	150,800		Depreciation	23,200
31/12/2008	Balance c/d	175,200	1/1/2007	Land & Blgs.	96,000
				Depreciation	33,600
			1/1/2008	Land & Blgs.	90,000
				Depreciation	13,200
		356,000			356,000

Revenue Reserve

			1/1/2005	Reval Res.	30,000
			1/1/2008	Reval Res.	150,800
					180,800

Balance Sheet (extract) as at 31/12/2008

Fixed Assets	750,000	15,000	735,000
Land & Buildings			
Capital and Reserves			
Revaluation Reserve			175,200
Revenue Reserve			180,800

8 JOHNO

On 1/1/2006 Johno Ltd owned freehold property and land which cost €570,000, consisting of land valued at €210,000 and buildings valued at €360,000. The company depreciates its buildings at the rate of 2% per annum straight-line method. It is the company's policy to apply a full year's depreciation in the year of acquisition and no depreciation in the year of sale. The property had been purchased on 1/1/1998 and depreciation had been charged against profits in each of the 8 years. (Land is not depreciated.)

The following details were taken from the firm's books:

1/1/2006 Revalued land and buildings at €660,000. Of this revalued amount €240,000 was attributable to land.

1/1/2007 Sold land for €270,000 which cost €210,000 but was since revalued on 1/1/2006.

1/1/2008 Purchased buildings for €150,000. During the year 2008, €54,000 was paid to a building contractor for an extension to the newly purchased buildings. The company's own employees also worked on this extension and they were paid wages amounting to €24,000 by Johno for this work.

1/1/2009 Revalued buildings owned at €712,800 (a 10% increase in respect of each building).

1/1/2010 Sold for €468,000 the buildings owned on 1/1/2006. The remaining buildings were revalued at €360,000.

You are required to:

(a) Prepare the relevant ledger accounts in respect of the above transactions for each of the years ended 31/12/2006 to 31/12/2010. (Bank account and Profit and Loss account not required.)

(b) Show the relevant extract from the Balance Sheet as at 31/12/2010.

9 U. CULLEN

On 1/1/2005 Una Cullen and Associates owned freehold property and land which cost €868,000, consisting of land valued at €196,000 and buildings valued at €672,000. The company depreciates its buildings at the rate of 2% per annum straight-line method. It is the company's policy to apply a full year's depreciation in the year of acquisition and no depreciation in the year of sale. The property had been purchased on 1/1/1999 and depreciation had been charged against profits in each of the 6 years. (Land is not depreciated.)

The following details were taken from the firm's books:

1/1/2005 Revalued land and buildings at €1,064,000. Of this revalued amount €308,000 was attributable to land.

1/1/2006 Sold land for €392,000 which cost €196,000 but was since revalued on 1/1/2005.

1/1/2007 Purchased buildings for €504,000. During the year 2002, €406,000 was paid to a building contractor for an extension to the newly purchased buildings. The company's own employees also worked on this extension and they were paid wages amounting to €84,000 by Una Cullen and Associates for this work.

1/1/2008 Revalued buildings owned at €1,925,000 (a 10% increase in respect of each building).

1/1/2009 Sold the buildings owned on 1/1/2005 for €952,000. The remaining buildings were revalued at €1,190,000.

You are required to:

(a) Prepare the relevant ledger accounts in respect of the above transactions for each of the years ended 31/12/2005 to 31/12/2009. (Bank account and Profit and Loss account not required.)

(b) Show the relevant extract from the Balance Sheet as at 31/12/2009.

10 Stuart Trainor

On 1/1/2006 Stuart Trainor Ltd purchased freehold property and land which cost €250,000, consisting of land at €50,000 and buildings at €200,000. The company depreciates its buildings at the rate of 2% per annum straight-line method. It is the company's policy to apply a full year's depreciation in the year of acquisition and no depreciation in the year of disposal. (Land is not depreciated.)

The following details were taken from the firm's books:

1/1/2006 Revalued land and buildings at €480,000. Of this revalued amount €120,000 was attributable to land.

1/1/2007 Sold land for €140,000 which cost €50,000 but was since revalued on 1/1/2006.

1/1/2008 Purchased buildings for €150,000. During the year 2008, €30,000 was paid to a building contractor for an extension to the newly purchased buildings. The company's own employees also worked on this extension and they were paid wages amounting to €20,000 by Stuart Trainor for this work.

1/1/2009 Revalued buildings owned at €700,000. (A 25% increase in respect of each building.)

1/1/2010 Sold for €510,000 the buildings owned on 1/1/2006. The remaining buildings were revalued at €300,000.

You are required to:

(a) Prepare the relevant ledger accounts in respect of the above transactions for each of the years ended 31/12/2006 to 31/12/2010. (Bank account and Profit and Loss account not required.)

(b) Show the relevant extract from the Balance Sheet as at 31/12/2010.

TOPIC

6

Tabular Statements

Confidence is what you feel when you understand.

Proverb

1 NSL – Sample Exam Question

Balance Sheet as at 1/1/2005

	Cost €	Acc. Depc €	Net €
Fixed Assets – Land and buildings	260,000	25,000	235,000
– Equipment	50,000	20,000	30,000
	310,000	45,000	265,000
Current Assets – Stock		70,000	
– Debtors (less 5% provision)		85,500	
		155,500	
Less Creditors Falling Due Within 1 Year			
Creditors	61,000		
Bank	23,000		
Expenses due	3,500	87,500	
Net Current Assets			68,000
			333,000
Financed by			
Capital and reserves			
Authorised – 400,000 Ordinary shares at €1			
Issued – 290,000 Ordinary shares at €1			290,000
Share premium			14,000
Profit and loss balance			29,000
			333,000

The following transactions took place during 2005:

Jan. NSL Ltd bought an adjoining business which included buildings €120,000, debtors €10,000 and creditors €38,000. The purchase price was discharged by granting the seller 80,000 shares in NSL Ltd at a premium of 20c per share.

Feb. NSL Ltd decided to revalue land and buildings at €550,000 (which includes land valued at €70,000) on 28/2/2005.

Mar. Management decided that the provision for bad debts should be raised to 6% of debtors.

Apr. Goods previously sold for €800 were returned. The selling price of these goods was cost plus 25%. A credit note was issued showing a deduction of 10% of the selling price as a restocking charge.

May Received a bank statement on 31 May showing a credit transfer received of €4,800 to cover 10 months rent in advance from 1 May and a direct debit of €2,000 to cover fire insurance for the year ended 31/3/2006.

June A payment of €630 was received from a debtor whose debt had been previously written-off and who now wishes to trade with NSL Ltd again. This represents 70% of the original debt and the debtor had undertaken to pay the remainder of the debt by January 2006.

July A creditor, who was owed €500 by NSL Ltd, accepted equipment, the book value of which was €400, in full settlement of the debt. The equipment cost €900.

Aug. An interim dividend of 5c per share was paid on all paid-up shares.

Oct. Received €40,000 from the issue of the remaining shares.

Nov. Received balance of previously written-off bad debt as agreed in June.

Dec. The buildings are to be depreciated at the rate of 2% per annum of value at 28/2/2005. The total depreciation charge on equipment for the year was €9,700.

You are required to:

Record on a tabular statement the effect each of the above transactions had on the relevant asset, liability and capital accounts and ascertain the total assets and liabilities on 31/12/2005. (100 marks)

Tabular Statement Solution – NSL Ltd

	1/1/2005	Jan	Feb	Mar	Apr	May	June	July	Aug	Oct	Nov	Dec	31/12/2005
Land and buildings	260,000	120,000	170,000										550,000
Depreciation	(25,000)		25,000									(8,000)	(8,000)
Equipment	50,000							(900)					49,100
Depreciation	(20,000)							500				(9,700)	(29,200)
Goodwill		4,000											4,000
Stock	70,000				640								70,640
Debtors	90,000	10,000			(720)		270				(270)		99,280
Bad debts provision	(4,500)			(1,500)									(6,000)
Insurance						2,000						(1,500)	500
	420,500	134,000	195,000	(1,500)	(80)	2,000	270	(400)	–	–	(270)	(19,200)	730,320
Ordinary shares	290,000	80,000								30,000			400,000
Share premium	14,000	16,000								10,000			40,000
P & L balance	29,000			(1,500)	(80)		900	100	(18,500)			(17,700)	
												(1,500)	
												3,840	(5,440)
Creditors	61,000	38,000						(500)					98,500
Bank	23,000					(2,800)	(630)		18,500	(40,000)	(270)		(2,200)
Expenses due	3,500												3,500
Revaluation reserve			195,000										195,000
Rent received						4,800						(3,840)	960
	420,000	134,000	195,000	(1,500)	(80)	2,000	270	(400)	–	–	(270)	(19,200)	730,320

❷ MERCANTILE

Balance Sheet as at 1/1/2012

	Cost €	Acc. Depc €	Net €
Fixed Assets – Land and buildings	252,000	15,000	237,000
– Delivery vans	70,000	28,000	42,000
	322,000	43,000	279,000
Current Assets – Stock		68,400	
– Debtors		53,000	
– Insurance prepaid		600	
		122,000	
Less Creditors Falling Due Within 1 Year			
Creditors	29,000		
Bank	19,500		
Expenses due	2,500	51,000	
Net Current Assets			71,000
			350,000
Financed By			
Capital and reserves			
Authorised – 350,000 Ordinary shares at €1			
Issued – 250,000 Ordinary shares at €1			250,000
Share premium			25,000
Profit and Loss balance			75,000
			350,000

The following transactions took place during 2012:

Jan. Mercantile Plc decided to revalue land and buildings at €380,000 (which includes land valued at €100,000). The buildings depreciation for the year is to be 2% of book value.

Feb. Mercantile Plc bought an adjoining business which included buildings at €90,000, vans at €45,000 and creditors €15,000. The purchase price was discharged by granting the seller 100,000 shares in Mercantile at a premium of 25 cent per share.

Mar. Goods previously purchased for €2,000 were returned. A credit note was issued showing a deduction of 8% of the invoice price as a restocking charge.

May. Received a bank statement on 31 May showing a direct debit of €1,680 to cover fire insurance for the year ended 31/5/2013.

June An interim dividend of 5 cent per share was paid

July A payment of €600 was received from a debtor whose debt had been previously written-off and who now wishes to trade with Mercantile Plc again. This represents 60% of the original debt and the debtor had undertaken to pay the remainder of the debt by January 2013.

Dec. A delivery van cost €12,000 and was traded in against a new van costing €20,000. An allowance of €5,500 was made for the old van. Depreciation to date on the old van was €7,200 and the depreciation charge for the year was €17,000.

You are required to:

Record on a tabular statement the effect each of the above transactions had on the relevant asset, liability and capital accounts and ascertain the total assets and liabilities on 31/12/2012.

3 NORDIC

Balance Sheet as at 1/1/2012

	Cost €	Acc. Depc €	Net €
Fixed Assets – Land and buildings	300,000	24,000	276,000
– Equipment	48,000	18,000	30,000
	348,000	42,000	306,000
Current Assets – Stock		78,000	
– Debtors (less 5% provision)		91,200	
		169,200	
Less Creditors Falling Due Within 1 Year			
Creditors	70,800		
Bank	25,200		
Expenses due	2,400	98,400	
Net Current Assets			70,800
			376,800
Financed by			
Capital and reserves			
Authorised – 450,000 Ordinary shares at €1			
Issued – 336,000 Ordinary shares at €1			336,000
Share premium			14,400
Profit and Loss balance			26,400
			376,800

The following transactions took place during 2012:

Jan. Nordic Ltd bought an adjoining business which included buildings at €110,000, debtors €15,000 and creditors €35,000. The purchase price was discharged by granting the seller 80,000 shares in Nordic Ltd at a premium of 25c per share.

Feb. Nordic Ltd decided to revalue land and buildings at €550,000 (which includes land valued at €50,000) on 28/2/2012.

Mar. A payment of €900 was received from a debtor whose debt had been previously written-off and who now wishes to trade with Nordic Ltd again. This represents 60% of the original debt and the debtor had undertaken to pay the remainder of the debt by January 2013.

Apr. Goods previously sold for €720 were returned. The selling price of these goods was cost plus 20%. A credit note was issued showing a deduction of 10% of the selling price as a restocking charge.

May Received a bank statement on 31 May showing a direct debit of €1,800 to cover vehicle insurance for the year ending 31/3/2013 and a credit transfer received of €3,600 representing 9-months rent in advance from 1 May.

June A creditor, who was owed €400 by Nordic Ltd, accepted equipment (the book value of which was €300) in full settlement of the debt. The equipment cost €800.

Aug. An interim dividend of 4c per share was paid on all paid-up shares.

Oct. Received €45,000 from the issue of the remaining shares.

Nov. Received balance of previously written-off bad debt as agreed in March.

Dec. The buildings are to be depreciated at the rate of 2% per annum of value at 31/12/12 for a full year.

You are required to:

(a) Record on a tabular statement the effect that each of the above transactions had on the relevant asset, liability and capital accounts and ascertain the total assets and liabilities on 31/12/2012.

(b) Name 3 groups of people who would be interested in a company's financial affairs and identify the main reason why.

4 OTHELLO

Balance Sheet as at 1/1/2012

	Cost €	Acc. Depc €	Net €
Fixed Assets – Land and buildings	590,000	35,000	555,000
– Delivery vans	88,000	28,000	60,000
	678,000	63,000	615,000
Current Assets – Stock		36,000	
– Debtors (less 4% provision)		72,000	
– Insurance prepaid		800	
		108,800	
Less Creditors Falling Due Within 1 Year			
Creditors	65,000		
Bank	22,400		
Expenses due	1,800	89,200	
Net Current Assets			19,600
			634,600
Financed by			
Capital and reserves			
Authorised – 700,000 Ordinary shares at €1			
Issued – 560,000 Ordinary shares at €1			560,000
Share premium			37,000
Profit and Loss balance			37,600
			634,600

The following transactions took place during 2012:

Jan. Othello Plc decided to revalue land and buildings at €675,000 (which includes land valued at €55,000) on 1/1/2012. The buildings depreciation charge for the year is to be 2% of book value from date of valuation and purchase. The depreciation charge for the year on vehicles was €16,800.

Feb. Othello Plc bought an adjoining business which included land and buildings at €180,000, debtors €18,000 and creditors €23,000. The purchase price was discharged by granting the seller 130,000 shares in Othello Ltd at a premium of 40c per share.

Mar. A payment of €900 was received from a debtor whose debt had been previously written-off and who now wishes to trade with Othello Plc again. This represents 60% of the original debt and the debtor had undertaken to pay the remainder of the debt by January, 2013.

Apr. Goods previously purchased for €900 were returned. A credit note was issued showing a deduction of 10% of the invoice price as a restocking charge.

May Received a bank statement on 31 May showing a direct debit of €6,600 to cover insurance for year ending 31/5/2013 and a credit transfer received of €2,700 representing 9-months rent in advance from 1 May.

June A creditor, who was owed €12,000 by Othello Plc, accepted a vehicle, the book value of which was €10,800, in full settlement of the debt. The vehicle had cost €16,000.

Aug. An interim dividend of 7c per share was paid on all paid-up shares.

Sept. A delivery van costing €18,000 was traded in against a new van costing €22,000. An allowance of €13,000 was made for the new van. Depreciation to date on the old van was €6,500.

Oct. Received €13,500 from the issue of the remaining shares.

Nov. Received a first and final payment of €750 from a debtor who was declared bankrupt. This amounted to 30c in the €.

You are required to:

Record on a tabular statement the effect each of the above transactions had on the relevant asset, liability and capital accounts and ascertain the total assets and liabilities on 31/12/2012.

5 POLAR

Balance Sheet as at 1/1/2012

	Cost €	Acc. Depc €	Net €
Fixed Assets – Land and buildings	160,000	8,000	152,000
– Furniture and equipment	76,000	22,000	54,000
– Goodwill			25,000
	166,000	30,000	231,000
Current Assets – Stock		61,000	
– Debtors (less 5% provision)		57,000	
		118,000	
Less Creditors Falling Due Within 1 Year			
Creditors	61,000		
Bank	19,000		
Expenses due	3,000	83,000	
Net Current Assets			35,000
			266,000
Financed by			
Capital and reserves			
Authorised – 260,000 Ordinary shares at €1			
Issued – 180,000 Ordinary shares @ €1			180,000
Share premium			35,000
Profit and Loss balance			51,000
			266,000

The following transactions took place during 2012:

Jan. Polar Plc bought an adjoining business which included buildings at €80,000, debtors €18,000 and creditors €25,000. The purchase price was discharged by granting the seller 60,000 shares in Polar Plc at a premium of 25c per share.

Mar. A payment of €480 was received from a debtor whose debt had been previously written-off and who now wishes to trade with Polar Plc again. This represents 20% of the original debt and the debtor had undertaken to pay the remainder of the debt by December 2012.

Apr. Goods previously sold for €600 were returned. The selling price of these goods was cost plus 20%. A credit note was issued showing a deduction of 10% of the selling price as a restocking charge.

May Received a bank statement on 31 May showing a direct debit of €1,200 to cover annual fire insurance for the first 3 months of next year and a credit transfer was received of €810 representing 9-months rent in advance from 1 May.

June A creditor, who was owed €400 by Polar Plc accepted furniture, the book value of which was €240, in full settlement of the debt. The equipment cost €700.

Aug. An interim dividend of 5c per share was paid on all paid-up shares.

Oct. Received €25,000 from the issue of the remaining shares.

Nov. Received balance of previously written-off bad debt as agreed in March.

Dec. Polar Plc decided to revalue the land and buildings at €300,000 of which land is valued at €50,000. The buildings are to be depreciated at the rate of 2% per annum of the new valuation for the year.

You are required to:

(a) Record on a tabular statement the effect each of the above transactions had on the relevant asset, liability and capital accounts and ascertain the total assets and liabilities on 31/12/2012.

(b) Explain, with the aid of an example, how the principle of **double entry** works.

6 REMUS

Balance Sheet as at 1/1/2012

	Cost €	Acc. Depc €	Net €
Fixed Assets – Land and buildings	364,000	35,000	329,000
– Equipment	70,000	28,000	42,000
	334,000	63,000	371,000
Current Assets – Stock		98,000	
– Debtors (less 5% provision)		119,700	
		217,700	
Less Creditors Falling Due Within 1 Year			
Creditors	85,400		
Bank	32,200		
Expenses due	4,900	122,500	
Net Current Assets			95,200
			466,200
Financed by			
Capital and reserves			
Authorised – 560,000 Ordinary shares at €1			
Issued – 406,000 Ordinary shares at €1			406,000
Share premium			19,600
Profit and Loss balance			40,600
			466,200

The following transactions took place during 2012:

Jan. Remus Ltd bought an adjoining business which included buildings at €168,000, debtors €14,000 and creditors €53,200. The purchase price was discharged by granting the seller 112,000 shares in Remus Ltd at a premium of 20c per share.

Feb. Remus Ltd decided to revalue land and buildings at €770,000 (which includes land valued at €98,000) on 28/2/2012.

Mar. Management decided that the provision for bad debts should be raised to 6% of debtors.

Apr. Goods previously sold for €1,120 were returned. The selling price of these goods was cost plus 25%. A credit note was issued showing a deduction of 10% of the selling price as a restocking charge.

May Received a bank statement on 31 May showing a credit transfer received of €6,720 to cover 10 months rent in advance from 1 May and a direct debit of €2,800 to cover fire insurance for the year ended March next year.

June A payment of €882 was received from a debtor whose debt had been previously written-off and who now wishes to trade with Remus Ltd again. This represents 70% of the original debt and the debtor had undertaken to pay the remainder of the debt by January of next year.

July A creditor, who was owed €700 by Remus Ltd, accepted equipment (the book value of which was €560) in full settlement of the debt. The equipment cost €1,260.

Aug. An interim dividend of 5c per share was paid on all paid-up shares.

Oct. Received €56,000 from the issue of the remaining shares.

Nov. Received balance of previously written-off bad debt as agreed in June.

Dec. The buildings are to be depreciated at the rate of 2% per annum of value at 28/2/2012. The total depreciation charge on equipment for the year was €13,580.

You are required to:

(a) Record on a tabular statement the effect that each of the above transactions had on the relevant asset, liability and capital accounts and ascertain the total assets and liabilities on 31/12/2012.

(b) What is meant by **overtrading**? How can it be corrected?

7 SONATA

Balance Sheet as at 1/1/2012

	Cost €	Acc. Depc €	Net €
Fixed Assets – Land and buildings	290,000	24,000	266,000
– Equipment	20,000	10,000	10,000
– Goodwill			40,000
	310,000	34,000	316,000
Current Assets – Stock		86,000	
– Debtors (less 5% provision)		85,500	
		171,500	
Less Creditors Falling Due Within 1 Year			
Creditors	19,000		
Bank	54,000		
Expenses due	1,500	74,500	
Net Current Assets			97,000
			413,000
Financed by			
Capital and reserves			
Authorised – 600,000 Ordinary shares at €1			
Issued – 350,000 Ordinary shares at €1			350,000
Share premium			20,000
Profit and Loss balance			43,000
			413,000

The following transactions took place during 2012:

Jan. Sonata Ltd bought an adjoining business which included buildings at €190,000, debtors €24,000 and creditors €16,000. The purchase price was discharged by granting the seller 160,000 shares in Sonata Ltd at a premium of 25c per share.

Feb. Purchased goods on credit to value €25,000.

Mar. A payment of €600 was received from a debtor whose debt had been previously written-off and who now wishes to trade with Sonata Ltd again. This represents 20% of the original debt and the debtor had undertaken to pay the remainder of the debt by January of next year.

Apr. Received €96,000 from the issue of the remaining shares.

May Goods previously sold on credit for €1,500 were returned. The selling price of those goods was cost plus 25%. Owing to a delay in their return, a credit note was issued showing a 10% reduction of selling price.

June Received a bank statement on 31 May showing a credit transfer received of €1,800 to cover 9-months rent in advance from 1 May and a direct debit of €1,400 to cover fire insurance for the year ended March next year.

July Received balance of debt previously written-off as agreed in March.

Aug. An interim dividend of 8c per share was paid on all paid-up shares.

Sept. A creditor who was owed €600 by Sonata accepted equipment (the book value of which was €500) in full settlement of the debt. The equipment had cost €800.

Oct. Equipment costing €12,000 was traded in against new equipment costing €20,000. An allowance of €5,500 was made for the old equipment. Depreciation to date on the old equipment was €7,200.

Dec. 1. The land and buildings are to be revalued at €600,000 which includes land valued at €120,000.
2. The buildings are to be depreciated at the rate of 3% of the new valuation for the year.
3. All equipment to be depreciated by 10% of net book value.
4. Provision for bad debts to be adjusted to 7% of debtors.

You are required to:

(a) Record on a tabular statement the effect that each of the above transactions had on the relevant asset, liability and capital accounts and ascertain the total assets and liabilities on 31/12/2012.

(b) Name and explain 3 fundamental accounting concepts.

8 TERTIUS

Balance Sheet as at 1/1/2012

	Cost €	Acc. Depc €	Net €
Fixed Assets – Land and buildings	82,500	10,000	72,500
– Delivery vehicles	24,500	4,500	20,000
	107,000	14,500	92,500
Intangible – Goodwill			10,000
Current Assets – Stock		32,500	
– Debtors (less provision for bad debts 4%)		26,400	
– Insurance prepaid		600	
		59,500	
Less Creditors Falling Due Within 1 Year			
Creditors	22,550		
VAT	1,750		
Bank	14,750		
Expenses due	375	39,425	
Net Current Assets			20,075
			122,575
Financed by			
Capital and reserves			
Authorised – 350,000 Ordinary shares at €1			
Issued – 100,000 Ordinary shares at €1			100,000
Share premium			12,500
Profit and loss balance			10,075
			122,575

The following transactions took place during 2012:

Jan. On 1 Jan Tertius Plc revalued their land and buildings to €100,000, including land valued at €37,500. The depreciation charge for this year is 2% of book value on buildings on 31/12/2012.

Feb. On 1/1/2012 Tertius Plc purchased a business made up of the following: buildings €30,000, vehicles €7,500, stock €1,750 and creditors €3,250. The purchase price was discharged by granting the seller 30,000 shares in Tertius Plc at a premium of 20c per share.

Mar. Paid all outstanding expenses due at face value. In March it was also decided to increase bad debts provision to 5% of debtors.

Apr. Sold goods on credit for €5,280 which included VAT at 10%. These goods were marked up at 20% of cost.

June Paid insurance by cheque for €3,000 for the year ending 31 March of next year. The bank statement also showed a credit transfer receipt of €750 as a bad debt recoverable.

July Received a cheque from a debtor for €525 and allowed discount of €75.

Aug. Goods previously sold in April for €396 including VAT were returned to Tertius Plc. Owing to a delay in returning these goods a credit note for only €376 was issued.

Sept. An interim dividend of 6c per share was paid.

Oct. A payment of €250 was received from a debtor whose debt had been previously written-off. This represents 20% of the original debt, and the debtor has undertaken to pay the remainder in January of next year.

Nov. A delivery motor bike costing €2,500 was traded in against a new bike costing €8,000. A trade-in allowance of €1,500 was given on the old bike, which had been depreciated by €600 at the date of disposal. The annual charge for depreciation on delivery vehicles was €1,125.

You are required to:

(a) Record on a **tabular statement** the effect that each of the above transactions had on the relevant assets and liabilities showing the total assets and liabilities on 31/12/2012.

(b) Has Tertius got **liquidity** problems? Explain your answer.

9 QUALTER

Balance Sheet as at 1/1/2012

	Cost €	Acc. Depc €	Net €
Intangible – Goodwill			50,000
Fixed Assets – Land and buildings	160,000	16,000	144,000
– Equipment	91,000	21,000	70,000
	251,000	37,000	264,000
Current Assets – Stock		48,000	
– Debtors (less 5% provision)		57,000	
– Insurance prepaid		2,000	
		107,000	
Less Creditors Falling Due Within 1 Year			
Creditors	22,000		
Bank	47,000		
VAT	5,600		
Rent receivable prepaid	4,000	78,600	
Net Current Assets			28,400
			292,400
Financed by			
Capital and reserves			
Authorised – 340,000 Ordinary shares at €1			
Issued – 200,000 Ordinary shares at €1			200,000
Share premium			50,000
Profit and Loss balance			42,400
			292,400

The following transactions took place during 2012:

Jan. Qualter Ltd bought an adjoining business which included buildings at €170,000, debtors €10,000 and creditors €26,200. The purchase price was discharged by granting the seller 140,000 shares in Qualter Ltd at a premium of 20c per share.

Feb. Qualter Ltd decided to revalue land and buildings at €400,000 (which includes land valued at €50,000) on 28/2/2012.

Mar. Management decided that the provision for bad debts should be raised to 6% of debtors.

Apr. Goods previously sold for €1,120 were returned. The selling price of these goods was cost plus 25%. A credit note was issued showing a deduction of 10% of the selling price as a restocking charge.

May Received a bank statement on 31 May showing:

1. A credit transfer received of €8,000 to cover 10-months rent in advance from 1 May .
2. A direct debit of €5,600 to cover fire insurance for the year ended March next year.
3. Bank charges and interest €350.
4. Bad debt recovered €500 was received. This was 20% of original debt and the customer guaranteed to pay the remainder in full before the year end.

June An extension was added to the new buildings. Materials of €10,000 from trading stock was used, as was business labour of €15,000. A contractor was paid €30,000 and architect's fees for the extension amounted to €1,500.

July A creditor, who was owed €1,600 by Qualter Ltd, accepted equipment (the book value of which was €1,120) in full settlement of the debt. The equipment cost €2,520.

Aug. Sales on credit for €12,000 included VAT at 25%. These goods were marked up at 50% on cost.

Sept. The remainder of bad debt recoverable, as agreed in May, was paid up less a 5% discount.

Nov. Equipment costing €10,000 was traded in against new equipment costing €25,000. The depreciation to date on the old equipment was €4,500, and a loss on disposal/trade-in of €1,500 was incurred. The depreciation charge on equipment for the year was €14,500.

Dec. The buildings are to be depreciated at the rate of 2% per annum of value at 31/12/2012.

You are required to:

(a) Record on a tabular statement the effect that each of the above transactions had on the relevant asset, liability and capital accounts. Ascertain the total assets and liabilities on 31/12/2012.

(b) What is meant by **leaning on the trade**? Name 3 dangers associated with this practice.

TOPIC 7

Club a/c's

I refuse to join any club that would have me as a member.

Groucho Marx

1 BARDS VALLEY – SAMPLE EXAM QUESTION

Included in the assets and liabilities of the Bards Valley Golf Club on 1/1/2007 were: Clubhouse and Course €750,000, Bar stock €7,000, Equipment at cost €26,000, Life membership €40,000, Bar Debtors €535, Bar Creditors €6,000, Wages due €2,500, Levy Reserve Fund €50,000, Subscriptions in advance €1,600 and Investment interest due €400.

The following Receipts and Payment account was prepared for the year ending 31/12/2007

Receipts	**€**	**Payments**	**€**
Bank current account	14,000	Catering costs	8,000
Interest on 5% investments	1,600	Sundry expenses	186,400
Bar receipts	110,460	Bar purchases	78,500
Catering receipts	14,000	Golf lessons for teams	4,600
Entrance fees	15,000	Equipment	45,000
Annual sponsorship	25,000	Transfer to Building Society	60,000
Subscriptions	250,000	Repayment of €30,000 loan on 31/5/07 with 18-months' interest	33,600
		Balance	13,960
	430,060		430,060

The following information is also available:

(i) Bar stock €8,500 on 31/12/2007.
(ii) Bar debtors €275, Bar creditors €3,220, on 31/12/2007.
(iii) Equipment owned on 31/12/2007 is to be depreciated at 20% on cost.
(iv) Clubhouse to be depreciated at 2% on cost.
(v) Subscriptions include:
   1. One life, bringing the total up to 21.
   2. Subscriptions for 2008 of €2,600.
   3. Levy of €250 on all 200 members for the year 2007.
   4. Levy of €250 on 10 members due from 2006.
(vi) Life membership is to be credited to income over a 10-year period commencing in 2007.

You are required to:

(a) Show the club's Accumulated Fund on 1/1/2007.
(b) Show the Income and Expenditure account for the year ending 31/12/2007.
(c) Show the club's Balance Sheet on 31/12/2007.
(d) Explain with an example what is meant by a Special Purpose Profit and Loss Account.
(e) If it were to introduce a further 4-year levy to fund a €250,000 extension, what points would you as an ordinary member make?

Sample Solution Bards Valley

(a) Accumulated Fund 1/1/2007

Assets:		
Clubhouse	750,000	
Bar stock	7,000	
Equipment	26,000	
Bar debtors	535	
Investments	24,000	
Investment interest due	400	
Bank current account	14,000	
Levy due	2,500	824,435
Liabilities:		
Life membership	40,000	
Bar creditors	6,000	
Levy reserve fund	50,000	
Wages due	2,500	
Loan	30,000	
Loan interest due	2,600	
Subscriptions prepaid	1,600	(132,700)
Accumulated fund		691,735

(b) Income And Expenditure Account for year ending 31/12/2007

Income		
Bar profit	35,980	
Investment interest	1,200	
Entrance fees	15,000	
Catering profit (14,000 − 8,000)	6,000	
Annual sponsorship	25,000	
Subscriptions	194,500	
Life membership	4,200	281,880
Less Expenditure		
Sundry expenses (186,400 − 2,500)	183,900	
Golf lessons	4,600	
Loan interest	1,000	
Depreciation – equipment	14,200	
Depreciation – clubhouse	15,000	(218,700)
Surplus income over expenditure		63,180

(c) Balance Sheet on 31/12/2007

Fixed Assets			
Clubhouse	750,000	15,000	735,000
Equipment	71,000	14,200	56,800
	821,000	29,200	
Financial			
5% investments	24,000		
Building society	60,000		84,000
			875,800
Current Assets			
Closing stock of bar	8,500		
Bar debtors	275		
Bank	13,960	22,735	
Creditors falling due for less than 1 year			
Bar creditors	3,220		
Subscriptions prepaid	2,600	(5,820)	16,915
			892,715
Financed by			
Accumulated fund		691,735	
Surplus income over expenditure		63,180	
Life subscriptions		37,800	
Levy fund		100,000	892,715

Notes to Accounts

1. Bar Profit							
Sales	110,460 +	275	−535				= **110,200**
Purchases	78,500 +	3,220 −	6,000				= **75,720**
Bar profit	7,000 +	75,720 −	8,500	=	74,220 −	110,200 =	**35,980**
2. Subscriptions	250,000 −	2,000 −	2,600 −	50,000 −	2,500 +	1,600 =	**194,500**
3. Loan interest	13 months	=	2,600	Acc Fund			= **2,600**
4. Investment interest	1,600 −	400					= **1,200**
5. Life subs	40,000 +	2,000 =	42,000 −	**4,200**			= **37,800**

(d) Special Purpose Profit and Loss account

Sometimes non-profit making organisations prepare a Profit and Loss a/c for activities carried out to make a profit, e.g. lottery, dances, bar etc. All expenses and revenue relating to that activity are entered in a special Profit and Loss account and then transferred to the Income and Expenditure a/c.

(e) Introduction of Proposed Levy

Club has surplus of €63,180
Cash balance of €13,960
Building society investment of €60,000
5% government investments €24,000
Loan repaid and equipment of €45,000
So in my view there is no need to introduce a levy as all of these will provide almost €100,000 of available funds.

2 ATHLONE ATHLETICS

Included in the assets and liabilities of the Athlone Athletics Club on 1/1/2012 were: Clubhouse €850,000, Bar stock €4,600, Equipment at cost €54,000, Life membership €30,000, Bar Debtors €900, Bar Creditors €2,650, Levy Reserve Fund €24,000, Subscriptions prepaid €2,000, Investment interest due €150 and Wages due €1,600.

The following Receipts and Payment account was prepared for the year ending 31/12/2012

Receipts	€	Payments	€
Bar receipts	115,780	Balance	1,560
Catering receipts	5,160	Bar purchases	75,200
Annual sponsorship	40,000	Equipment	32,000
Investment income	3,000	Transfer to building society	100,000
Subscriptions	275,920	Catering costs	3,610
Entrance fees	17,600	Repayment of €35,000 loan on 30/6/2012 with 21-months' interest	38,780
		Sundry expenses	97,600
		Balance	108,710
	457,460		457,460

The following information is also available:

(i) Bar stock €5,200 on 31/12/2012.
(ii) Bar debtors €430, Bar creditors €3,270 on 31/12/2012.
(iii) Equipment owned on 31/12/2012 is valued at €85,000.
(iv) Subscriptions include:
  1. 3 Life memberships of €5,000 each.
  2. Subscriptions for 2013 of €2,500.
  3. Levy of €250 on all 300 members for the year 2012.
  4. Levy of €250 on 5 members due from 2011.
(v) Life membership is to be written-off over a 10-year period commencing in 2012.
(vi) Investment income is on 7.5% government investments.
(vii) The club depreciates the clubhouse at 3% per annum.
(viii) On 31/12/2012 decided to revalue the clubhouse to €1,200,000.

You are required to:

(a) Show the club's Accumulated Fund on 1/1/2012.
(b) Show the Income and Expenditure account for the year ending 31/12/2012.
(c) Show the club's Balance Sheet on 31/12/2012.
(d) Advise the club on how the purchase of extra land of €250,000 could be funded.

3 Bray Boxing

Included in the assets and liabilities of the Bray Boxing Club on 1/1/2012 were: Clubhouse €340,000, Land €180,000, Bar stock €10,700, Machinery at cost €34,000, Life membership €6,000, Bar Debtors €700, Bar Creditors €1,780, Levy Reserve Fund, €13,000, Investment interest due €250, Subscriptions due €750, 8% Investment €12,000.

The following Receipts and Payment account was prepared for the year ending 31/12/2012

Receipts	€	Payments	€
Bank current account	2,400	Catering costs	15,480
Interest on 8% investments	960	Sundry expenses	61,420
Bar receipts	109,000	Bar purchases	90,800
Catering receipts	28,640	Machinery	34,000
Sale of machinery (cost €8,000)	2,700	Purchase of 5% Investment on 1/7/2012	25,000
Subscriptions	103,000	Repayment of €20,000 loan on 31/12/2012 with 18-months' interest	23,600
Balance	3,600		
	250,300		250,300

The following information is also available:

(i) Bar stock €12,800 on 31/12/2012.

(ii) Bar debtors €850, bar creditors €3,900 on 31/12/2012.

(iii) Machinery owned on 31/12/2012 is to be depreciated at 20% on cost. Also note that all machinery is given at cost and depreciation has been accumulated for 2 years by 1/1/2012.

(iv) Clubhouse to be depreciated at 2% on cost.

(v) Subscriptions include:
1. 4 life of €5,000 each.
2. Subscriptions for 2013 of €880.
3. Levy of €60 on all 300 members for the year 2012.
4. Levy of €420 due from members for 2011.

(vi) Life membership is to be written-off over a 5-year period commencing in 2012.

You are required to:

(a) Show the club's Accumulated Fund on 1/1/2012.

(b) Show the Income and Expenditure account for the year ending 31/12/2012.

(c) Show the club's Balance Sheet on 31/12/2012.

(d) The club intends to undertake capital expenditure of €80,000 in 2013. Would you anticipate any difficulties in funding of such a project?

4 CLARA CURLING

Included in the assets and liabilities of the Clara Curling Club on 1/1/2012 were: Clubhouse and Rink €290,000, Bar stock €4,100, Equipment at cost €15,000, Life membership €36,000, Bar Debtors €260, Bar Creditors €1,450, Levy Reserve Fund €40,000, Subscriptions prepaid €1,050, Investment interest due €420, Wages due €200.

The following Receipts and Payment account was prepared for the year ending 31/12/2012

Receipts	€	Payments	€
Bar receipts	12,400	Balance	1,850
Catering receipts	10,200	Bar purchases	9,230
Annual sponsorship	4,800	Equipment	8,000
8% investment interest	1,700	Coaching	1,600
Subscriptions	36,200	Catering costs	8,500
Entrance fees	700	Repayment of 5% loan on 30/6/12 with 18-months' interest	17,200
		Balance	19,620
	66,000		66,000

The following information is also available:

(i) Bar stock of €2,800 on 31/12/2012.
(ii) Bar debtors €140, bar creditors €250 on 31/12/2012.
(iii) Equipment owned on 31/12/2012 is to be depreciated at 10% on cost.
(iv) Clubhouse and Courts to be depreciated at 2% on cost.
(v) Subscriptions include:
  1. Three life of €2,000 each.
  2. Subscriptions for 2013 of €1,800.
  3. Levy of €50 on all 40 members for the year 2012.
  4. Levy of €50 on 20 members due from 2011.
(vi) Life membership is to be written-off over a 10-year period commencing in 2012.
(vii) Wages due on 1/1/2012 were owed to the club coach.
(viii) The club decided to revalue the clubhouse and rink to €450,000 on 31/12/2012.

You are required to:

(a) Show the club's Accumulated Fund on 1/1/2012.
(b) Show the Income and Expenditure account for the year ending 31/12/2012.
(c) Show the club's Balance Sheet on 31/12/2012.
(d) Indicate the points you, as treasurer, would make to a proposal to reduce the subscriptions by 10%.

5 DUNSHAUGHLIN DRAUGHTS

Included in the assets and liabilities of the Dunshaughlin Draughts Club on 1/1/2012 were: Clubhouse and Land €560,000, Bar stock €29,000, Equipment at cost €36,000, Book value of equipment €16,000, Life membership €40,000, Bar Debtors €100, Bar Creditors €7,700, Levy Reserve Fund €8,000, Investment interest due €250, Insurance prepaid €400, Stock of heating oil €400, Catering stock €1,000.

The following Receipts and Payment account was prepared for the year ending 31/12/2012

Receipts	€	Payments	€
Bar debtors	1,200	Bank current account	1,300
Interest on 7.5% investments	1,750	Catering costs	1,500
Bar receipts	98,700	Insurance paid to 31/1/2013	2,200
Catering receipts	4,500	Extension	80,000
Sale of equipment (on 1/7/2012)	4,000	Bar purchases	64,700
		Equipment 1/7/2012	14,000
Subscriptions	49,200	Purchase of prize bonds	20,000
Disco receipts	40,400	Light and heat	5,400
Annual grant	3,000	Loan interest at 11.5% for 10 months paid 30/10/2012	1,150
Balance	1,600	Disco expenses	14,100
	204,350		204,350

The following information is also available:

(i) Bar stock €22,000, catering stock €700, stock of heating oil €600, and electricity due €700 on 31/12/2012.

(ii) Bar debtors €300, bar creditors €6,100 on 31/12/2012.

(iii) The Equipment sold during the year cost €10,000 and was purchased on 1/7/2007. All equipment is depreciated by 10% per annum on cost.

(iv) Insurance on 1/1/2012 was paid up to 28/2/2012, Investment interest on 1/1/2012 was for 2 months.

(v) Subscriptions include:
1. Subscriptions for 2013 of €1,000 paid in advance by 10 members.
2. Levy of €20 on all 400 members for the year 2012.
3. Levy due from 10 members for 2011.

(vi) The 11.5% loan was acquired in 2011 and all interest payments during 2011 were paid.

You are required to:

(a) Show the club's Accumulated Fund on 1/1/2012.

(b) Show the Income and Expenditure account for the year ending 31/12/2012.

(c) Prepare the Balance Sheet on 31/12/2012.

(d) What are the main differences between a **levy** and a **subscription**?

(e) List 3 duties of the treasurer of a club.

6 ELPHIN EQUESTRIAN

Included in the assets and liabilities of the Elphin Equestrian Club on 1/1/2012 were: Clubhouse €350,000, Land and stables €400,000, Bar stock €11,700, Machinery at cost €44,000, Life membership €16,000, Bar Debtors €1,250, Bar Creditors €5,550, 8% Investment €20,000, Levy Reserve Fund €20,000, Subscriptions due €1,200, Investment interest due €620.

The following Receipts and Payment account was prepared for the year ending 31/12/2012

Receipts	**€**	**Payments**	**€**
Annual grant	17,500	Bank current	4,400
Interest on investments	1,200	Catering costs	13,300
Bar receipts	127,500	Sundry expenses	85,900
Catering receipts	23,300	Bar purchases	71,200
Sale of machinery (cost €9,000)	2,000	Machinery	50,000
Subscriptions	124,400	Purchase of 6% Investment on 1/10/2012	25,000
		Repayment of €24,000 loan on 31/12/12 with 16-months' interest	27,520
		Balance	18,580
	295,900		295,900

The following information is also available:

(i) Bar stock €9,700 on 31/12/2012.
(ii) Bar debtors €1,540, Bar creditors €8,800 on 31/12/2012.
(iii) Machinery owned on 31/12/2012 is to be depreciated at 20% on cost.
(iv) Clubhouse to be depreciated at 2% on cost.
(v) Subscriptions include:
  1. One life bringing the total up to 5.
  2. Subscriptions for 2013 of €640.
  3. Levy of €50 on all 300 members for the year 2012.
  4. Levy of €300 due from 2011.
(vi) Life membership is to be credited to income over a 4-year period commencing in 2012.

You are required to:

(a) Show the club's Accumulated Fund on 1/1/2012.
(b) Show the Income and Expenditure account for the year ending 31/12/2012.
(c) Show the club's Balance Sheet on 31/12/2012.
(d) Explain, with an example, what is meant by a Special Purpose Profit and Loss account.
(e) What is the main difference between **annual subscriptions** and **levy reserve fund**?

7 FERBANE FENCING

Included in the assets and liabilities of Ferbane Fencing Club on 1/1/2012 were: Clubhouse and Land €194,000, Bar stock €6,700, Equipment at cost €18,600, Life membership €20,000, Bar Debtors €240, Bar Creditors €5,280, Levy Reserve Fund €6,840, Provision for depreciation €5,000.

The following Receipts and Payment account was prepared for the year ending 31/12/2012

Receipts	**€**	**Payments**	**€**
Bank current account	3,400	Bar purchases – cash	12,500
Bank deposit account	15,000	Equipment	4,000
7% investment interest	2,100	Bar creditors	42,100
(over 2 years)		Sundry expenses	19,840
Sale of equipment		Purchase on 1/7/2012 of	
(cost €2,600, NBV €1,000)	1,100	8% investments	60,000
Disco receipts	24,600	Repayment of €12,000	
Bar receipts	84,900	Loan on 30/6/2012 with	
Subscriptions	39,440	2-years' interest	14,000
Interest on deposit a/c	500	Balance – Deposit a/c	15,000
		– Current a/c	3,600
	171,040		171,040

The following information is also available:

(i) Bar stock €5,300 on 31/12/2012.

(ii) Bar Debtors €510, Bar creditors €4,900.on 31/12/2012.

(iii) Equipment owned on 31/12/2012 is to be depreciated at 10% on cost.

(iv) Interest on Deposit a/c is 5%.

(v) Subscriptions include:

1. Another Life bringing total to 41.
2. Subscriptions for 2013 of €340.
3. Levy of €10 on all 700 members for the year 2012.
4. Levy of €600 due from 2011.

You are required to:

(a) Show the Club's Accumulated Fund on 1/1/2012.

(b) Show the Income and Expenditure account for the year ending 31/12/2012.

(c) Show the clubs Balance Sheet on 31/12/2012.

(d) The club intends to undertake capital expenditure of €60,000 in 2013. What advice would you give for the funding of such a project?

8 GALWAY GOLF

Included in the assets and liabilities of the Galway Golf Club on 1/1/2012 were: Clubhouse and Course €300,000, Bar stock €6,000, Equipment and machinery at cost €20,000, Life membership €35,000, Bar Debtors €566, Bar Creditors €6,500, Levy Reserve Fund €40,000, Subscriptions due €750, Investment interest due €400, Wages due €3,500.

The following Receipts and Payment account was prepared for the year ending 31/12/2012

Receipts	**€**	**Payments**	**€**
Bank current	2,000	Catering costs	18,870
Interest on 5% investments	1,600	Sundry expenses	45,000
Bar receipts	99,870	Bar purchases	72,000
Catering receipts	43,542	Equipment	32,000
Sale of machinery (cost €9,600)	4,700	Purchase of 6% investment on 1/6/2012	30,000
Subscriptions	105,600	Repayment of 8% loan on 30/6/2012 with 18-months' interest	33,600
		Balance	25,842
	257,312		257,312

The following information is also available:

(i) Bar stock €5,600 on 31/12/2012.
(ii) Bar debtors €348, bar creditors €7,890 on 31/12/2012.
(iii) Equipment owned on 31/12/2012 is to be depreciated at 20% on cost. Also note that all equipment is given at cost and depreciation has been accumulated for 3 years by 1/1/2012.
(iv) Clubhouse to be depreciated at 2% on cost.
(v) Subscriptions include:
  1. Four life of €5,000 each.
  2. Subscriptions for 2013 of €950.
  3. Levy of €400 on all 40 members for the year 2012.
  4. Levy of €450 due from members for 2011.

Life membership is to be written-off over a 10-year period commencing in 2012.

You are required to:

(a) Show the club's Accumulated Fund on 1/1/2012.
(b) Show the Income and Expenditure account for the year ending 31/12/2012.
(c) Show the club's Balance Sheet on 31/12/2012.
(d) The club intends to undertake capital expenditure of €120,000 in 2013. What advice would you give for the funding of such a project?

TOPIC

8

Service Firm a/c's (Including Farm Accounts)

Thinking is the hardest work there is, which is probably the reason why so few engage in it.

Henry Ford

1 ELMS NURSING – SAMPLE EXAM QUESTION

The following were included in the assets and liabilities of Elms Nursing Home Ltd on 1/1/2009: Buildings at cost €550,000, Equipment at cost €45,000, Minibus at cost €50,000, Stock in shop €3,300, Heating oil €1,600, Creditors for supplies to nursing home €1,000, 5% Investments €30,000, Contract cleaning prepaid €200, Clients' fees paid in advance €4,000, Authorised Capital €450,000, Issued Capital €320,000.

All fixed assets have 3-years' accumulated depreciation on 1/1/2009.

The following is the Receipts and Payments account for year ended 31/12/2009

Balance at bank on 1/1/2009	8,250	Wages and salaries	85,500
Investment income	1,000	Insurance	6,400
Clients' fees	340,000	Equipment	15,000
Shop receipts	40,000	Repayment of €40,000 loan on 1/05/2009 with 18 months interest	48,100
Balance at bank 31/12/2009	75,450	Extension	200,000
		Contract cleaning	3,500
		Light and heat	3,100
		Telephone and stationery	1,600
		Purchases – shop	28,000
		Purchases – supplies	35,900
		Laundry	2,000
		New minibus	35,000
		Dishonoured cheque fee	600
	464,700		464,700

The following information and instructions are to be taken into account:

(i) Closing stock at 31/12/2009: shop €1,500, heating oil €300.

(ii) Clients' fees include fees for 2010 of €5,000. Clients' fees in arrears for 2009 are €500.

(iii) Cleaning is done under contract, payable monthly, and includes a payment of €400 for January 2010.

(iv) The dishonoured cheque was not recovered and was written-off as a bad debt.

(v) Wages and salaries include €18,000 paid to a secretary who also runs the shop. It is estimated that 40% of this salary, €250 of the light and heat, €800 of the insurance, and €350 of the telephone are attributable to the shop.

(vi) Creditors for supplies to the nursing home at 31/12/2009 are €1,800.

(vii) Electricity due on 31/12/2009 is €320.

(viii) On 31/12/2009 it was decided to revalue the buildings at €900,000.

(ix) Depreciation to be provided as follows:
1. Buildings 2% of cost for the full year.
2. Equipment at 15% of cost per annum.
3. Minibus at 20% of cost per annum from date of purchase to date of sale.

The minibus held on 1/1/2009 was purchased on 1/1/2006 and was traded in on 1/7/2009 against a new minibus. The trade-in allowance was €7,000 against a new minibus valued at €42,000.

You are required to:

(a) Calculate the company's reserves on 1/1/2009.

(b) Calculate the profit/loss from the health shop for the year ended 31/12/2009.

(c) Prepare a Profit and Loss account for the year ended 31/12/2009.

(d) Prepare a Balance Sheet on 31/12/2009.

(e) The management of the home is considering an increase of 10% in clients' fees. What advice would you give? Explain your answer.

Sample Solution Elms Nursing Home

(a) Reserves on 1/1/2009

Assets		
Buildings (550,000 − 33,000)	517,000	
Equipment (45,000 − 20,250)	24,750	
Minibus (50,000 − 30,000)	20,000	
Stock	3,300	
Oil	1,600	
Cleaning prepaid	200	
5% investments	30,000	
Bank	8,250	605,100
Liabilities		
Clients prepaid	4,000	
Creditors	1,000	
Loan	40,000	
Loan interest due	6,300	
Capital	320,000	(371,300)
Reserves		233,800

(b) Profit and Loss Account of Shop for Year Ending 31/12/2009

Receipts		40,000
Less cost of sales		
Opening stock	3,300	
Purchases	28,000	
Less closing stock	(1,500)	(29,800)
Gross profit		10,200
Less wages	7,200	
Insurance	800	
Light and heat	250	
Telephone	350	8,600
Profit on shop		1,600

(c) Profit and Loss Account for Year Ending 31/12/2009

Income		
Shop profit	**1,600**	
Investment interest	**1,500**	
Clients' fees	**339,500**	342,600
Less expenditure		
Laundry	2,000	
Insurance (800)	5,600	
Telephone (350)	1,250	
Wages (7,200)	78,300	
Loan interest	**1,800**	
Cleaning	**3,300**	
Bad debt	600	
Light and heat	**4,470**	
Purchases of supplies	**36,700**	
Depreciation – buildings	15,000	
Derpreciation – equipment	9,000	
Depreciation – minibus	9,200	
Loss on sale of minibus	8,000	175,220
Profit		167,380
Add reserves 1/1/2009		233,800
Profit and Loss 31/12/2009		401,180

(d) Balance Sheet on 31/12/2009

Fixed Assets	Cost	Depc	Value
Buildings	900,000		900,000
Equipment	60,000	29,250	30,750
Minibus	42,000	4,200	37,800
Financial	1,002,000	33,450	968,550
5% investments			30,000
			998,550
Current Assets			
Closing stock (1,500 + 300)	1,800		
Cleaning prepaid	400		
Clients' fees due	500		
Interest due	500	3,200	
Creditors Falling Due for Less Than 1 Year			
Creditors	1,800		
Fees prepaid	5,000		
Bank overdraft	75,450		
Electricity due	320	82,570	79,370
Total Net Assets			919,180
Financed by		Authorised	Issued
Share capital		450,000	320,000
Profit and Loss balance			401,180
Revenue reserve			198,000
			919,180

Notes to Accounts

Loan interest	14 months	=		6,300		so 4 months	=	**1,800**
Fees	340,000	+	4,000	−	5,000 +	500	=	**339,500**
Investment interest	1,500	−				1,000	=	**500**
Cleaning	3,500	+			200 −	400	=	**3,300**
Light and heat	3,100 + 1,600	−	250	−	300 +	320	=	**4,470**
Purchases of supplies	35,900	−	1,000		+	1,800	=	**36,700**
Minibus	50,000	−	50,000		+	42,000	=	**42,000**
Accumulated depreciation	30,000	+	9,200		−	35,000	=	**4,200**
Disposal	50,000	−	35,000		−	7,000	=	**8,000**
Depreciation this year	5,000	+				4,200	=	**9,200**
Revaluation	150,000	+			15,000 +	33,000	=	**198,000**
Depreciation of equipment	45,000	+	15,000			× 15%	=	**9,000**

(e) 10% Increase in Clients' fees would increase income by €33,950

No need to increase fees.
Business is profitable with return on capital of 18.4%.
Loan of €40,000 repaid, equipment €15,000 purchased and minibus purchased.
58% of a new extension financed also from cash receipts.
In today's climate profit and cash flow are excellent while competition is increasing and costs are falling.
Charges should not be increasing.

2 Anderson Clinic

The following were included in the assets and liabilities of The Anderson Clinic on 1/1/2012: Surgery at cost €280,000, Equipment at cost €70,000, Vehicle at cost €22,000, Owed from medical insurance scheme €3,800, 9% Mortgage €100,000, Stock of supplies €4,600, Creditors for supplies €1,400, 8% Investments €120,000, Capital €368,600.

Fixed assets are given at cost and have 2 years' accumulated depreciation written-off by 1/1/2012.

The following is the Receipts and Payments account for year ended 31/12/2012

Balance at bank on 1/1/2012	10,600	Wages and salaries	15,200
Investment income	4,000	Car expenses	5,200
Receipts from patients	94,300	Stationery	3,980
Sale of equipment	14,200	Interest on mortgage	11,000
(cost €18,000)		Investment bonds 31/12/2012	25,000
Medical insurance scheme	46,800	Drawings	35,800
		Sponsorship	3,100
		Light and heat	12,820
		Insurance	11,400
		Medical supplies	26,400
		Balance	20,000
	169,900		169,900

The following information and instructions are to be taken into account:

(i) Stock of medical supplies on 31/12/2012 is €5,200.

(ii) The closing figure for cash drawings includes wages at €1,800 for 2 weeks paid to a substitute and you are required to provide for a further week's wages due.

(iii) The closing figure for the bank does not take into account a standing order of €300 for insurance paid and a dishonoured cheque of €180 from a private patient.

(iv) 40% of light and heat and insurance is for private use.

(v) Fees due from a medical insurance scheme are €4,100 and private patients at €380.

(vi) Depreciation to be provided as follows:
1. Surgery 2% of cost for the full year.
2. Equipment 15% of cost per annum.
3. Vehicle 20% of cost per annum.

You are required to:

(a) Prepare a Profit and Loss account for the year ended 31/12/2012.

(b) Prepare a Balance Sheet on 31/12/2012.

3 Beautiful Body

The following were included in the assets and liabilities of The Beautiful Body Centre Ltd on 1/1/2012: Buildings at cost €420,000, Equipment at cost €80,000, Furniture at cost €90,000, Stock of health food for sale €2,400, Heating oil €540, Creditors for supplies to health centre €3,680, Investments €30,000, Contract cleaning prepaid €480, Clients' fees paid in advance €5,400, Authorised Capital €600,000, Issued Capital €400,000.

All fixed assets have 3-years' accumulated depreciation on 1/1/2012.

The following is the Receipts and Payments account for the year ended 31/12/2012

Balance at bank on 1/1/2012	4,200	Wages and salaries	91,400
Investment income	4,250	Laundry	2,300
Clients' fees	221,000	Equipment	12,000
Shop receipts	68,400	Repayment of €40,000 loan on 1/5/2012 with 15-months' interest	43,000
Balance at bank 31/12/2012	21,650	Extension	70,000
		Contract cleaning	4,800
		Light and heat	3,400
		Insurance	7,800
		Telephone and stationery	2,400
		Purchases – shop	39,600
		Purchases – supplies	42,800
	319,500		319,500

The following information and instructions are to be taken into account:

(i) Closing stock at 31/12/2012: shop €3,200, heating oil €720.

(ii) Clients' fees include fees for next year of €5,200. Clients' fees in arrears for 2012 are €670.

(iii) Cleaning is done under contract payable monthly and includes a payment of €700 for January next year.

(iv) The closing figure for the bank does not take into account a dishonoured cheque of €110 received from a client and lodged in late December.

(v) Wages and salaries include €18,000 per annum paid to the receptionist, who also runs the shop. It is estimated that 40% of this salary, €330 of the light and heat, €900 of the insurance and €200 of the telephone are attributable to the shop.

(vi) On 31/12/2012 it was decided to revalue buildings at €650,000.

(vii) Electricity due 31/12/2012 was €480.

(viii) Creditors for supplies to the health centre at 31/12/2012 are €2,200.

(ix) Depreciation to be provided as follows:
1. Buildings 2% of cost for the full year.
2. Equipment at 20% of cost per annum.
3. Furniture at 20% of cost per annum.

(x) All investment interest due for 2012 was received.

You are required to:

(a) Calculate the company's reserves on 1/1/2012.

(b) Calculate the profit/loss from the health shop for the year ended 31/12/2012.

(c) Prepare a Profit and Loss account for the year ended 31/12/2012.

(d) Prepare a Balance Sheet on 31/12/2012.

(e) Explain the purpose of preparing Service Firm accounts.

4 OVERWEIGHT HEALTH

The following were included in the assets and liabilities of Overweight Health Centre Ltd on 1/1/2012: Buildings at cost €200,000, Equipment at cost €100,000, Furniture at cost €50,000, Stock of health food for sale €1,000, Heating oil €580, Creditors for supplies to health centre €4,500, 5% Investments €75,000, Investment interest due €500, Contract cleaning prepaid €500, Members' fees due €3,000, Members' fees paid in advance €5,800, Authorised Capital €400,000, Issued Capital €200,000.

All fixed assets have 2-years' accumulated depreciation on 1/1/2012.

The following is the Receipts and Payments account for year ended 31/12/2012

Balance at bank on 1/1/2012	7,450	Wages and salaries	111,250
Investment income	600	Insurance	4,250
Members' fees	120,000	Equipment (1/10/2012)	10,000
Shop receipts	15,400	Repayment of €30,000 loan on 30/06/2012 with 18-months' interest	36,000
Balance at Bank 31/12/2012	89,400	4% Bonds 1/7/2012	20,000
		Extension	20,000
		Contract cleaning	3,350
		Light and heat	950
		Telephone and stationery	1,450
		Purchases – shop	14,350
		Purchases – supplies	11,250
	232,850		232,850

The following information and instructions are to be taken into account:

(i) Closing stock at 31/12/2012: shop €1,730, heating oil €200, health supplies €1,100.

(ii) Members' fees include fees for next year of €2,250. Clients' fees in arrears for 2012 are €800.

(iii) Cleaning is done under contract payable monthly and includes a payment of €250 for January next.

(iv) The closing figure for bank does not take into account bank charges of €100 and a dishonoured cheque. €200 received from a member and lodged in late December.

(v) Wages and salaries include €400 attributable to the shop. It is estimated that 10% of the insurance and telephone are attributable to the shop.

(vi) Creditors for the health centre at €650, and shop €400, at 31/12/2012.

(vii) On 31/12/2012 it was decided to revalue buildings at €350,000.

(viii) Depreciation to be provided as follows:

1. Buildings 2% of cost for the full year.
2. Equipment at 20% of cost per annum.
3. Furniture at 20% of cost per annum.

You are required to:

(a) Calculate the company's reserves on 1/1/2012.

(b) Calculate the profit/loss from the health shop for the year ended 31/12/2012.

(c) Prepare a Profit and Loss account for the year ended 31/12/2012.

(d) Prepare a Balance Sheet on 31/12/2012.

(e) Explain what is meant by **enterprise analysis account**.

5 WEIGHT WATCHERS

The following were included in the assets and liabilities of Weight Watchers Health Centre Ltd on 1/1/2012: Buildings at cost €240,000, Equipment at cost €30,000, Furniture at cost €12,000, Stock of health food for sale €3,100, Heating oil €240, Creditors for supplies to health centre €3,450, 4% Investments €40,000, Contract cleaning prepaid €640, Clients' fees paid in advance €1,800, Authorised Capital €325,000, Issued Capital €270,000.

All fixed assets have 3-years accumulated depreciation on 1/1/2012.

The following is the Receipts and Payments Account for year ended 31/12/2012

Balance at bank on 1/1/2012	10,600	Wages and salaries	45,325
Investment income	1,600	Laundry	2,600
Clients' fees	92,400	Equipment	4,500
Shop receipts	38,150	Repayment of €12,500 loan on 1/3/2012 with 20-months' interest	14,375
		Extension	20,000
		Contract cleaning	7,310
		Light and heat	3,100
		Insurance	6,400
		Telephone and stationery	1,840
		Purchases – shop	20,050
		Purchases – supplies	7,450
		Balance on 31/12/2012	4,200
	142,750		142,750

The following information and instructions are to be taken into account:

(i) Closing stock at 31/12/2012: shop €3,700, heating oil €180.
(ii) Clients' fees include fees for next year of €2,400. Clients' fees in arrears for 2012 are €475.
(iii) Cleaning is done under contract payable monthly and includes a payment of €700 for January next year.
(iv) The closing figure for the bank does not take into account a dishonoured cheque of €110 received from a client and lodged in late December.
(v) Wages and salaries include €14,000 per annum paid to the receptionist, who also runs the shop. It is estimated that 40% of this salary, €600 of the light and heat, €450 of the insurance and €320 of the telephone are attributable to the shop.
(vi) On 31/12/2012 it was decided to revalue buildings at €290,000.
(vii) Electricity due 31/12/2012 at €90.
(viii) Creditors for supplies to the health centre at 31/12/2012 are €3,250.
(ix) Depreciation to be provided as follows:
   1. Buildings at 2% of cost for the full year.
   2. Equipment at 20% of cost per annum.
   3. Furniture at 15% of cost per annum.

You are required to:

(a) Calculate the company's reserves on 1/1/2012.
(b) Calculate the profit/loss from the health shop for the year ended 31/12/2012.
(c) Prepare a Profit and Loss account for the year ended 31/12/2012.
(d) Prepare a Balance Sheet on 31/12/2012.
(e) What factors would a bank manager consider before granting or not granting a €50,000 loan to the above business for refurbishing of existing premises.

6 FAT FREDDIES

The following were included in the assets and liabilities of Fat Freddies Centre Ltd on 1/1/2012: Buildings at cost €600,000, Equipment at cost €300,000, Furniture at cost €150,000, Stock of health food for sale €3,000, Heating oil €1,740, Creditors for supplies to health centre €13,500, 5% Investments €225,000, Investment interest due €1,500, Contract cleaning prepaid €1,500, Members' fees due €9,000, Members' fees paid in advance €17,400, Authorised Capital €900,000, Issued Capital €600,000.

All fixed assets have 2-years' accumulated depreciation on 1/1/2012.

The following is the Receipts and Payments account for year ended 31/12/2012

Balance at bank on 1/1/2012	22,350	Wages and salaries	153,750
Investment income	1,800	Insurance	12,600
Members' fees	350,000	Equipment (1/10/2012)	20,000
Shop receipts	146,200	Repayment of €90,000 loan on 30/06/2012 with 18-months' interest	108,000
Annual grant	10,000	4% investments 1/7/2012	30,000
		Extension	65,000
		Contract cleaning	5,200
		Light and heat	2,560
		Telephone and stationery	4,800
		Purchases – shop	42,750
		Purchases – supplies	31,870
		Balance	53,820
	530,350		530,350

The following information and instructions are to be taken into account:

(i) Closing stock at 31/12/2012: shop €1,730, heating oil €200, health supplies €1,100.

(ii) Members' fees include fees for next year of €9,500. Clients' fees in arrears for 2012 €5,150.

(iii) Cleaning is done under contract payable monthly and includes a payment of €550 for January next year.

(iv) The closing figure for the bank does not take into account bank charges of €100 and a dishonoured cheque €200 received from a member and lodged in late December.

(v) Wages and salaries include €8,000 attributable to the shop. It is estimated that 10% of the insurance and telephone costs are attributable to the shop.

(vi) Creditors for the health centre at €9,560 and shop €400 at 31/12/2012.

(vii) On 31/12/2012 it was decided to revalue buildings at €850,000.

(viii) Depreciation to be provided as follows:
1. Buildings at 2% of cost for the full year.
2. Equipment at 20% of cost per annum.
3. Furniture at 20% of cost per annum.

You are required to:

(a) Calculate the company's reserves on 1/1/2012.

(b) Calculate the profit/loss from the health shop for the year ended 31/12/2012.

(c) Prepare a Profit and Loss account for the year ended 31/12/2012.

(d) Prepare a Balance Sheet on 31/12/2012.

(e) Would a bank loan of €100,000 be granted for capital investment to Fat Freddie's based on your accounts? Give reasons for your answer.

7 LIVE LONGER

The following were included in the assets and liabilities of Live Longer Health Centre Ltd on 1/10/2010: Buildings at cost €350,000, Equipment at cost €80,000, Furniture at cost €30,000, Stock of health food for sale €2,800, Heating oil €800, Creditors for supplies to health centre €8,800, 4 % Investments €60,000, Investment interest due €600, Contract cleaning prepaid €400, Members' fees due €2,600, Members' fees paid in advance €8,300, Authorised Capital €400,000, Issued Capital €180,000.

All fixed assets have 2-years' accumulated depreciation on 1/10/2010.

The following is the Receipts and Payments Account for year ended 30/9/2011

Balance at bank on 1/10/2010	25,000	Wages and salaries	122,500
Investment income	1,200	Insurance	8,500
Members' fees	242,500	Equipment (30/9/2011)	20,000
Shop receipts	28,300	Repayment of 8% loan on 30/9/2011 with 18 months' interest	56,000
		4% bonds 31/12/2010	40,000
		Contract cleaning	6,700
		Light and heat	1,900
		Telephone and stationery	2,900
		Purchases – shop	14,700
		Purchases – supplies	22,500
		Balance	1,300
	297,000		297,000

The following information and instructions are to be taken into account:

(i) Closing stock at 30/9/2011: shop €3,700, heating oil €400, health supplies €2,200.

(ii) Members' fees include fees for next year at €4,500. Clients' fees in arrears on 30/9/2011 are €1,600.

(iii) Cleaning is done under contract payable monthly and includes a payment of €500 in advance.

(iv) The closing figure for the bank does not take into account bank charges at €360 and a dishonoured cheque €480 is received from a member and lodged in late September.

(v) Wages and salaries include €6,000 attributable to the shop and an advance of €18,000 to an employee for the purchase of a private house. It is estimated that 10% of the cost of insurance and telephone are attributable to the shop.

(vi) Creditors for the health centre at €1,300 and shop €900 at 30/9/2011.

(vii) On 30/9/2011 it was decided to revalue buildings at €500,000.

(viii) Depreciation to be provided as follows:
1. Buildings at 2% of cost for the full year.
2. Equipment at 20% of cost per annum.
3. Furniture at 20% of cost per annum.

You are required to:

(a) Calculate the company's reserves on 1/10/2010.

(b) Calculate the profit/loss from the health shop for the year ended 31/9/2011.

(c) Prepare a Profit and Loss account for the year ended 31/9/2011.

(d) Prepare a Balance Sheet on 31/9/2011.

Note: Account year 1/10/2010 to 30/9/2011.

8 JUMPING UP'N DOWN EXERCISE CENTRE

The following were the assets and liabilities of The Jumping Up'n Down Exercise Centre Ltd on 1/1/2012: Buildings at cost €660,000, Equipment at cost €54,000, Vehicle at cost €60,000, Stock in shop €3,960, Heating oil €1,920, Creditors for supplies to centre €1,200, 5% Investments €36,000, Contract cleaning prepaid €240, Clients' fees paid in advance €4,800, Authorised Capital €500,000, Issued Capital €384,000.

All fixed assets have 3-years' accumulated depreciation on 1/1/2012.

The following is the Receipts and Payments account for the year ended 31/12/2012

Balance at bank on 1/1/2012	9,900	Wages and salaries	102,600
Investment income	1,200	Insurance	7,680
Clients' fees	408,000	Equipment	18,000
Shop receipts	48,000	Repayment of €48,000 loan on 1/5/2012 – with 18-months' interest	57,720
Balance at Bank 31/12/2012	90,540	New premises	240,000
		Contract cleaning	4,200
		Light and heat	3,720
		Telephone and stationery	1,920
		Purchases – shop	33,600
		Purchases – supplies	43,080
		Laundry	2,400
		New vehicle	42,000
		Dishonoured cheque fee	720
	557,640		557,640

The following information and instructions are to be taken into account:

(i) Closing stock at 31/12/2012: shop €1,800, heating oil €360.
(ii) Clients' fees include fees for next year of €6,000. Clients' fees in arrears for 2012 are €600.
(iii) Cleaning is done under contract payable monthly and includes a payment of €480 for January next year.
(iv) The dishonoured cheque was not recovered and was written-off as a bad debt.
(v) Wages and salaries include €21,600 paid to a secretary who also runs the shop. It is estimated that €40% of this salary, €300 of the light and heat, €960 of the insurance and €420 of the telephone are for the shop.
(vi) Creditors for supplies to the centre at 31/12/2012 are €2,160.
(vii) Electricity due on 31/12/2012 at €384.
(viii) On 31/12/2012 it was decided to revalue buildings at €1,080,000.
(ix) Depreciation to be provided as follows:
   1. Buildings 2% of cost for the full year.
   2. Equipment at 15% of cost per annum.
   3. Vehicles at 20% of cost per annum from date of purchase to date of sale.

The vehicle held on 1/1/2012 was purchased on 1 Jan, three years prior, and was traded in on 1/7/2012 against a new vehicle. The trade-in allowance was €8,400 against the new minibus valued at €50,400.

You are required to:

(a) Calculate the company's reserves on 1/1/2012.
(b) Calculate the profit/loss from the health shop for the year ended 31/12/2012.
(c) Prepare a Profit and Loss account for the year ended 31/12/2012.
(d) Prepare a Balance Sheet on 31/12/2012.
(e) Comment on the liquidity position of the centre.

9 McGUIRE

Farm Account

Among the assets and liabilities of Maggie and Mick McGuire (who carry on a mixed farming business) on 1/1/2012 are: Land and Buildings at cost €560,000, Machinery at cost €100,000, Stock of fuel €1,400, Value of Cattle €112,000, Value of sheep €34,000, Light and heat due €700, Milk cheque due €4,400.

The following is a summary taken from their cheque payments and lodgment books for the year

Lodgments	€	**Payments**	€
Balance	5,000	Cattle	30,000
Sheep	42,000	Sheep	36,000
Milk	54,000	Dairy wages	3,400
Lambs	24,800	Fertiliser	5,800
Calves	11,600	General farm expenses	29,600
Ewe premium	7,600	Light, heat and fuel	6,700
Wool	2,800	Repairs	12,200
Forestry premium	3,600	Vet expenses	3,300
Beef premium	4,600	Drawings	15,400
6-months' interest on 8% investment	1,600	Bank loan plus 15-months' interest at 8% on 31/3/2012	33,000
Cattle	22,000	Balance	4,200
	179,600		179,600

The following information and instructions are to be taken into account:

(i) Value of livestock on 31/12/2012 was cattle €114,000 and sheep €38,000.
(ii) Farm produce used by the family during the year milk: €1,320, lamb €500.
(iii) General farm expenses, fertiliser and vet's fees are to be apportioned at 60% to cattle and milk, and 40% to sheep.
(iv) Other expenses are to be apportioned 80% to farm and 20% to household.
(v) Depreciation is to be provided on machinery at 20% on cost.
(vi) Vet's fees include a cheque to Quinn Health Insurance for €1,200.
(vii) On 31/12/2012 a milk cheque due was €3,900, creditors for fertilisers €600 and a stock of fuel at €1,100.

You are required to prepare:

(a) A Statement of Capital for the farm on 1/1/2012.
(b) An Enterprise Analysis account for 'Cattle and milk' and 'Sheep' for the year ended 31/12/2012.
(c) A General Profit and Loss account for the year.
(d) 1. Which account, other than **drawings**, is affected by farm produce used by the family?
2. Prepare McGuire's drawings account.

10 DONAL POWER

Farm Account

Donal Power farms 300 acres of mixed farm land and has the following Trial Balance on 31/12/2012.

8% bank loan on 1/10/2012		200,000
Bank current a/c	172,800	
Capital		1,180,000
Land and buildings at cost	1,280,000	
Acc. depreciation		100,000
Plant and equipment	300,000	
Acc. depreciation		160,000
Creditors		44,000
Stocks 1/1/2012		
Cattle	50,000	
Fertilisers	6,000	
Sheep	24,000	
Foodstuffs	5,000	
Purchases		
Cattle	88,000	
Fertilisers	18,000	
Foodstuffs	8,600	
Bedding plants	11,000	
Sales		
Cattle		180,000
Milk		52,000
Plants		54,000
Sheep		26,400
Rent of land		10,200
Repairs	3,800	
Wages	14,400	
Vet expenses	6,600	
Rates	8,200	
Insurance	10,200	
	2,006,600	2,006,600

You are also given the following information:

(i) Closing stocks on 31/12/2012.

Cattle	€58,000
Fertilisers	€10,000
Sheep	€8,200
Foodstuff	€4,600

(ii) EU subsidy on beef was €5,000 and sheep €2,400, due on 31/12/2012.

(iii) Vet's expenses to be allocated two-thirds to cattle and one-third to sheep.
Fertilisers allocated: cattle three-sevenths, sheep three-sevenths, and plants one-seventh.
Foodstuff allocated: cattle two-fifths, sheep three-fifths.

(iv) The Power family used produce during the year as follows: beef €1,800, milk €1,400, plants €1,600.

(v) Rent receivable due on 31/12/2012 was €1,800, also tax due was €24,000 on 31/12/2012.

(vi) The milk cheque for December (€6,000) had not been received on 31/12/2012.

(vii) Bank charges of €400 were not recorded in the books, also a cheque for €460 was recorded on the incorrect side of both the bank and ledger accounts.

(viii) Depreciation is to be written-off on buildings at 2% and machinery at 25% on cost.
Land and Buildings were revalued to €1.4 million on 31/12/2012.

(ix) Provide for interest due on loan.

(x) Of the 300 acres, 260 acres were used for cattle, 35 acres for bedding plants and 5 acres for sheep.

You are required to prepare:

(a) Enterprise Analysis accounts for (i) Cattle and milk, (ii) Sheep, and (iii) Bedding plants.

(b) An overall Trading Profit and Loss account for the entire farm.

(c) Balance Sheet on 31/12/2012.

(d) How might Power improve the overall profitability of the farm?

(e) Write a brief comment on the profitability of this business.

TOPIC

9

Cash Flow Statements

Perseverance is not a long race, it is many short races one after the other.

Elliot

1 Hayes – Sample Exam Question

The following are the Balance Sheets of Hayes Plc as at 31/12/2006 and 31/12/2007.

	31/12/2007		31/12/2006	
Fixed Assets – Cost	620,000		490,000	
Less depreciation	(220,000)	400,000	(100,000)	390,000
Financial Fixed Assets – Investments at cost		200,000		300,000
Current Assets – Stocks	360,000		252,000	
– Debtors	170,000		110,000	
– Government securities	70,000			
– Cash	50,000		70,000	
	650,000		432,000	
Less Creditors Falling Due Within 1 Year				
Trade creditors	214,000		247,000	
Bank	20,000		34,000	
Taxation	48,000		39,000	
	282,000	368,000	320,000	112,000
		968,000		802,000
Financed by				
Creditors Falling Due After More Than 1 Year				
10% debentures		170,000		120,000
Capital and Reserves				
Ordinary shares at €1 each	290,000		230,000	
Share premium	18,000			
Profit and Loss account	490,000	798,000	452,000	682,000
		968,000		802,000

The following information is also available:

(i) 60,000 shares were issued at €1.30 per share.
(ii) Fixed assets which cost €60,000, on which depreciation of €30,000 had been provided, were sold for €40,000.
(iii) €50,000 debentures were issued on 1/1/2007.
(iv) Dividends paid during the year amounted to €54,000.
(v) Taxation charge on profits for the year 2007 was €60,000.
(vi) Investments which cost €100,000 were sold for cash at their book value.

You are required to:

(a) 1. Prepare an abridged Profit and Loss account to ascertain profit for the year ending 31/12/2007.
2. Prepare the Cash Flow statement for Hayes Plc for the year ending 31/12/2007 including Reconciliation statements.

(b) 1. Explain why earning profit does not always result in a corresponding increase in cash balances.
2. Write a note on the Accounting Standards Board. In your answer refer to the main activity of the Board and how it has influenced the preparation of Cash Flow statements.

Hayes Solution

Abridged Profit and Loss for Year Ending 31/12/2007

Operating profit	169,000
Less interest	(17,000)
Profit before tax	152,000
Taxation	(60,000)
Profit after tax	92,000
Dividends for year	(54,000)
Retained profit	38,000
Profit and Loss balance 1/1/2007	452,000
Profit and Loss balance 31/12/2007	490,000

Reconciliation of Operating Profit to Net Cash Flow from Operating Activities

Operating profit	169,000
Depreciation for year	**150,000**
Profit on sale of fixed assets	**(10,000)**
Increase in stock	(108,000)
Increase in debtors	(60,000)
Decrease in creditors	(33,000)
Net cash flow from operating activities	108,000

Cash Flow Statement of Hayes Plc for the Year Ended 31/12/2007 (ORTCEMF)

Operating Activities		
Net cash flow from operating activities		108,000
Return on Investment and Servicing of Finance		
Interest paid		(17,000)
Taxation		
Tax paid		**(51,000)**
Capital Expenditure and Financial Investment		
Sale of fixed assets	40,000	
Purchase of fixed assets	**(190,000)**	
Sale of investments	100,000	(50,000)
Equity Dividends		
Dividends paid		(54,000)
Net cash flow before liquid resources and financing		(64,000)
Management of Liquid Resources		
Government securities		(70,000)
Financing		
Issue of debentures	50,000	
Issue of ordinary shares	60,000	
Share premium	18,000	128,000
Decrease in cash		(6,000)

Reconciliation of Net Cash to Movement in Net Debt

Decrease in cash	(6,000)
Plus cash to purchase liquid resources	70,000
– Cash received from debentures	(50,000)
– Change in net debt	14,000
Net debt at 1/1/2007	**(84,000)**
Net debt at 31/12/2007	(70,000)

Workings

Tax	39,000	+	60,000	–	48,000	=	**51,000**
Depreciation	100,000	–	30,000	–	220,000	=	**150,000**
Disposal profit	60,000	–	30,000	–	40,000	=	**10,000**
Purchase of fixed asset	490,000	–	60,000	–	620,000	=	**190,000**
Net debt 1/1	120,000	–	70,000	+	34,000	=	**84,000**

1. Credit sales and purchases affect profit but not cash. Non-cash losses and gains affect profit but not cash. Purchase and sale of fixed assets by cash affect cash but not profit. Introduction or withdrawal of capital in cash affect cash but not profit.
2. The **Accounting Standards Board** issues new accounting standards called **Financial Reporting Standards** (FRS). It also amends and withdraws old accounting standards. FRS1 (issued in 1991 and revised in 1996) requires large companies to prepare a Cash Flow Statement for each activity period. It requires that individual cash flows should be entered under standard headings that give rise to them.

2 MARY T

The following are the Balance Sheets of Mary T. Plc as at 31/12/2012 and 31/12/2011 together with an abridged Profit and Loss account for year ending 2012.

Abridged Profit and Loss Account for Year Ending 31/12/2012

Operating profit	164,400
Interest	(14,400)
Profit before taxation	150,000
Taxation	(64,800)
Profit after tax	85,200
Dividends	(62,400)
Retained profit for year	22,800
Profit and Loss balance on 1/1/2012	43,200
Profit and Loss balance 31/12/2012	66,000

Balance Sheet as at	**31/12/2012**		**31/12/2011**	
Fixed Assets – Land and buildings	468,000		516,000	
Less depreciation	(90,000)	378,000	(85,200)	430,800
Machinery	354,000		300,000	
Less depreciation	(117,600)	236,400	(90,000)	210,000
		614,400		640,800
Financial Assets – Quoted investments		45,600		30,000
Current Assets – Stocks	57,700		38,500	
– Debtors	151,100		134,300	
– Bank	105,600		86,400	
	314,400		259,200	
Less Creditors Falling Due Within 1 Year				
Trade creditors	163,200		182,400	
Taxation	50,400		58,800	
Dividends	40,800		45,600	
	254,400	60,000	286,800	(27,600)
		720,000		643,200
Financed by				
Creditors Falling Due After More Than 1 Year				
8% debentures		108,000		144,000
Capital and Reserves				
Ordinary shares at €1 each	528,000		456,000	
Share premium	18,000			
Profit and Loss account	66,000	612,000	43,200	499,200
		720,000		643,200

The following information is available:

(i) There were no disposals of machinery during the year but new machinery was acquired.
(ii) There were no additions to buildings during the year. Buildings were disposed of for €74,400.
(iii) Depreciation charged for the year on buildings in arriving at the operating profit was €21,600.

You are required to:

(a) Prepare the Cash Flow statement for Mary T Plc for the year ended 31/12/2012 including Reconciliation statements.

(b) 1. Outline the benefits of preparing a Cash Flow statement.
2. Distinguish between a **cash** expense and a **non-cash** expense.

3 MAGS

The following are the Balance Sheets of Mags Plc as at 31/12/2012 and 31/12/2011.

Abridged Profit and Loss Account for Year Ending 31/12/2012

Operating profit	210,000
Interest	(12,000)
Profit before taxation	198,000
Taxation	(67,500)
Profit after tax	130,500
Dividends	(99,000)
Retained profit for year	31,500
Profit and Loss balance on 1/1/2012	286,500
Profit and Loss balance 31/12/2012	318,000

Balance Sheet as at	**12/31/2012**		**12/31/2011**	
Fixed Assets – Land and buildings	1,237,500		1,125,000	
Less depreciation	(142,500)	1,095,000	(120,000)	1,005,000
Machinery	600,000		705,000	
Less depreciation	(303,000)	297,000	(270,000)	435,000
		1,392,000		1,440,000
Financial Assets – Quoted investments		195,000		150,000
Current Assets – Stocks	330,000		307,500	
– Debtors	300,000		285,000	
– Bank			15,000	
– Government securities	18,000			
– Cash	3,000		1,500	
	651,000		609,000	
Less Creditors Falling Due Within 1 Year				
Trade creditors	375,000		342,000	
Taxation	75,000		64,500	
Dividends	67,500		51,000	
Bank	10,200			
Interest	1,800			
	529,500	121,500	457,500	151,500
		1,708,500		1,741,500
Financed By				
Creditors Falling Due After More Than 1 Year				
9% debentures		112,500		270,000
Capital and Reserves				
Ordinary shares at €1 each	1,245,000		1,185,000	
Share premium	33,000			
Profit and Loss account	318,000	1,596,000	286,500	1,471,500
		1,708,500		1,741,500

The following information is available:

(i) There were no disposals of buildings during the year but new buildings were acquired.
(ii) There were no additions to machinery during the year. Machinery was disposed of for €52,500.
(iii) Depreciation charged for the year on machinery in arriving at the operating profit was €90,000.

You are required to:

(a) Prepare the Cash Flow statement for Mags Plc for the year ended 31/12/2012 including Reconciliation statements.

(b) 1. Explain the term **Solvency**.
2. Identify a **non-cash expense** and a **non-cash gain**.

4 NASH

The following are the Balance Sheets of G. Nash Plc as at 31/12/2012 and 31/12/2011.

Abridged Profit and Loss Account for Year Ending 31/12/2012

Operating profit	168,000
Interest	(9,600)
Profit before taxation	158,400
Taxation	(54,000)
Profit after tax	104,400
Dividends	(79,200)
Retained profit for year	25,200
Profit and Loss balance on 1/1/2012	229,200
Profit and Loss balance 31/12/2012	254,400

Balance Sheet as at	**31/12/2012**		**31/12/2011**	
Fixed Assets – Land and buildings	990,000		900,000	
Less depreciation	(114,000)	876,000	(96,000)	804,000
Machinery	480,000		564,000	
Less depreciation	(242,400)	237,600	(216,000)	348,000
		1,113,600		1,152,000
Financial Assets – Quoted investments		156,000		120,000
Current Assets – Stocks	264,000		246,000	
– Debtors	240,000		228,000	
– Bank			12,000	
– Government securities	14,400			
– Cash	2,400		1,200	
	520,800		487,200	
Less Creditors Falling Due Within 1 Year				
Trade creditors	300,000		273,600	
Taxation	60,000		51,600	
Dividends	54,000		40,800	
Bank	8,160			
Interest	1,440			
	423,600	97,200	366,000	121,200
		1,366,800		1,393,200
Financed by				
Creditors Falling Due After More Than 1 Year				
9% debentures		90,000		216,000
Capital and Reserves				
Ordinary shares at €1 each	996,000		948,000	
Share premium	26,400			
Profit and Loss account	254,400	1,276,800	229,200	1,177,200
		1,366,800		1,393,200

The following information is available:

(i) There were no disposals of buildings during the year but new buildings were acquired.
(ii) There were no additions to machinery during the year. Machinery was disposed of for €42,000.
(iii) Depreciation charged for the year on machinery in arriving at the operating profit was €72,000.

You are required to:

(a) Prepare the Cash Flow statement for G. Nash for the year ended 31/12/2012 including Reconciliation statements.

(b) 1. Explain the term **Accounting standard**.
2. Identify 2 **Accounting bodies**.

5 On Line

The following are the Balance Sheets of On Line Plc as at 31/12/2012 and 31/12/2011.

	31/12/2012		31/12/2011	
Intangible Assets – Patents		100,000		120,000
Fixed Assets – Land and buildings	1,960,000		1,620,000	
Less depreciation	(136,000)	1,824,000	(70,000)	1,550,000
Financial Assets – Investments		420,000		180,000
		2,344,000		1,850,000
Current Assets – Stocks	110,000		194,000	
– Debtors	130,000		192,000	
– Government securities	20,000			
– Cash	24,000		42,000	
	284,000		428,000	
Less Creditors Falling Due Within 1 Year				
Trade creditors	84,000		24,000	
Interest	18,000		20,000	
Taxation	46,000		30,000	
Dividends	48,000		42,000	
Bank	12,000		32,000	
	208,000	76,000	148,000	280,000
		2,420,000		2,130,000
Financed by				
Creditors Falling Due After More Than 1 Year				
10% debentures		800,000		600,000
Capital and Reserves				
Ordinary shares at €1 each	1,000,000		920,000	
Profit and Loss account	620,000	1,620,000	610,000	1,530,000
		2,420,000		2,130,000

The following information is also available:

(i) Fixed Assets which cost €140,000, on which depreciation of €54,000 had been provided, were sold for €100,000.

(ii) 80,000 shares were issued at €1 per share.

(iii) €200,000 debentures were issued on 1/1/2012.

(iv) Dividends due and taxation due at 31/12/2011 were paid.

You are required to:

(a) 1. Prepare an abridged Profit and Loss account to ascertain profit for the year ending 31/12/2012.

2. Prepare the Cash Flow statement for On Line Plc for the year ending 31/12/2012 including Reconciliation statements.

(b) 1. What do the letters **ASB** and **FRS** stand for?

2. Name 2 other agencies that regulate company accounts.

6 RELIHAN

The following are the Balance Sheets of Relihan Plc as at 31/12/2012 and 31/12/2011.

	31/12/2012		31/12/2011	
Fixed Assets – Cost	496,000		392,000	
Less depreciation	(176,000)	320,000	(80,000)	312,000
Financial Fixed Assets – Investments at cost		160,000		240,000
Current Assets – Stocks	288,000		201,600	
– Debtors	136,000		88,000	
– Government securities	56,000			
– Cash	40,000		56,000	
	520,000		345,600	
Less Creditors Falling Due Within 1 Year				
Trade creditors	171,200		197,600	
Bank	16,000		27,200	
Taxation	38,400		31,200	
	225,600	294,400	256,000	89,600
		774,400		641,600
Financed by				
Creditors Falling Due After More Than 1 Year				
10% debentures		136,000		96,000
Capital and Reserves				
Ordinary shares at €1 each	232,000		184,000	
Share premium	14,400			
Profit and Loss account	392,000	638,400	361,600	545,600
		774,400		641,600

The following information is also available:

(i) 48,000 shares were issued at €1.30 per share.

(ii) Fixed assets which cost €48,000, on which depreciation of €24,000 had been provided, were sold for €32,000.

(iii) €40,000 debentures were issued on 1/1/2012.

(iv) Dividends paid during the year amounted to €43,200.

(v) Taxation charge on profits for the year 2012 was €48,000.

You are required to:

(a) 1. Prepare an abridged Profit and Loss account to ascertain profit for the year ending 31/12/2012.

2. Prepare the Cash Flow statement for Relihan Plc for the year ending 31/12/2012 including Reconciliation statements.

(b) 1. Explain why earning profit does not always result in a corresponding increase in cash balances.

2. Write a note on the Accounting Standards Board. In your answer refer to the main activity of the Board and how it has influenced the preparation of Cash Flow statements.

7 PINNACLE

The following are the Balance Sheets of Pinnacle Plc as at 31/12/2012 and 31/12/2011.

	31/12/2012		31/12/2011	
Intangible Assets – Patents		112,000		126,000
Fixed Assets – Land and buildings	546,000		616,000	
Less depreciation	(112,000)	434,000	(140,000)	476,000
Equipment	532,000		420,000	
Less depreciation	(119,000)	413,000	(98,000)	322,000
		959,000		924,000
Current Assets – Stocks	364,000		350,000	
– Debtors	324,800		344,400	
– Bank	63,000		43,400	
– Government securities	21,000			
– Cash	1,400		2,800	
– Prepaids	5,600		4,200	
	779,800		744,800	
Less Creditors Falling Due Within 1 Year				
Trade creditors	238,000		266,000	
Interest	4,200			
Taxation	229,600		210,000	
Dividends	56,000		77,000	
	527,800	252,000	553,000	191,800
		1,211,000		1,115,800
Financed By				
Creditors Falling Due After More Than 1 Year				
8% debentures		126,000		210,000
Capital and Reserves				
Ordinary shares at €1 each	770,000		630,000	
Share premium	14,000			
Profit and Loss account	301,000	1,085,000	275,800	905,800
		1,211,000		1,115,800

The following information is also available:

(i) Buildings were disposed of during the year for €98,000. The profit on the sale of these buildings was €35,000.
(ii) There were no disposals of equipment during the year but new equipment was acquired costing €112,000.
(iii) Depreciation charged for the year was €63,000.
(iv) Patents are being written-off over 9 years.
(v) Dividends due and taxation due at 31/12/2011 were paid.
(vi) Redemption of debentures took place on 1/9/2012.

You are required to:

(a) 1. Prepare an abridged Profit and Loss account to ascertain profit for the year ending 31/12/2012.
2. Prepare the Cash Flow statement for Pinnacle Plc for the year ending 31/12/2012 including Reconciliation statements.

(b) 1. What is the purpose of preparing Cash Flow statements?
2. Explain the term **non-cash items** and give two examples.

8 QUIGLEY

The following are the Balance Sheets of Quigley Plc as at 31/12/2012 and 31/12/2011.

	31/12/2012		31/12/2011	
Intangible Assets – Patents		134,400		153,600
Fixed Assets – Land and buildings	720,000		600,000	
Less depreciation	(56,000)	664,000	(44,800)	555,200
Equipment	416,000		360,000	
Less depreciation	(83,200)	332,800	(57,600)	302,400
		1,131,200		1,011,200
Financial Assets – Investments		64,000		80,000
		1,195,200		1,091,200
Current Assets – Stocks	200,000		172,800	
– Debtors (less 4% provision)	122,880		119,808	
– Bank	9,600			
– Government securities	48,000		32,000	
– Cash	3,200		1,600	
– Prepaids	7,200		5,600	
	390,880		331,808	
Less Creditors Falling Due Within 1 Year				
Trade creditors	124,800		134,400	
Interest	25,600		22,400	
Taxation	104,000		84,800	
Dividends	72,000		48,000	
Bank			20,800	
	326,400	64,480	310,400	21,408
		1,259,680		1,112,608
Financed By				
Creditors Falling Due After More Than 1 Year				
8% debentures		320,000		416,000
Capital and Reserves				
Ordinary shares at €1 each	800,000		640,000	
Revaluation reserve	80,000			
Profit and Loss account	59,680	939,680	56,608	696,608
		1,259,680		1,112,608

The following information is also available:

(i) Equipment which had cost €112,000 was sold for €88,000.
(ii) There was no disposal of buildings during the year but an extension was built by the company.
(iii) Dividends and taxation due on 31/12/2011 were paid during the year.
(iv) The redemption of debentures took place on 30/6/2012.
(v) Revaluation of land (increased by €80,000) took place during the year.
(vi) The total depreciation charge for the year was €83,200.
(vii) Patents are being amortised over an 8-year period.

You are required to:

(a) 1. Prepare an abridged Profit and Loss account to ascertain profit for the year ending 31/12/2012.
2. Prepare the Cash Flow statement for Quigley Plc for the year ending 31/12/2012 including Reconciliation statements.

(b) Explain why earning profit does not always result in a corresponding increase in cash balances.

TOPIC

10

Correction of Errors (Suspense a/c's)

There is no elevator to success. Just take the stairs like everyone else.

Unknown

1 O'Shea – Sample Exam Question

The Trial Balance of O'Shea, a boutique owner, failed to agree on 31/12/2007. The difference was entered in a suspense account and the following Balance Sheet was prepared.

Balance Sheet as at 31/12/2007

Fixed Assets	€	€	€
Premises		400,000	
Motor vehicles		20,000	
Furniture and equipment		16,000	436,000
Current Assets			
Stock		17,000	
Debtors		5,600	
Cash		3,200	
		25,800	
Less Creditors Falling Due Within 1 Year			
Creditors (incl. suspense)	12,200		
Bank	5,600	(17,800)	
Net Current Assets			8,000
			444,000
Financed by			
Capital		441,000	
Add net profit		15,000	
		456,000	
Less drawings		12,000	444,000
			444,000

On checking the books the following errors were discovered:

(i) An overdraft of €400 in the bank account had been brought down on the incorrect side of the Nominal Ledger and consequently had been entered on the incorrect side of the Trial Balance.

(ii) O'Shea sold privately owned jewellery to a debtor of the business on credit for €2,800. This sale had been treated in error as a cash sale of stock. O'Shea intended that the proceeds of this sale were to be retained in the business.

(iii) A debtor who owed O'Shea €700 sent a cheque for €550 and €100 in cash in full settlement. This was correctly entered in the books. However, no entry had been made in the books of the subsequent dishonouring of this cheque or of the writing-off of the remaining debt in full because of bankruptcy.

(iv) O'Shea won a motor vehicle valued at €20,000 in a grand prize draw. O'Shea gave the vehicle to the business and took an old van from the business valued at €8,000 which was to be used for private purposes. The only entry made in the firm's books regarding both motor vehicles was a debit in the cash book of €8,000.

(v) Cash payments of €160 for repairs to the business motor vehicle, and €100 for repairs to private motor vehicles, had both been credited to the creditors and also credited to the motor vehicles account only.

You are required to:

(a) Journalise the necessary corrections.

(b) Show the **suspense** account.

(c) Prepare a statement showing the correct **net profit**.

(d) Prepare a corrected Balance Sheet.

(e) Explain with examples what is meant by:

1. Error of Commission.
2. Error of Principle.

Solution

(a) Journal

		€	€
(i)	Suspense	800	
	Bank		800
	(Overdraft brought down on incorrect side)		
(ii)	Sales	2,800	
	Cash		2,800
	Debtors	2,800	
	Capital		2,800
	(Private sale treated as business sale)		
(iii)	Debtor	600	600
	Bank		550
	Discount allowed/disallowed		50
	Bad debts	600	
	(Record of dishonoured cheque and bad debt)		
(iv)	Suspense	8,000	
	Bank		8,000
	Vehicle	12,000	
	Capital		12,000
	(Capital introduced)		
(v)	Creditors	260	
	Vehicles	260	
	Suspense		520
	Repairs	160	
	Drawings	100	
	Bank		260
	(Repairs and drawings omitted)		

(b) Suspense

	Dr	Cr
Bank	800	
Bank	8,000	
Creditors		520
Balance – original difference		**8,280**

(c) O'Shea Net Profit

Statement of corrected net profit

		€
Original net profit		15,000
Add discount disallowed		50
		15,050
Less Sales	2,800	
Bad debts	600	
Repairs	160	3,560
Corrected Net Profit		**11,490**

(d) Corrected Balance Sheet

Fixed Assets	€	€	€
Premises		400,000	
Motor vehicles (+12,000 + 260)		32,260	
Furniture and equipment		16,000	448,260
Current Assets			
Stock		17,000	
Debtors (+2,800 + 600 − 600)		8,400	
Cash (−2,800)		400	
		25,800	
Less Creditors Falling Due Within 1 Year			
Creditors (−260 − 8280)	3,660		
Bank (+800 + 550 + 8,000 + 260)	15,210	18,870	
Net Current Assets			6,930
			455,190
Financed by			
Capital (+2,800 + 12,000)		455,800	
Add net profit		11,490	
		467,290	
Less drawings (+100)		12,100	455,190
			455,190

Error of Commission occurs when the correct amount is posted to the correct side of the incorrect account, e.g. goods sold on credit to Cullen were debited in error to Carroll.

Error of Principle arises when an item is posted to the incorrect class of account, e.g. a computer supplier purchased a vehicle and entered it in the purchases account.

2 O'BRIEN

The Trial Balance of O'Brien, a garage owner, failed to agree on 31/12/2012. The difference was entered in a suspense account and the Balance Sheet was prepared.

Balance Sheet as at 31/12/2012

Fixed Assets	€	€	€
Premises		270,000	
Furniture and equipment		99,000	369,000
Current Assets			
Stock (incl. suspense)		130,500	
Debtors		91,500	
		222,000	
Less Creditors Falling Due Within 1 Year			
Creditors	118,500		
Bank	52,500	171,000	
Net Current Assets			51,000
			420,000
Financed by			
Capital		360,000	
Add net profit		78,000	
		438,000	
Less drawings		(18,000)	420,000
			420,000

On checking the books the following errors were discovered:

(i) Car parts previously sold on credit for €825 had been returned to O'Brien. These returns had been incorrectly entered as €75 on the credit of equipment account and as €83 on the debit of purchases account.

(ii) O'Brien had returned a car previously purchased on credit for €14,700 and had entered this transaction in the relevant ledger accounts incorrectly as €13,350. However, a credit note subsequently arrived from the supplier showing a restocking charge of €300. The only entry made in respect of this credit note was a credit entry of €14,400 in the creditors account.

(iii) A car purchased on credit from Allen for €18,000 had been entered on the incorrect side of Allen's account and credited as €1,800 in the equipment account.

(iv) A private debt for €1,448 owed by O'Brien had been offset in full against a business debt of €1,500 owed to the firm for work carried out. No entry had been made in the books in respect of this offset.

(v) O'Brien won a private holiday prize for two worth €9,000. One ticket had been given to a salesperson as commission on sales and the other to a creditor as payment in full of a debt of €5,100. No entries had been made in the books.

You are required to:

(a) Journalise the necessary corrections.

(b) Prepare a suspense a/c showing the original difference.

(c) Prepare a statement showing the correct net profit.

(d) Prepare a corrected Balance Sheet.

(e) Explain with examples:

1. Error of Commission.
2. Error of Original Entry.

❸ O'CONNELL

The Trial Balance of **O'Connell** a retailer failed to agree on 31/12/2012. The difference was entered in a suspense account and the following Balance Sheet was prepared.

Balance Sheet as at 31/12/2012

Fixed Assets	€	€	€
Premises		700,000	
Motor vehicles		35,000	
Furniture and equipment		28,000	763,000
Current Assets			
Stock		29,750	
Debtors		9,800	
Cash		5,600	
		45,150	
Less Creditors Falling Due Within 1 Year			
Creditors (incl. suspense)	21,350		
Bank	9,800	31,150	
Net Current Assets			14,000
			777,000
Financed by			
Capital		771,750	
Add net profit		26,250	
		798,000	
Less drawings		(21,000)	777,000
			777,000

On checking the books the following errors were discovered:

(i) An overdraft of €700 in the bank account had been brought down on the incorrect side of the Nominal Ledger and consequently had been entered on the incorrect side of the Trial Balance.

(ii) O'Connell sold privately owned computer equipment to a debtor of the business on credit for €4,900. This sale had been treated in error as a cash sale of stock. O'Connell intended that the proceeds of this sale were to be retained in the business.

(iii) A debtor who owed O'Connell €1,225 sent a cheque for €963 and €175 in cash in full settlement. This was correctly entered in the books. However, no entry had been made in the books of the subsequent dishonouring of this cheque or of the writing-off of the remaining debt in full because of bankruptcy.

(iv) O'Connell won a motor vehicle valued at €35,000 in a local credit union raffle. O'Connell gave the vehicle to the business and took an old van from the business valued at €14,000 which was to be used for private purposes. The only entry made in the firm's books regarding both motor vehicles was a debit in the cash book of €14,000.

(v) Cash payments of €280 for repairs to the business motor vehicle and €175 for repairs to private vehicles had both been credited to the creditors, and also credited to the motor vehicles account only.

You are required to:

(a) Journalise the necessary corrections.

(b) Show the suspense account.

(c) Prepare a statement showing the correct net profit.

(d) Prepare a corrected Balance Sheet.

(e) What is a suspense account and why does it arise?

4 O'DRISCOLL

The Trial Balance of O'Driscoll, a garage owner, failed to agree on 31/12/2012. The difference was entered in a suspense account and the final accounts were prepared.

Balance Sheet as at 31/12/2012

Fixed Assets	€	€	€
Premises		1,040,000	
Furniture and equipment		170,000	1,210,000
Current Assets			
Stock (incl. suspense)		144,800	
Debtors		90,400	
Cash		16,200	
		251,400	
Less Creditors Falling Due Within 1 Year			
Creditors	127,400		
Bank	64,000	191,400	
Net Current Assets			60,000
			1,270,000
Financed by			
Capital		1,190,000	
Add net profit		116,000	
		1,306,000	
Less drawings		(36,000)	1,270,000
			1,270,000

On checking the books the following errors were discovered:

(i) Repairs to premises of €3,800 and repairs to private dwelling house of €1,920 were paid out of the business bank account and credited to premises.

(ii) O'Driscoll had returned a car previously purchased on credit for €57,600, and had entered this transaction in the relevant ledger accounts incorrectly as €57,760. However, a credit note subsequently arrived from the supplier showing a transport charge of €1,200. The only entry made in respect of this credit note was a credit entry of €56,400 in the creditors account.

(iii) A credit note received from a creditor for €3,440 had been incorrectly entered in the Nominal Ledger as €3,224 and entered twice on the incorrect side of the creditors account.

(iv) A debtor who owed O'Driscoll €8,000 sent a cheque for €4,800 and €2,800 cash in full settlement. This was correctly entered in the books. However, no entry had been made in the books of the subsequent dishonouring of this cheque or of the writing-off of the remaining debt in full because of bankruptcy.

(v) O'Driscoll sold a private car for cash to the business for €25,200. This sale had been treated in error as a credit sale of stock. O'Driscoll intended that the proceeds of the sale be retained in the business.

You are required to:

(a) Journalise the necessary corrections.

(b) Prepare a statement showing the corrected net profit.

(c) Show the suspense account.

(d) Prepare the corrected Balance Sheet.

(e) 1. Why do all errors not affect the suspense account?
2. Identify 2 errors that do not affect the suspense account.

5 O'FARRELL

The Trial Balance of O'Farrell, a haulage supplier, failed to agree on 31/12/2012. The difference was entered in a suspense account and the final accounts were prepared.

Balance Sheet as at 31/12/2012

Fixed Assets	€	€	€
Premises		170,000	
Furniture and equipment		40,000	210,000
Current Assets			
Stock (incl. suspense)		34,000	
Debtors		16,000	
		50,000	
Less Creditors Falling Due Within 1 Year			
Creditors	30,000		
Bank	3,500	33,500	
Net Current Assets			16,500
			226,500
Financed by			
Capital		188,500	
Add net profit		46,500	
		235,000	
Less drawings		(8,500)	226,500
			226,500

On checking the books the following errors were discovered:

(i) A private debt for €3,400 owed to O'Farrell had been offset against a business debt of €3,150 owed by the firm. The only entry made in the books in respect of this offset was a credit of €3,400 in the creditors account.

(ii) O'Farrell had returned a container previously purchased on credit for €18,200 and had entered this transaction in the relevant ledger accounts incorrectly as €18,220. However, a credit note subsequently arrived from the supplier showing a restocking charge of €320. The only entry made in respect of this credit note was a credit entry of €17,880 in the creditors account.

(iii) O'Farrell won a private holiday prize for two worth €4,500. One ticket had been given to a salesperson as part payment of sales commission for the year, and the other to a creditor as payment in full of a debt of €2,700. No entry had been made in the books.

(iv) Repairs to premises of €800 and repairs to private dwelling house of €480 were paid out of the business bank account and both credited to the premises account.

(v) O'Farrell sent a cheque for €780 in full settlement of a business debt of €820 and this was recorded correctly in the books. However, no entry had been made of the subsequent dishonouring of this cheque and the payment on account of €400 cash by O'Farrell.

You are required to:

(a) Journalise the necessary corrections.

(b) Show the suspense account.

(c) Prepare a statement showing the corrected net profit.

(d) Prepare the corrected Balance Sheet.

(e) Name 4 different types of errors that do not affect the Trial Balance.

6 O'GRADY

The Trial Balance of O'Grady, a computer software company, failed to agree on 31/12/2012. The difference was entered in a suspense account and the following Balance Sheet was prepared.

Balance Sheet as at 31/12/2012

Fixed Assets	€	€	€
Premises		900,000	
Equipment		45,000	
Motor vehicles		90,000	1,035,000
Current Assets			
Stock (incl. suspense)		273,600	
Debtors		57,300	
Cash		1,500	
		332,400	
Less Creditors Falling Due Within 1 Year			
Creditors	84,000		
Bank	46,500	130,500	
Net Current Assets			201,900
			1,236,900
Financed by			
Capital		1,125,000	
Add net profit		121,800	
		1,246,800	
Less drawings		(9,900)	1,236,900
			1,236,900

On checking the books the following errors were discovered:

(i) O'Grady sent a cheque for €930 in full settlement of a business debt of €990 and this was recorded correctly in the books. However, no entry had been made in the books of the subsequent dishonouring of this cheque and the payment on account of €450 cash by O'Grady.

(ii) O'Grady won a vehicle valued at €45,000 in a draw. He gave this vehicle to the business and took an old vehicle from the business valued at €33,750 which was to be used for private purposes. The only entry in the firm's books regarding both vehicles was a debit in the bank account of €33,750.

(iii) A cheque for €7,875 paid by O'Grady out of a private bank account for 15-months' consultancy contract work up to 31/12/2013 had not been entered in the books.

(iv) Cash payments of €675 for repairs to equipment had been credited to the creditors account and also credited to the motor vehicles account.

(v) O'Grady had returned software previously purchased on credit for €23,400 from a supplier. O'Grady entered this transaction as €24,300 on the correct sides of the correct accounts in the ledger. A credit note subsequently arrived from the supplier showing a restocking charge of €900. The only entry made in respect of this credit note was a credit of €22,500 in the creditors account.

You are required to:

(a) Journalise the necessary corrections.

(b) Show the suspense account.

(c) Prepare a statement showing the correct net profit.

(d) Prepare a corrected Balance Sheet.

(e) What are the limitations of **final accounts** as a means of presentation?

7 O'HALLORAN

The Trial Balance of O'Halloran, a small garage owner, failed to agree on 31/12/2012. The difference was entered in a suspense account and the following Balance Sheet was prepared.

Balance Sheet as at 31/12/2012

Fixed Assets	€	€	€
Premises		1,580,000	
Equipment		1,000,000	
			2,580,000
Current Assets			
Stock (incl. suspense)		940,000	
Debtors		260,000	
Cash		10,000	
		1,210,000	
Less Creditors Falling Due Within 1 Year			
Creditors	460,000		
Bank	310,000	770,000	
Net Current Assets			440,000
			3,020,000
Financed by			
Capital		2,660,000	
Add net profit		490,000	
		3,150,000	
Less drawings		(130,000)	3,020,000
			3,020,000

On checking the books the following errors were discovered:

(i) An overdraft of €600 in the bank account had been brought down on the incorrect side of the Nominal Ledger and consequently had been entered on the incorrect side of the Trial Balance.

(ii) New equipment purchased on credit from Carberry for €11,000 had been entered on the incorrect side of the Carberry account and credited as €1,100 in the equipment account.

(iii) O'Halloran had returned a vehicle previously purchased on credit from a supplier for €10,500 and had entered this transaction in the books as €15,100. However, a credit note later arrived from a supplier showing a restocking charge of €400 to cover the cost of the return. The only entry made in respect of the credit note was a credit entry of €10,100 in the creditors account.

(iv) Car parts previously sold on credit for €230 had been returned to O'Halloran. These goods had been incorrectly entered as €30 on the credit of the equipment account and as €23 on the debit of the purchases account.

(v) €1,400 cash received from the sale of an old computer (book value €1,200) which was privately owned and had not been entered in the books.

(vi) A private debt of €220 owed by the owner to a creditor had been offset in full against a bill for €250 owed by this creditor to O'Halloran for car repairs previously carried out.

(vii) Wages due to an employee of €560 were not entered in the books.

(viii) O'Halloran had sold a private car for cash to a debtor of the business for €15,600. This sale had been treated in error as a credit sale of stock. The owner had intended that the proceeds of the sale were to be retained in the business.

You are required to:

(a) Journalise the necessary corrections.

(b) Show the suspense account.

(c) Prepare a statement showing the correct net profit.

(d) Prepare a corrected Balance Sheet.

8 O'LEARY

The Trial Balance of O'Leary, a baker, failed to agree on 31/12/2012. The difference was entered in a suspense a/c and the following Balance Sheet was prepared.

Balance Sheet as at 31/12/2012

Fixed Assets	€	€	€
Premises		440,000	
Furniture and equipment		40,000	480,000
Current Assets			
Stock (incl. suspense)		32,000	
Debtors		24,000	
Cash		200	
		56,200	
Less Creditors Falling Due Within 1 Year			
Creditors	40,000		
Bank	8,200	48,200	
Net Current Assets			8,000
			488,000
Financed by			
Capital		400,000	
Add net profit		100,000	
		500,000	
Less drawings		(12,000)	488,000
			488,000

On checking the books the following errors were discovered:

(i) A cheque paid to a creditor in full settlement of a debt of €1,550 was dishonoured. No entry was made for this, nor for the subsequent payment on account of €500 by O'Leary.

(ii) O'Leary purchased goods on credit for €5,000 on 31/12/2012. As delivery did not arrive until 31 December, O'Leary did not enter this in the books or include it in the closing stock.

(iii) A private debt of €340 owed to the owner by a creditor had been offset in full settlement against a business debt of €320 owed by the owner. No entries were made.

(iv) Wages due of €210 and rent receivable prepaid €480 were both omitted from the books.

(v) Goods previously sold for €6,000 at a margin of 20% were returned on 31/12/2012. O'Leary applied a restocking charge of 5% to the credit note. No entries were made in respect of the returns in either the books or the stocktake.

(vi) Payments from the business bank account of €350 and €1,200 for delivery van repairs and private van repairs respectively were entered correctly in the bank account, but €1,500 was debited to a supplier's account.

(vii) O'Leary sold equipment with a book value of €3,200 on credit for €2,800, while replacing it with machinery at €7,300 purchased through a hire purchase loan taken out on 31/12/2012. The only entries made were €2,300 debited to the purchases account and €400 credited to a supplier's account.

You are required to:

(a) Journalise the necessary corrections.

(b) Show the suspense account.

(c) Prepare the corrected net profit.

(d) Show the Balance Sheet.

TOPIC

11

Interpretation of a/c's

Kites rise highest against the wind, not with it.

Winston Churchill

The following are the ratios needed for Question 5 on the Leaving Certificate Higher Level paper.

Liquidity

Current Ratio	Current Assets : Current Liabilities (This shows solvency for the year/ability to pay debts.)
Acid Test	Current Assets − Closing stock : Current Liabilities (Can business pay debts in the short term?)

Activity

Credit to Debtors	Credit Sales/Debtors (The number of times a year Debtors settle their accounts.)
Credit from Creditors	Credit Purchases/Creditors (The number of times we pay Creditors p.a.)
Stock Turnover	Cost of Sales/Average Stock (Number of times p.a. we sell our stock.)

Profitability

Mark-up/(Margin)	Gross Profit × 100/Cost of Sales/Sales (Profit as a percentage of Cost/Sales.)
Return on Investment	Net Profit + Interest × 100/Total Capital Employed (Profit as a percentage of total capital employed.)
Return on Equity	Net Profit − Preference Dividend × 100/Equity (Return on ordinary shareholders' investment.)
Dividend per Share (DPS)	Ordinary Dividend/Number of Ordinary Shares (Shows cash return per ordinary share.)
Gearing Ratio	Debt × 100/Total Capital Employed (What percentage of the business is owned by outsiders.)
Interest Cover	Net Profit + Interest/Interest (The number of times the company is able to pay interest.)
Dividend Cover	Net Profit − Preference Dividend/Ordinary Dividend (Number of times the business can pay ordinary dividends.)

Performance

Earnings per Share (EPS)	Net Profit − Pref. Dividend/Number of Ordinary Shares (This is the profit earned per ordinary share.)
Price Earnings Ratio	(i) Earnings Rate = Market Price/EPS (ii) Payout Rate = Market Price/DPS (These show the number of years it takes a share to recover/recoup its share price at (i) Earnings Rate (ii) Dividend Rate.)
Dividend Yield	DPS × 100/Market Price
Earnings Yield	EPS × 100/Market Price
Real Return	Dividend Yield × Dividend Cover (Both yields and real rate of return are stock exchange indicators of performance.)

Note:
- Use Net Profit after tax if the tax is given in the question.
- Financed by = Equity (Ordinary Share Capital + Reserves 31/12) + Debt (Debentures + Preference Shares)
- Operating Profit − Debenture Interest = Net Profit

1 WATSON – SAMPLE EXAM QUESTION

Watson Plc is a manufacturing firm in the construction industry that has an authorised capital of 500,000 Ordinary shares at €1each and 100,000 6% Preference shares of €1 each.

Trading Profit and Loss account for year ending 31/12/2008.

Sales	980,000
Cost of sales	(785,000)
Operating expenses	(125,000)
Interest	(25,000)
Net profit	45,000
Dividends	(37,000)
Retained profit	8,000
Profit and Loss balance 1/1	40,000
Profit and Loss balance 31/12	48,000

Ratios and Information for Year Ended 31/12/2007

Earnings per share	19.05c
Dividend per ordinary share	12.7c
Interest cover	4 times
Quick ratio	0.98:1
Return on capital employed	10.6%
Market value of an ordinary share	€1.30
Gearing	34%

Balance Sheet as at 31/12/2008

Fixed Assets		670,000
Investments (market value €140,000)		190,000
		860,000
Current Assets (incl. Stock €29,500, Debtors €100,000)	147,000	
Less Creditors Falling Due Within 1 Year		
Creditors	(159,000)	(12,000)
		848,000
Financed by		
10% debentures (2012 secured)		250,000
Capital and Reserves		
Ordinary shares at €1 each	450,000	
6% Preference shares at €1 each	100,000	
Profit and Loss balance	48,000	598,000
		848,000

Market value of share €1.20

You are required to calculate the following:

(i) 1. The cash sales, if the period of credit given to debtors is 2 months.
2. Return on capital employed.
3. The earnings per share
4. The dividend yield.
5. How long it would take one ordinary share to recover its value at the present payout rate?

(ii) Indicate if the Ordinary shareholders would be satisfied with the performance, state of affairs and prospects of the company. Use relevant ratios and other information to support your answer.

(iii) Having assessed Watson Plc what actions would you advise the company to take?

Watson Solution

(a) Cash Sales

$\frac{\text{Credit sales}}{\text{Debtors}} = 6$ times, i.e. 6 times debtors = 600,000 = Credit sales

Cash sales = 980,000 − 600,000 = **380,000**

Return on Capital Employed

$$\frac{\text{Net Profit} + \text{Debenture interest} \times 100}{\text{Capital employed}} = \frac{45{,}000 + 25{,}000 \times 100}{848{,}000} = \mathbf{8.25\%}$$

Earnings per Share

$$\frac{\text{Net Profit} - \text{preference dividend}}{\text{No. of ordinary shares}} = \frac{39{,}000}{450{,}000} = \mathbf{8.66c}$$

Dividend Yield

$$\frac{\text{Dividend per share} \times 100}{\text{Market price}} = \frac{6.89 \times 100}{120} = \mathbf{5.74\%}$$

Period to Recoup Share

$$\frac{\text{Market price}}{\text{Dividend per share}} = \frac{120}{6.89c} = \mathbf{17.42\ years}$$

(DPS = Ordinary dividend/No. of Ordinary shares)
= 37,000 − 6,000/450,000 = **6.89c**

(b) Performance

Profitability

- ROCE for 2008 is 8.25% which is 3 to 4 times the return from risk-free investment in the bank. However, this profitability has deteriorated from 10.6% last year which shows a less efficient use of resources.
- Return on equity to the ordinary shareholders specifically is only 7.8% which does not compare favourably with the 10% return being given to debenture holders.
- While Watson Plc is a profitable business able to generate profits for ordinary dividends the trend of declining return on capital employed of 20% would certainly worry shareholders

Dividend Policy

- DPS for 2008 is 6.89c which is down 45% from last year's 12.7c and that would not please shareholders.
- Dividend cover is also down from 1.5 to a very delicate 1.2 cover of dividends by profit with less profit retained. Dividend yield has also fallen from 9.77% last year to 5.47% this year as has the real rate of return from 14.65% to 6.89%.
- These falling dividend ratios are a very worrying trend as they would not reassure shareholders of Watson's ability to pay generous dividends going forward.

State of Affairs

Liquidity

- Watson has a liquidity problem as the current ratio of 0.92 indicates that the company is unable to pay its debts for the year. This ratio is well down the on the recommended figure of 2:1. (Although technically solvent as total assets are greater than total debts.)
- The Acid Test, down from 0.92 last year, shows that Watson is also illiquid and has only 74c in every €1 available to pay short-term debts.
- Watson has serious cash flow problems with the ability to pay dividends being a very immediate worry.

Gearing

- The company is lowly geared at 41.27% which would please ordinary shareholders as it increases their chance of getting a dividend and there is little risk from outsiders. It has worsened, however, from 34% last year which would worry shareholders.
- Interest cover has also fallen from 4 times last year to 2.8 times in 2008.
- Gearing/interest cover is satisfactory though not exceptional and shareholders would be concerned that both figures do not deteriorate further.

Investment Policy

- Investments which cost the company €190,000 are now only worth €140,000 – a drop of 26% of their value. This would not please ordinary shareholders although one must take into account the economic downturn globally in 2008.

Prospects

Share Price/Stock exchange performance

- Market price has fallen from €1.30 to €1.20, a fall of 7.7% which would displease shareholders as it shows a lack of confidence in the company by the market. When you factor in other indicators such as EPS falling from 19.05c to 8.66c in 2008 and a very poor P/E ratio of 17 years', the prospects and market sentiment for Watson are not positive.

Sector

- The construction industry is not a good sector to be in at the moment as prices have fallen by over 40% nationally. Property developers are finding it hard to sell as there is oversupply in the market. This has a knock-on effect for companies in the building industry so prospects here are not positive.

(c) Watson has a serious liquidity problem as the Acid Test has fallen from 0.98 to 0.74 to 1.

It can raise cash and improve liquidity by using the following methods:

1. Reduce dividends.
2. Sell investments and raise €140,000.
3. Issue the remaining 50,000 shares at €1.20 which should generate €60,000.
4. Improve gross profit percentage (currently 19.9%) by reducing cost of sales.
5. Diversify into other areas.
6. Collect debts quicker.
7. Sale and leaseback of fixed assets could yield over half a million.
8. Issue further debentures as gearing ratio is low.

2 ARTISAN

Artisan Plc is a manufacturing firm in the medical equipment industry. It has an authorised capital of 500,000 Ordinary shares at €1 each and 200,000 8% Preference shares at €1 each.

Trading Profit and Loss Account for Year Ending 31/12/2012

Sales	890,000
Cost of sales (opening stock €42,000)	(670,000)
Operating expenses	(156,000)
Interest	(14,000)
Net profit	50,000
Dividends	(34,250)
Retained profit	15,750
P&L 1/1	60,750
P&L 31/12	76,500

Balance Sheet as at 31/12/2012

Goodwill		160,000
Fixed Assets		570,000
		730,000
Current Assets (closing stock €37,000 and debtors €18,000)	85,000	
Less Creditors Falling Due Within 1 Year		
Trade creditors	(54,250)	
Proposed dividends	(34,250)	(3,500)
		726,500
Financed by		
7% debentures (2013/2014)		200,000
Capital and Reserves		
Ordinary shares at €1 each	350,000	
8% Preference shares at €1 each	100,000	
Profit and Loss balance	76,500	526,500
		726,500
Market value of one ordinary share	€2.60	

Ratios and Information for Year Ended 31/12/2011

Earnings per share	14c
Dividend per ordinary share	5c
Quick ratio	0.75 : 1
Return on capital employed	10.0%
Martket value of one ordinary share	€2.80
Gearing	44%
Interest cover	6 times
Return on equity	16%
Gross profit percentage	28%

You are required to calculate the following:

(a) 1. The cash purchases if the average period of credit from creditors is 1.5 months.
2. Ordinary dividend cover.
3. Dividend yield.
4. Interest cover.
5. How long it would take one ordinary share to recover its market price.

(b) Consider whether the debenture holders would be satisfied with the policy and state of affairs of the above company. Use available relevant information to support your answer.

(c) 1. Is a rising liquidity ratio always a sign of good management?
2. Identify 4 reasons for a declining **gross** profit percentage.

3 BOCASAN

Bocasan Plc is an internet travel company in the tourist industry. It has an authorised capital of 500,000 Ordinary shares at €1 each and 200,000 6% Preference shares of €1 each.

Trading Profit and Loss Account for Year Ending 31/12/2012

Sales	600,000
Cost of sales (closing stock €32,000)	(350,000)
Operating expenses	(159,000)
Interest	(18,000)
Net profit	73,000
Dividends	(33,000)
Retained profit	40,000
P&L 1/1	90,000
P&L 31/12	130,000

Ratios and Information for Year Ended 31/12/2011

Quick ratio	0.9 to 1
Return on capital employed	10.5%
Market value of one ordinary share	€2.60
Gearing	49%
Interest cover	4.8 times
Return on equity	12%
Current ratio	1.3 to 1

Balance Sheet as at 31/12/2012

Goodwill		300,000
Fixed Assets		495,000
		795,000
Current Assets	90,000	
Less Creditors Falling Due Within 1 Year		
Trade creditors	(37,000)	
Proposed dividends	(33,000)	20,000
		815,000
Financed by		
10% debentures (2015)		185,000
Capital and Reserves		
Ordinary shares at €1 each	300,000	
6% Preference shares at €1 each	200,000	
Profit and Loss balance	130,000	630,000
		815,000
Market price of one ordinary share	€2.85	

You are required to calculate the following:

(a) 1. Cash purchases if the average period of credit is 1.5 months and the opening stock is €40,000.
2. Ordinary dividend cover.
3. Dividend yield.
4. Interest cover.
5. How long it would take one ordinary share to recoup its value at the present payout rate.

(b) Bocasan Plc has applied to its bank for a €200,000 loan. Advise the bank manager whether this loan at 10% should be granted for further expansion. Use appropriate ratios, percentages and any other information from the above to support your conclusion.

(c) What action would you advise Bocasan to take?

4 CONDOR

Condor Plc is a consultancy firm in the quantity surveying industry for construction. It has an authorised capital of 600,000. Ordinary shares at €1 each and 300,000 6% Preference shares of €1 each.

Trading Profit and Loss Account for Year Ending 31/12/2012

Sales	1,250,000
Cost of sales (opening stock €75,000)	(880,000)
Operating expenses	(265,000)
Interest	(15,000)
Dividends	(39,500)
Retained profit	50,500
P&L 1/1	9,500
P&L 31/12	60,000

Balance Sheet as at 31/12/2012

Intangible assets		259,000
Fixed Assets		830,000
		1,089,000
Current Assets (closing stock € 65,000 and debtors €45,000)	115,000	
Less Creditors Falling Due Within 1 Year		
Trade creditors	(155,000)	
Proposed dividends	(39,000)	(79,000)
		1,010,000
Financed by		
5% debentures (2013/2014)		300,000
Capital and Reserves		
Ordinary shares at €1 each	450,000	
6% Preference shares at €1 each	200,000	
Profit and Loss balance	60,000	710,000
		1,010,000
Market value of one ordinary share	€3.60	

Ratios and information for year ended 31/12/2011

Earnings per share	14c
Dividend per ordinary share	5.2c
Quick ratio	0.75 : 1
Return on capital employed	12.9%
Market value of one ordinary share	€3.60
Gearing	44%
Interest cover	8.8 times
Gross profit percentage	33%

You are required to calculate the following:

(a) 1. The cash sales if the average period of credit allowed to debtors is 8 times.
2. Ordinary dividend cover.
3. Dividend yield.
4. Stock turnover rate.
5. How long it would take for one ordinary share to recover its market price.

(b) Indicate if the **ordinary** shareholders would be satisfied with the performance, state of affairs and prospects of the company. Use relevant ratios and other information to support your answer.

(c) Advise the bank manager as to whether a loan of €150,000 at 10% interest should be granted to Condor for future expansion.

5 DELGADO

Delgado Plc is a manufacturing firm in the computer software industry. It has an authorised capital of 800,000 Ordinary shares at €1 each and 200,000 6% preference shares of €1 each.

Trading Profit and Loss Account for Year Ending 31/12/2012

Sales	975,000
Opening stock	50,000
Purchases	630,000
Closing stock	(52,000)
Operating expenses	(216,000)
Interest	(13,500)
Net profit	117,500
Dividends	(52,000)
Retained profit	65,500
P&L 1/1	29,500
P&L 31/12	95,000

Ratios and Information for Year Ended 31/12/2011

Earnings per share	20c
Current ratio	1.45 : 1
Dividend per ordinary share	12.2c
Quick ratio	1.09 : 1
Return on capital employed	13.4%
Market value of an ordinary share	€1.58
Return on equity	15.6%

Balance Sheet as at 31/12/2012

Goodwill		176,000
Fixed Assets		700,000
Investments (market value €95,000)		135,000
		1,011,000
Current Assets (Debtors 65,000)	102,000	
Less Creditors Falling Due Within 1 Year		
Trade creditors	(36,000)	
Proposed dividends	(52,000)	14,000
		1,025,000
Financed by		
9% debentures (2013 secured)		150,000
Capital and Reserves		
Ordinary shares at €1 each	580,000	
8% Preference shares at €1 each	200,000	
Profit and Loss balance	95,000	875,000
		1,025,000
Share price	€1.45	

You are required to calculate the following:

(a) 1. The cash sales if the credit to debtors is 2 months.
2. Ordinary dividend cover.
3. The Earnings per share.
4. The Dividend yield.
5. How long it would take one ordinary share to recover its value assuming current performance is maintained.

(b) Indicate if the ordinary shareholders would be satisfied with the performance, state of affairs and prospects of the company. Use relevant ratios and other information to support your answer.

(c) The Net profit percentage was 12.5% in 2010. Calculate the percentage figure for 2011 and give 3 reasons for any change.
How can a falling Net profit percentage be corrected?

6 ELIZA

Eliza Plc, a manufacturing firm in the pharmaceutical industry has an authorised capital of 650,000 Ordinary shares at €1 each and 250,000 6% Preference shares of €1 each.

Trading Profit and Loss Account for Year Ending 31/12/2012

Sales	900,000
Opening stock	55,000
Closing stock	60,000
Cost of sales	(675,000)
Operating expenses	(160,000)
Interest	(27,000)
Dividends	(31,000)
Retained profit	7,000
P&L 1/1	35,000
P&L 31/12	42,000

Projected ratios and information for year ended 31/12/2013

Earnings per share	4c
Dividend per ordinary share	2.4c
Quick ratio	0.8
Return on capital employed	8.9%
Price earnings	24 times
Gearing	66%
Interest cover	1.4 times

Balance Sheet as at 31/12/2012

Fixed Assets		700,000
Investments (market value €200,000)		168,000
		868,000
Current Assets	187,000	
Less Creditors Falling Due Within 1 Year		
Trade creditors	(102,000)	
Proposed dividends	(31,000)	54,000
		922,000
Financed by		
9% debentures (2015 secured)		280,000
Capital and Reserves		
Ordinary shares at €1 each	340,000	
8% Preference shares at €1 each	260,000	
Profit and Loss balance	42,000	642,000
		922,000

Market price of one ordinary share €1.20

You are required to calculate the following:

(a) 1. The cash purchases if the credit from creditors is 5 times.
2. Interest cover.
3. The Dividend yield for 2012.
4. How long it would take one ordinary share to recover its value at the present payout rate.
5. The projected market price of the share in 2013.

(b) Indicate if the ordinary shareholders would be satisfied with the performance, state of affairs and prospects of the company. Use relevant ratios and other information to support your answer.

(c) What are the limitations of final accounts as a means of presentation.

7 FULCUM

Fulcum Plc is a service provider in the tourist industry. It has an authorised capital of 700,000 Ordinary shares at €1 each and 200,000 10% Preference shares of €1 each.

Trading Profit and Loss Account for Year Ending 31/12/2012

Sales	589,000
Opening stock	9,000
Closing stock	(60,000)
Cost of sales	(274,000)
Operating expenses	(201,000)
Interest	(22,500)
Dividends	(67,000)
Retained profit	24,500
P&L 1/1	44,500
P&L 31/12	69,000

Balance Sheet as at 31/12/2012

Goodwill		140,000
Fixed Assets		810,000
		950,000
Current Assets	171,000	
Less Creditors Falling Due Within 1 Year		
Trade creditors	(35,000)	
Proposed dividends	(67,000)	69,000
		1,019,000
Financed by		
9% debentures (2015 secured)		250,000
Capital and Reserves		
Ordinary shares at €1 each	500,000	
10% Preference shares at €1 each	200,000	
Profit and Loss balance	69,000	769,000
		1,019,000
Share price	€1.55	

Ratios and Information for Year Ended 31/12/2011

Earnings per share	24c
Current ratio	1.67 : 1
Dividend per ordinary share	9c
Quick ratio	0.9 : 1
Return on capital employed	9.2%
Market value of an ordinary share	€1.20
Return on equity	8%
Gearing	45%
Interest cover	10 times

You are required to calculate the following:

(a) 1. The cash purchases if the average period of credit from creditors is 1.5 months.
2. Return on capital employed.
3. Earnings per share.
4. Interest cover.
5. How long it would take one ordinary share to recover its market price based on the payout rate.

(b) A friend of yours has been given the opportunity to buy ordinary shares in Fulcum at €1.35, but before doing so they ask your opinion. What advice would you give? Use ratios, percentages and any other information from the above to support your conclusions.

(c) Outline three main users of financial statements of companies. Explain why the user has an interest in the accounts.

8 GABLE

Gable Plc, a service provider in the transport haulage industry has an authorised capital of 500,000 Ordinary shares at €1 each and 200,000 4% Preference shares of €1 each.

Trading Profit and Loss Account for Year Ending 31/12/2012

Sales	800,000
Cost of sales (closing stock €74,000)	440,000
Operating expenses	(200,000)
Interest	(14,000)
Net profit	146,000
Dividends	(44,000)
Retained profit	102,000
P&L 1/1	(20,000)
P&L 31/12	82,000

Balance Sheet as at 31/12/2012

Goodwill		100,000
Fixed Assets		539,000
		639,000
Current Assets	135,000	
Less Creditors Falling Due Within 1 Year		
Trade creditors	(44,000)	
Proposed dividends	(44,000)	47,000
		686,000
Financed by		
9% debentures (2015 /2016)		140,000
Capital and Reserves		
Ordinary shares at €1 each	304,000	
10% Preference shares at €1 each	120,000	
Profit and Loss balance	82,000	
Debenture redemption reserve	40,000	546,000
		686,000
Market price of share	€2.05	

Projected Ratios and Information for Year Ended 31/12/2013

Earnings per share	36c
Dividend per ordinary share	8.2c
Quick ratio	0.59
Return on capital employed	8.9%
Martket value of one ordinary share	€1.90
Gearing	44%
Interest cover	8 times
Return on equity	16%
Gross profit percentage	60%

You are required to calculate the following:

(a) 1. The opening stock if the rate of stock turnover is 10 times.
2. Dividend yield.
3. Return on capital employed.
4. Real rate of return.
5. How long it would take one ordinary share to recover its market price.

(b) Consider whether the debenture holders would be satisfied with the policy and state of affairs of the above company. Use available relevant information to support your answer.

(c) 1. When is a company **highly geared**?
2. What are the problems associated with this form of capital structure?

TOPIC 12

Published a/c's

Motivation is what gets you started. Habit is what keeps you going.

Jim Ryun

1 Zodiac – Sample Exam Question

Zodiac Plc has an authorised capital of 650,000 Ordinary shares of €1 each and 300,000 8% Preference shares of €1 each.

The following Trial Balance was extracted from the books on 31/12/2008.

	€	€
Vehicles	280,000	
Vehicles account, depreciation on 1/1		112,000
7% investments	320,000	
Investment income		5,600
Buildings at cost	860,000	
Accumulated depreciation on 1/1		52,800
Debtors and creditors	243,000	191,000
Stock at 1/1/2008	81,000	
Patents at 1/1/2008	28,000	
Administration expenses	212,000	
Distribution expenses	198,000	
Purchases and sales	1,340,000	2,005,000
Rental income		48,000
6% debentures 2013/2014		300,000
Profit on sale of land		72,000
Bank	62,900	
VAT		66,000
Dividends paid	72,000	
Profit and Loss 1/1/2008		84,000
Issued capital		
– Ordinary shares		600,000
– Preference shares		150,000
Provision for bad debts		14,500
Debenture interest paid	15,000	
Patent royalties		11,000
	3,711,900	3,711,900

The following information and instructions are to be taken into account:

(i) Stock 31/12/2008 is €89,000.

(ii) The Patent was acquired on 1/1/2004 for €84,000. It is amortised over 6 years in equal instalments. The amortisation is to be included in the cost of sales.

(iii) Provide for debenture interest due, investment interest due, auditors' fees €7,400, directors' fees €40,000 and corporation tax €62,000.

(iv) Depreciation is to be provided for on buildings, at the rate of 2% straight-line and is to be allocated 40% distribution costs and 60% administration expenses. There was no purchase or sale of buildings during the year. Vehicles are to be depreciated at the rate of 20% of cost.

(v) During the year land adjacent to the company's premises, which had cost €60,000 was sold for €132,000. At the end of the year the company revalued its buildings to €950,000. The company wishes to incorporate this value in this year's accounts.

(vi) Included in administration expenses is the receipt of €17,000 for discount.

You are required:

(a) To prepare the **published** Profit and Loss account for the year 31/12/2008 and a Balance Sheet as at that date in accordance with the Companies Acts and the appropriate accounting standards showing the following notes:
1. Accounting policy note for tangible fixed assets and stock.
2. Operating profit.
3. Interest payable.
4. Tangible fixed assets.

(b) 1. State 3 items of information that must be included in a **directors' report**.
2. Explain the term **exceptional item** and give an example.

Zodiac Published Solution

Profit and Loss for Year Ended 31/12/2008	€
Turnover	2,005,000
Less cost of sales	**(1,346,000)**
Gross Profit	659,000
Less distribution costs	**(260,880)**
Less administration costs	**(286,720)**
	111,400
Other operating income	**76,000**
Operating profit	187,400
Investment income	22,400
Profit on sale of land	72,000
	281,800
Interest payable	(18,000)
Profit on ordinary activities before tax	263,800
Taxation	(62,000)
	201,800
Dividends paid	(72,000)
	129,800
Profit brought forward at 1/1/2008	84,000
Profit carried forward at 31/12/2008	213,800

Balance Sheet at 31/12/2008			
Fixed assets			
Intangible assets			**14,000**
Tangible fixed assets			**1,062,000**
Financial fixed			320,000
			1,396,000
Current Assets			
Stock	89,000		
Debtors	**245,300**		
Bank	62,900	397,200	
Creditors Falling Due Within 1 Year			
Trade creditors	191,000		
Taxation	**128,000**		
Other creditors	**50,400**	(369,400)	27,800
			1,423,800
Creditors Falling Due After More Than 1 Year			
6% debentures			300,000
Capital and Reserves			
Issued shares		750,000	
Revaluation reserve		**160,000**	
Profit carried forward		213,800	1,123,800
			1,423,800

Workings

Cost of sales	81,000	+	1,340,000	+	14,000	−	89,000		=	**1,346,000**
Distribution costs	198,000	+	6,880	+	56,000				=	**260,880**
Administration expenses	212,000	+	7,400	+	40,000	+	10,320	+ 17,000	=	**286,720**
Other operating income	48,000	+	11,000	+	17,000				=	**76,000**
Tangible fixed assets	950,000	+	280,000	−	112,000	−	56,000		=	**1,062,000**
Debtors	243,000	−	14,500	+	16,800				=	**245,300**
Other creditors	7,400	+	40,000	+	3,000				=	**50,400**
Taxation	62,000	+	66,000						=	**128,000**
Revaluation reserve	90,000	+	52,800	+	17,200				=	**160,000**

Notes to Published Accounts

Notes to Accounts for Zodiac

(i) **Accounting policy on tangible fixed assets and stock**

Depreciation is calculated in order to write-off tangible fixed assets over their useful economic life as follows:

- Buildings are depreciated at 2% p.a. on cost and revalued at the end of 2008. Vehicles are depreciated at 20% on cost.
- Stocks are valued on a FIFO basis at whichever is the lowest: cost or book value.

(ii) **Operating profit is arrived at after charging**

Depreciation on Tangible Assets	73,200
Patents amortised	14,000
Auditors' fees	7,400
Directors' remuneration	40,000

(iii) **Interest payable on debenture** (repayable by 2013/2014) 18,000

(iv) **Tangible fixed assets.**

Tangible Fixed Assets	Land/Blgs	Vehicles
1/1/2008	920,000	280,000
Disposal	(60,000)	
Revaluation	90,000	
Value 31/12/2008	950,000	280,000
Accumulated Depreciation		
Depreciation on 1/1	52,800	112,000
This year	17,200	56,000
Revaluation	(70,000)	
	Nil	168,000
Net Book Value 1/1	867,200	168,000
Net Book Value 31/12	950,000	112,000

Directors' report must contain the following:

(a) Amounts to be transferred to reserves.
(b) Report of any changes in the nature of the business for the year.
(c) The principal activities of the business any proposed changes.
(d) Recommendation of dividends to be paid.
(e) Details of directors' holding and dealing for the year.
(f) Significant changes in fixed assets.
(g) Review on yearly activities.
(h) A list of the company's subsidiaries and affiliations.

Exceptional Item

This is a material item of significant size. It is a profit or loss that must be shown separately in the Profit and Loss account because of its size, e.g. profit on the sale of a fixed asset or a large bad debt.

2 ANNEXE

Annexe Plc has an authorised capital of 250,000 6% Preference and 475,000 Ordinary shares of €1 each. The following Trial Balance was extracted from its books on 31/12/2012.

	€	€
Revaluation reserve		240,000
Vehicles at cost	132,000	
Vehicles – accumulated depreciation on 1/1/2012		86,000
8% investments	180,000	
Investment income		11,100
Land and buildings at cost (revalued 1/7/2012)	760,000	
Debtors and creditors	106,000	68,000
Directors' fees	73,000	
Stock at 1/1/2012	84,000	
Patent	40,000	
Salaries and general expenses	136,000	
Discount		8,400
Advertising	19,000	
Purchases and sales	544,000	896,000
Rent	27,000	
8% debentures 2015 (including €90,000 issued on 1/5/2012)		225,000
Profit on sale of land		62,000
Bank		24,950
VAT		11,250
Dividends paid	33,000	
Profit and Loss at 1/1/2012		36,300
Issued capital		
– Ordinary shares		335,000
– Preference shares		130,000
	2,134,000	2,134,000

The following information and instructions are to be taken into account:

(i) Stock on 31/12/2012 is €79,000.

(ii) The patent was acquired on 1/1/2007 for €80,000. It is amortised over 10 years in equal instalments. The amortisation is to be included in the cost of sales.

(iii) Provide for debenture interest due, investment interest due, auditors' fees €11,000, and corporation tax €24,000.

(iv) Depreciation is to be provided for on buildings, at the rate of 2% straight-line until the date of revaluation and thereafter at 2% of the revalued figure. Vehicles are to be depreciated at the rate of 20% of cost.

(v) On 1/7/2012 the land adjacent to the company's premises, which had cost €78,000 was sold for €140,000. On this date the remaining land and buildings were revalued at €760,000. Included in this revaluation is land valued at €130,000 which originally cost €50,000. The revalued buildings had cost €520,000.

(vi) The market value of investments on 31/12/2012 is €150,000.

You are required:

(a) To prepare the **published** Profit and Loss account for the year 31/12/2012 and a Balance Sheet on that date in accordance with the Companies Acts and the appropriate accounting standards showing the following notes:

1. Accounting policy note for tangible fixed assets and stock.
2. Interest payable.
3. Operating profit.
4. Profit on sale of property.

(b) 1. Explain the purpose of an audit and the duties of an auditor.

2. What is the difference between a **qualified** and **unqualified** audit?

3 BOYCIE

Boycie Plc has an authorised capital of 200,000 7% Preference and 600,000 Ordinary shares of €1 each. The following Trial Balance was extracted from its books on 31/12/2012.

	€	€
Buildings (cost €690,000)	638,000	
Debenture interest paid	4,000	
Provision for bad debts		1,250
9% investments	48,000	
Investment income		3,500
Debtors and creditors	20,000	43,500
Stock at 1/1/2012	23,500	
Patent	27,000	
Salaries and general expenses	140,000	
Administration expenses	65,000	
Discount		14,200
Selling expenses	18,700	
Purchases and sales	480,000	740,000
Rent	9,200	
8% debentures 2015 (including €20,000 issued on 30/9/2012)		90,000
Profit on sale of land		40,000
Bank		15,600
VAT	13,000	
Dividends paid	13,250	
Profit and Loss at 1/1/2012		51,600
Issued capital		
– Ordinary shares		350,000
– Preference shares		150,000
	1,499,650	1,499,650

The following information and instructions are to be taken into account:

(i) Stock on 31/12/2012 is €24,400.

(ii) The patent was acquired 2 years previously for €36,000. It is amortised over 8 years in equal instalments. The amortisation is to be included in the cost of sales.

(iii) Provide for debenture interest due, investment interest due, auditors' fees €6,200, and corporation tax €26,000 directors' fees €10,000.

(iv) Depreciation is to be provided for on buildings, at the rate of 2% straight-line. During the year land adjacent to the company's premises which cost €70,000 was sold for €110,000. At year end buildings were revalued at €900,000 and the company wishes to incorporate this into the accounts.

(v) The market value of investments currently stands at €68,000.

(vi) The debentures are secured by a floating charge on the fixed assets.

You are required:

(a) To prepare the **published** Profit and Loss account for the year 31/12/2012 and a Balance Sheet on that date in accordance with the Companies Acts and the appropriate accounting standards showing the following notes:

1. Accounting policy note for tangible fixed assets and stock.
2. Operating profit.
3. Interest payable.
4. Debentures.
5. Tangible fixed assets.

(b) State and explain 4 important accounting concepts.

4 KIM CLAVIN

Kim Clavin Plc has an authorised capital of 250,000 7% redeemable Preference shares of €1 and 800,000 Ordinary shares at 50c. On 31/12/2012, the following balances were extracted from the books.

	€	€
Vehicles (cost €167,000)	137,000	
12% investments	560,000	
Investment income		50,000
Buildings (cost €640,000)	512,000	
Rental income		120,000
12% debentures 2013/2014		200,000
Profit on sale of land		85,000
Debtors and creditors	300,000	382,000
Stock at 1/1/2012	660,000	
Goodwill at 1/1/2012	320,000	
Administration expenses	504,000	
Distribution expenses	450,000	
Purchases and sales	6,300,000	8,100,000
Bank	24,000	
PRSI		46,000
Dividends paid	30,000	
Profit and Loss at 1/1/2012		226,000
Issued capital		
Ordinary shares at 50c		400,000
Preference shares		200,000
Debenture interest paid	12,000	
	9,809,000	9,809,000

The following information and instructions are to be taken into account:

(i) Stock on 31/12/2012 was €720,000.

(ii) The Goodwill was valued 4 years previously for €640,000. It is amortised over 8 years in equal instalments. The amortisation is to be included in the cost of sales.

(iii) Provide for debenture interest due, investment interest due, auditors' fees €12,000, and corporation tax €235,000, directors' fees at €126,000.

(iv) Depreciation is to be provided for on buildings, at the rate of 2% straight-line. This depreciation is to be allocated at 30% to distribution expenses and 70% to administration expenses. During the year, land adjacent to the company premises which cost €90,000 was sold for €175,000. At year end, buildings were revalued at €900,000 and the company wishes to incorporate this into the accounts.

(v) Vehicles are to be depreciated at 15% on cost.

(vi) Included in administration expenses is the receipt of €25,000 for the use of the company name by a start-up company.

(vii) A contingent liability exists in respect of a pending unfair dismissal claim of €50,000.

(viii) Debentures are secured by a floating charge on the company's fixed assets.

You are required:

(a) To prepare the **published** Profit and Loss account for the year 31/12/2012, and a Balance Sheet as at that date, in accordance with the Companies Acts and the appropriate accounting standards showing the following notes:

1. Accounting policy note for tangible fixed assets and stock.
2. Operating profit.
3. Interest payable.
4. Debentures.
5. Tangible fixed assets.

(b) 1. State the criteria that determines that a company is **medium-sized**.

2. What is a **qualified audit**?

5 DURACELL

Duracell Plc has an authorised capital of 125,000 9% Preference shares at €2 each and 600,000 Ordinary shares at €1 each. On 31/12/2012, the following balances were extracted from the books.

	€	€
Directors' fees	76,000	
Vehicles at cost	96,000	
Vehicles – accumulated depreciation on 1/1/2012		28,000
8% investments	150,000	
Investment income		9,000
Buildings at cost	960,000	
Accumulated depreciation on 1/1/2012		180,000
Debtors and creditors	76,500	58,000
Stock at 1/1/2012	35,000	
Patents at 1/1/2012	48,000	
Administration expenses	49,000	
Distribution expenses	36,000	
Salaries and general expenses	139,000	
Discount		9,500
Advertising	32,000	
Purchases and sales	525,000	950,200
Rent	12,000	
9% debentures 2015 (incl. €80,000 issued on 1/7/2012)		220,000
Profit on sale of land		65,000
Bank		5,900
VAT		12,400
Dividends paid	37,500	
Profit and Loss at 1/1/2012		84,000
Issued capital		
450,000 Ordinary shares at €1 each		450,000
100,000 9% Preference shares at €2 each		200,000
	2,272,000	2,272,000

The following information and instructions are to be taken into account:

(i) Stock on 31/12/2012 was €48,000.

(ii) The Patent was acquired 4 years previously for €96,000. It is being written-off to cost of sales over 8 years.

(iii) Provide for debenture interest due, investment interest due, auditors' fees due €9,800, and tax due €54,000.

(iv) Depreciation is to be provided for on buildings, at the rate of 2% straight-line. This depreciation is to be allocated with 20% to distribution expenses and 80% to administration expenses.

(v) During the year, land adjacent to the building (which cost €70,000) was sold for €135,000. At year end buildings were revalued at €1.2 million and the company wishes to incorporate this into the accounts.

(vi) Vehicles are to be depreciated at 20% of book value.

(vii) Included in advertising is the receipt of €6,000 for rental income.

(viii) A contingent liability exists in respect of a liability claim by an employee for injury incurred to the value of €75,000.

You are required:

(a) To prepare the **published** Profit and Loss account for the year 31/12/2012. Also a Balance Sheet as at that date in accordance with the Companies Acts and the appropriate accounting standards showing the following notes:

1. Accounting policy note for tangible fixed assets and stock.
2. Operating profit.
3. Debentures.
4. Tangible fixed assets.

(b) 1. Explain the difference between a **qualified** and an **unqualified** audit.

2. Identify 4 specific responsibilities of directors.

6 DRAGON

Dragon Plc has an authorised capital of 600,000 Ordinary shares of €1 each and 200,000 5% Preference shares of €1 each. The following Trial Balance was extracted from the books on 31/12/2012.

	€	€
Patent royalties		6,600
Vehicles at cost	168,000	
Vehicles – accumulated depreciation on 1/1/2012		67,200
7% investments	192,000	
Investment income		3,360
Buildings at cost	516,000	
Accumulated depreciation on 1/1/2012		31,680
Debtors and creditors	145,800	114,600
Stock at 1/1/2012	48,600	
Patents at 1/1/2012	16,800	
Salaries and general expenses	127,200	
Advertising and selling expenses	118,800	
Purchases and sales	804,000	1,203,000
Discount		28,800
6% debentures 2013/2014		180,000
Issued capital		
– Ordinary shares		360,000
– Preference shares		90,000
Profit on sale of land		43,200
Bank	37,740	
VAT		39,600
Dividends paid	43,200	
Profit and Loss at 1/1/2012		50,400
Provision for bad debts		8,700
Debenture interest paid	9,000	
	2,227,140	2,227,140

The following information and instructions are to be taken into account:

(i) Stock 31/12/2012 is €53,400.

(ii) The Patent was acquired for €50,400, and has been written-off for 4 years out of a total of 6 years. This amortisation is to be included in the cost of sales.

(iii) Provide for debenture interest due, investment interest due, auditors' fees €4,440, directors' fees €24,000 and corporation tax €37,200.

(iv) Depreciation is to be provided for on buildings, at the rate of 2% straight-line and is to be allocated with 40% to distribution costs and 60% to administration expenses. There was no purchase or sale of buildings during the year. Vehicles are to be depreciated at the rate of 20% of cost.

(v) During the year, land adjacent to the company's premises (which had cost €36,000) was sold for €79,200. At the end of the year the company revalued its buildings to €570,000. The company wishes to incorporate this value in this year's accounts.

(vi) Included in salaries and general expenses is the receipt of €10,200 for rental income.

(vii) A contingent liability exists in respect of a product liability claim made against Dragon Plc. This case is unlikely to be successful although legal fees of €30,000 may have to be paid.

You are required:

(a) To prepare the **published** Profit and Loss account for the year 31/12/2012 and a Balance Sheet as at that date in accordance with the Companies Acts and the appropriate accounting standards showing the following notes:

1. Accounting policy note for tangible fixed assets and stock.
2. Operating profit.
3. Interest payable.
4. Tangible fixed assets.

(b) 1. State how Dragon Plc would deal with the above **contingent liability** which is possible but unlikely.

2. What are the main objectives of **financial accounting**?

7 EQUINOX

Equinox Plc has an authorised capital of 700,000 Ordinary shares at €1.25 each and 400,000 5.5% Preference shares of €1 each. The following Trial Balance was extracted from the books on 31/12/2012.

	€	€
Buildings at cost	989,000	
Accumulated depreciation on 1/1/2012		60,720
Vehicles at cost	322,000	
Vehicles – accumulated depreciation on 1/1/2012		128,800
Debtors and creditors	279,450	219,650
Purchases and sales	1,541,000	2,305,750
7% investments	368,000	
Investment income		6,440
Patents (cost €96,600)	32,200	
General expenses	243,800	
Selling expenses	227,700	
Stock at 1/1/2012	93,150	
Rental income		55,200
6% debentures 2015/2016		345,000
Profit on sale of land		82,800
Bank	72,335	
Royalties		12,650
Debenture interest paid	17,250	
Provision for bad debts		16,675
Tax and PRSI		75,900
Dividends paid	82,800	
Profit and Loss at 1/1/2012		96,600
Issued capital		
– Ordinary shares of €1.25 each		690,000
– 5.5% Preference shares		172,500
	4,268,685	4,268,685

The following information and instructions are to be taken into account:

(i) Stock 31/12/2012 is €102,350.

(ii) The Patent is being written-off over 6 years to cost of sales.

(iii) Provide for debenture interest due, investment interest due, auditors' fees €8,510, directors' fees €46,000 and corporation tax €71,300.

(iv) Depreciation is to be provided for on buildings, at the rate of 2% straight-line and is to be allocated by 40% distribution costs and 60% administration expenses. There was no purchase or sale of buildings during the year.

(v) Vehicles are to be depreciated at the rate of 20% of cost.

(vi) During the year, land adjacent to the company's premises (which had cost €69,000) was sold for €151,800. At the end of the year the company revalued its buildings to €1,092,500. The company wishes to incorporate this value in this year's accounts.

(vii) Included in administration expenses is the receipt of €19,550 for royalties receivable.

(viii) The market value of investments on 31/12/2012 is €402,500.

(ix) Debentures are secured by a fixed charge on the tangible fixed assets of Equinox Plc.

(x) On 31/12/2012 preliminary contract agreements were entered into at a total cost of €500,000 and a further €150,000 capital improvements to existing premises is also envisaged for next year.

You are required:

(a) To prepare the **published** Profit and Loss account for the year 31/12/2012 and a Balance Sheet as at that date in accordance with the Companies Acts and the appropriate accounting standards showing the following notes:

1. Accounting policy note for tangible fixed assets and stock.
2. Operating profit.
3. Proposed capital expenditure.
4. Tangible fixed assets.

(b) 1. When is an item in the accounts considered **'material'**?

2. Explain what is meant by accounting concepts, bases and policies?

TOPIC

13

Incomplete Records

Never try to solve all the problems at once. Make them line up for you one-by-one.

Richard Sloma

1 LYNCH – SAMPLE EXAM QUESTION

On 1/1/2006 P. Lynch purchased a business for €590,000 consisting of the following tangible assets and liabilities: Premises €560,000, Stock €19,000, Debtors €12,000, 3-months' Premises insurance prepaid €1,600, Trade Creditors €18,200, Wages due €2,600 and Cash €200.

During 2006, Lynch did not keep a full set of accounts but was able to supply the following information on 31/12/2006:

Cash Payments:	Lodgments €116,000, General expenses €73,800, Purchases €105,200.
Bank Payments:	Light and heat €5,400, Annual premises insurance premium €6,800, Creditors €38,800, Interest €2,250, Furniture €14,000, Delivery van €28,400.
Bank Lodgments:	Debtors €61,000, Cash €116,000, Dividends €3,000.

Lynch took from stock goods to the value of €150, and cash of €200 per week for household use during the year. Lynch borrowed €180,000 on 1/9/2006 part of which was used to purchase an adjoining premises costing €155,000. It was agreed that Lynch would pay interest on the last day of each month at the rate of 5% per annum. The capital sum was to be repaid in one lump sum in the year 2016. To provide for this the bank was to transfer €1,200 on the last day of each month from Lynch's bank account into an investment fund starting on 30/9/2006. Lynch estimated that 25% of the furniture and light and heat **used**, as well as 20% of interest **payable** for the year, should be attributed to the private section of the premises.

Included in the assets and liabilities of the firm on 31/12/2006 were: Stock €16,400, Debtors €20,200, Trade Creditors €30,400, Cash €400, Electricity due €480 and €25 interest earned by the fund to date.

You are required to show, with workings:

(a) The Trading Profit and Loss account for the year ended 31/12/2006.

(b) The Balance Sheet as at 31/12/2006.

(c) 1. Explain the term **accounting concept**.
2. Name 2 fundamental accounting concepts.
3. Illustrate an accounting concept applying to the accounts of Lynch.

(a) Trading Profit and Loss Account for year ending 31/12/2006

Sales			374,800	
Less Cost of Sales				
Opening stock		19,000		
Purchases	W	148,400		
Less closing stock		(16,400)	151,000	
Gross profit			223,800	
Less expenses				
General expenses	W	71,200		
Insurance	W	6,700		
Interest	W	2,400		
Light and heat	W	4,410	84,710	
			139,090	
Add income from investment income			25	
Net profit			139,115	

(b) Balance Sheet on 31/12/2006

Intangible Fixed				
Goodwill	W			18,000
Tangible Fixed				
Buildings		715,000		
Delivery vans		28,400		
Furniture		10,500		753,900
Financial Assets				
Investment fund				4,825
Current Assets				776,725
Stock		16,400		
Debtors		20,200		
Bank	W	104,550		
Cash		400		
Insurance prepaid		1,700	143,250	
Creditors Falling Due Within 1 Year				
Creditors		30,400		
Interest due		750		
Electricity		480	(31,630)	111,620
				888,345
Financed by				
Creditors Falling Due for More Than 1 Year				
Loan				180,000
Capital		590,000		
Add capital introduced		3,000		
Net profit		139,115		
Less drawings	W	(23,770)		708,345
				888,345

Notes to Accounts

1. Expenses

	General	Light/Heat	Insurance	Interest
Paid	73,800	5,400	6,800	2,250
Adjustments	(2,600)	480	1,600	
			(1,700)	**750**
Cost/Used		5,880		3,000
Less drawings		(1,470)		(600)
	71,200	**4,410**	**6,700**	**2,400**

2. Drawings

(cash + goods + expenses + asset) 7,800 + 10,400 + 1,470 + 600 + 3,500 = **23,770**

3. Goodwill

(cost − value) 590,000 − 572,000 = **18,000**

4. Sales Credit

(pay + balance 31/12 − balance 1/1) 61,000 + 20,200 − 12,000 = 69,200

Cash (pay + drawings + balance 31/12 − balance 1/1) 295,000 + 10,400 + 400 − 200 = 305,600 = **374,800**

5. Purchases Credit

(pay + balance 31/12 − balance 1/1) 38,800 + 30,400 − 18,200 = **51,000**

(credit + cash − drawings of goods) 51,000 + 105,200 − 7,800 = **156,200**

6. Bank (payments + fund + asset − lodge − loan) 95,650 + 4,800 + 155,000 − 180,000 − 180,000 = **104,550**

(c) Concepts are practices or rules that are applied in the preparation of accounting financial statements.
Accruals, Going Concern, Consistency and Prudence are fundamental accounting concepts.
Accruals Concept means all expenses incurred in a particular period must be included in the accounts of that period whether paid or not. All revenue income included in the same fashion received or not.
Expenses due are included in this year's accounts although not paid until next year.
Insurance prepaid should not be included as the payment refers to the following year.

2 ARCHER

On 1/1/2012 A. Archer purchased a business for €200,000 consisting of the following tangible assets and liabilities: Premises €160,000, Stock €15,600, Debtors €18,000, 3-months' Insurance on premises prepaid €840, Trade Creditors €20,000, Wages due €1,400.

During 2012 Archer did not keep a full set of books but was able to supply the following information on 31/12/2012:

Cash Payments: Lodgments €89,600, General expenses €26,900, Purchases €45,200.

Bank Payments: Delivery vans €29,200, Creditors €31,200, Light and heat €5,600, Interest €1,400, Covenant for charitable organisation €2,600, Annual premises insurance premium €3,600, Furniture €15,000.

Bank Lodgments: Debtors €38,000, Cash €89,600, Dividends €1,900.

Archer took goods from stock to the value of €80 and cash of €50 per week for household use during the year. Archer borrowed €70,000 on 1/9/2012 part of which was used to purchase an adjoining premises costing €60,000. It was agreed that Archer would pay interest on the last day of each month at the rate of 12% per annum. The capital sum was to be repaid in a lump sum in the year 2020 and to provide for this the bank was to transfer €500 on the last day of each month from Archer's bank account into an investment fund. Archer estimated that one-third of furniture, 25% of light and heat **used** as well as 20% of interest **payable** for the year should be attributed to the private section of the premises.

Included in the assets and liabilities of the firm on 31/12/2012 were Stock €16,700, Debtors €19,500, Trade Creditors €12,800, Cash €400, Electricity due €600, and €55 Interest earned by the fund to date.

You are required to show, with workings:

(a) Trading Profit and Loss Account, for the year ended 31/12/2012.

(b) Balance Sheet as at 31/12/2012.

(c) Why is it important for sole traders to keep a double-entry system of bookkeeping.

3 BROPHY

On 1/1/2012 B. Brophy purchased a business for €390,000 consisting of the following tangible assets and liabilities: Premises €330,000, Stock €36,300, Debtors €54,600, 3-months' Premises insurance prepaid €1,080, Trade Creditors €42,450, Wages due €1,425.

During 2012 Brophy did not keep a full set of accounts but was able to supply the following information on 31/12/2012:

Cash Payments:	Lodgments €61,500, General expenses €49,200, Purchases €101,100.
Bank Payments:	Equipment €40,200, Light and heat €12,300, Annual premises insurance premium €6,120, Creditors €54,300, Interest €7,500, Furniture €24,000, Covenant for charitable organisation €5,250.
Bank Lodgments:	Debtors €68,100, Cash €61,500, Dividends €12,750.

Brophy took from stock goods to the value of €780 and cash of €1,170 per month for household use during the year. Brophy borrowed €180,000 on 1/4/2012 a part of which was used to purchase an adjoining premises costing €135,000. It was agreed that Brophy would pay interest on the last day of each month at the rate of 8% per annum. The capital sum was to be repaid in a lump sum in the year 2018. To provide for this the bank was to transfer €1,350 on the last day of each month from Brophy's bank account into an investment fund. Brophy estimated that 25% of furniture and light and heat **used** as well as 20% of interest **payable** for the year should be attributed to the private section of the premises.

Included in the assets and liabilities of the firm on 31/12/2012 were Stock €39,600, Debtors €57,150, Trade Creditors €37,800, Cash €1,050, Electricity due €450, and €195 Interest earned by the fund to date.

You are required to show, with workings:

(a) Trading Profit and Loss Account, for the year ended 31/12/2012.

(b) Balance Sheet as at 31/12/2012.

(c) Name 4 fundamental accounting concepts and explain one using an example.

4 CAREY

On 1/1/2012 Rita Carey purchased a business for €300,000 consisting of the following tangible assets and liabilities: Buildings €240,000, Stock €18,600, 8% Investments €30,000, Debtors €24,800, 4-months' Insurance on premises prepaid €1,160, Trade Creditors €18,900, Electricity due €160.

During 2012 Carey did not keep a full set of books but was able to supply the following information on 31/12/2012:

Cash Payments: Lodgments €128000, General expenses €46,500, Purchases €78,800.

Bank Payments: Vehicles €12,000, Creditors €65,400, Light and heat €8,400, Interest €3,200, Covenant for charitable organisation €3,500, Annual premises insurance premium €3,960, Machinery €18,000

Bank Lodgments: Debtors €84,300, Cash €128,000, Dividends €3,200, Investment interest €1,500.

Carey took goods from stock to the value of €360 and cash of €210 per month for household use during the year. Carey borrowed €135,000 on 1/8/2012, part of which was used to purchase an adjoining premises costing €115,000. It was agreed that Carey would pay interest on the last day of each month at the rate of 8% per annum. The capital sum was to be repaid in 12 equal 6 monthly instalments starting on 1 March of next year. Carey estimated that 25% of machinery, and light and heat **used**, as well as 20% of interest **payable** for the year should be attributed to the private section of the premises.

Included in the assets and liabilities of the firm on 31/12/2012 were Stock €22,400, Debtors €27,700, Trade Creditors €16,100, Cash €980, Electricity due €240.

You are required to show, with workings:

(a) Trading Profit and Loss Account for the year ended 31/12/2012.

(b) Balance Sheet as at 31/12/2012.

(c) Carey seeks your advice on how to finance a proposed update of new computer systems for €35,000. What advice would you give?

5 DUNICAN

On 1/1/2012, D. Dunican purchased a business for €354,000 consisting of the following tangible assets and liabilities: Premises €336,000, Stock €11,400, Debtors €7,200, 3-months' Premises insurance prepaid €960, Trade Creditors €10,920, Wages due €1,560 and Cash €120.

During 2012, Dunican did not keep a full set of accounts but was able to supply the following information on 31/12/2012.

Cash Payments	Lodgments €69,600, General expenses €44,280, Purchases €63,120.
Bank Payments	Furniture €8,400, Delivery van €17,040, Light and heat €3,240, Annual premises insurance premium €4,080, Creditors €23,280, Interest €1,350.
Bank Lodgments	Debtors €36,600, Cash €69,600, Dividends €1,800.

Dunican took goods from stock to the value of €90 and cash of €120 per week for household use during the year.

Dunican borrowed €108,000 on 1/9/2012 part of which was used to purchase an adjoining premises costing €93,000. It was agreed that Dunican would pay interest on the last day of each month at the rate of 5% per annum. The capital sum was to be repaid in a lump sum in the year 2020. To provide for this the bank was to transfer €720 on the last day of each month from Dunican's bank account into an investment fund commencing on 30/9/2012.

Dunican estimated that 25% of furniture, and light and heat **used**, as well as 20% of interest **payable** for the year should be attributed to the private section of the premises.

Included in the assets and liabilities of the firm on 31/12/2012 were Stock €9,840, Debtors €12,120, Trade Creditors €18,240, Cash €240, Electricity due €288, and €15 Interest earned by the fund to date.

You are required to show, with workings:

(a) Trading Profit and Loss Account, for the year ended 31/12/2012.

(b) Balance Sheet as at 31/12/2012.

(c) 1. Why are the records kept by Dunican unsatisfactory?

2. What additional information would be available if the firm's accounts were prepared using the double-entry system?

6 EDWARDS

On 1/1/2012, E. Edwards purchased a business for €390,000 consisting of the following tangible assets and liabilities: Buildings €324,000, Trade Creditors €37,400, Wages due €3,400, Stock €30,400, Debtors €34,000, 3-months' Insurance on premises prepaid €1,720.

During 2012, Edwards did not keep a full set of books but was able to supply the following information on 31/12/2012:

Cash Payments	Purchases €106,000, Lodgments €192,000, General expenses €47,400.
Bank Payments	Vehicle €52,000, Creditors €66,200, Light and heat €11,600, Interest €4,650, Standing order to Concern €6,400, Annual premises insurance premium €12,000, Equipment €44,000, Rent for one year €4,800.
Bank Lodgments	Debtors €68,000, Cash €192,000, Dividends €7,600.

Edwards took goods from stock to the value of €800 and cash of €700 per month for household use during the year.

Edwards borrowed €168,000 on 1/7/2012 part of which was used to purchase an adjoining building costing €140,000. It was agreed that that sum borrowed would be repaid in 12 equal instalments on 1 June each year. Interest was to be charged at the rate of 10% per annum on the initial sum, to be paid monthly at the end of each month.

The figure for rent was in respect of an adjoining business rented by Edwards on 01/10/12. It was payable in advance and Edwards estimated that one-third of the building was used as a private residence and that 20% of light and heat **used** should also be attributed to the private section of the premises.

Included in the assets and liabilities of the firm on 31/12/2012 were Cash €1,300, Stock €34,600 (including stock of heating fuel €600), Electricity due €1,440, Debtors €36,200, Trade Creditors €31,000.

You are required to show, with workings:
- **(a)** Trading Profit and Loss Account for the year ended 31/12/2012.
- **(b)** Balance Sheet as at 31/12/2012.
- **(c)** Explain the term **accounting concept** using 2 examples.

7 FOWLER

On 1/1/2012, F. Fowler lodged €448,000 to a business bank account and on the same day purchased a business for €413,000, including the following assets and liabilities: Buildings €322,000, Stock €36,960, 3-months' Rates prepaid €546, Debtors €59,360, Wages due €770, Trade Creditors €31,640.

Fowler did not keep a full set of books during 2012 but estimates that the gross profit was 40% of sales. He was able to supply the following information on 31/12/2012:

(i) Each week Fowler took from stock, goods to the value of €182 and cash of €84 for household expenses.

(ii) On 1/9/2012 Fowler borrowed €336,000, part of which would be used to purchase adjoining premises costing €294,000. It was agreed that Fowler would pay interest on the last day of the month at the rate of 6% per annum. The capital sum was to be repaid in one lump sum in the year 2019 and, to provide for this, the bank was instructed to transfer €3,640 on the last day of every month from Fowler's business account into an investment fund.

(iii) During the year, Fowler lodged a dividend of €4,480 to the business bank account and made the following payments: light and heat €21,280, interest €5,460, wages and general expenses €63,560, equipment €22,400, rates for twelve months €2,520, college fees €12,600.

(iv) Fowler estimated that 20% of the following: equipment, light and heat **used** and interest **payable** should be attributed to the private section of the premises. Fowler further estimates that 30% of college fees should be attributed to a family member and the remainder to an employee.

(v) Included in the assets and liabilities of the firm on 31/12/2012 were: Stock €33,740, Debtors €54,180, Trade Creditors €38,500, Cash at bank €115,360, Electricity due €420, Interest earned by the investment fund to date €119.

You are required to show, with workings:

(a) Statement/Balance Sheet showing Fowler's profit or loss for the year ended 31/12/2012.

(b) Trading Profit and Loss Account for the year ended 31/12/2012.

(c) Fowler is concerned about his high level of debtors. What are the dangers associated with increasing/high debtors and what actions would you advise in relation to their control?

8 GERAGHTY

On 1/1/2012 Ian Geraghty purchased a business for €480,000 which included the following assets and liabilities: Premises €350,400, Wages due €1,440, Stock €43,200, Debtors €38,640, Trade Creditors €42,840, 3-months' Rates prepaid €540, 5% Investments €60,000, Equipment €24,000.

During the year, Geraghty did not keep a full set of books but estimates that the gross profit was 20% of sales. He was able to supply the following information on 31/12/2012:

(i) Geraghty took from stock goods to the value of €416 per month and cash of €204 per week for household expenses.

(ii) On 1/8/2012 Geraghty borrowed €144,000 which, together with €36,000, of Geraghty's personal funds, was used to purchase an adjoining business premises. It was agreed that the sum borrowed would be repaid in 20 equal half-yearly instalments. The first instalment becomes due on 1 March of next year. Interest was to be charged at the rate of 6% per annum to be paid monthly at the end of each month.

(iii) During the year, Geraghty lodged to the business bank account an Enterprise Ireland assistance grant of €7,200 and investment interest of €3,000. Geraghty made the following payments from the business bank account during the year: light and heat €9,000, interest €2,400, equipment (purchased on 1/7/2012) €18,000, delivery vans (purchased on 1/9/2012) €36,000, wages and general expenses €96,000, rates for 12 months €8,400. The payment for wages and general expenses includes a €3,600 petrol bill for Geraghty's private use.

(iv) Geraghty estimated that 20% of rates **payable** for the year, 20% of light and heat **used** and 25% of interest **payable** should be attributed to private use.

(v) Geraghty decided to set up a provision for bad debts amounting to 3% of debtors on 31/12/2012, and for depreciation of 15% per annum on delivery vans as well as 10% on equipment held on 31/12/2012.

(vi) Included in the assets and liabilities of the firm on 31/12/2012 was Stock at €24,600, which includes stock of heating oil €360, Debtors €40,800, Bank overdraft €6,480, Electricity due €552 and Trade Creditors €42,480.

You are required to show, with workings:

(a) Statement/Balance Sheet showing Ian Geraghty's profit or loss for the year ended 31/12/2012.

(b) Trading Profit and Loss account for the year ended 31/12/2012.

(c) Calculate the following in relation to Geraghty:

1. Stock turnover.
2. Credit to debtors.
3. Credit from creditors.

(d) Write a brief comment on the cash flow of this business.

9 HENSHAW

Robbie Henshaw commenced business on 1/1/2012 when he lodged €325,000 to a business bank account. On the same day he purchased a business for €275,000 including the following tangible assets and liabilities: Buildings €200,000, 10% Investment €45,000, Stock €14,800, 3-months' Rates prepaid €1,200, Debtors €24,600, Wages due €1,600 and Trade Creditors €33,500.

Henshaw did not keep a full set of books during 2012 but estimates that the gross profit was 40% of sales. He was able to supply the following information on 31/12/2012.

(i) Henshaw took from stock goods to the value of €195 per month and cash of €65 per week for household expenses.
(ii) On 1/10/2012 Henshaw borrowed €150,000, part which was used to purchase an adjoining business premises costing €135,000. It was agreed that Henshaw would pay interest on the last day of the month at the rate of 9% per annum. The capital sum was to be repaid in one lump sum in the year 2020 and, to provide for this, the bank was instructed to transfer €1,500 on the last day of every month from Henshaw's business account into an investment fund.
(iii) During the year, Henshaw lodged income on 10% investments of €750 to the business bank account. He then made the following payments: equipment €22,500, light and heat €4,900, interest €2,100, wages and general expenses €50,500, rates for 12 months €5,100, college fees €1,700.
(iv) Henshaw estimated that 20% of the following: equipment, light and heat **used** and interest **payable** should be attributed to the private section of the premises. Henshaw further estimated that 60% of the college fees should be attributed to a family member and the remainder to an employee.
(v) Included in the assets and liabilities of the firm on 31/12/2012 were Stock €7,350, Debtors €23,000, Trade Creditors €10,750, Cash at bank €13,250, Electricity due €115 and €85 Interest earned by the investment fund to date.

You are required to show, with workings:

(a) Statement/Balance Sheet showing Henshaw's profit or loss for the year ended 31/12/2012.
(b) Trading Profit and Loss account for the year ended 31/12/2012.
(c) Assess the performance of Henshaw under the following headings:
  (i) liquidity
  (ii) profitability

10 JENNIFER ANN

Jennifer Ann commenced business on 1/1/2012 when she lodged €810,000 to a business bank account. On the same day she purchased a business for €738,000 including the following tangible assets and liabilities: Buildings €594,000, 9% Investment €108,000, Stock €28,080, 3-months' Rates prepaid €3,780, Debtors €68,760, Wages due €8,100 and Trade Creditors €77,400.

Jennifer Ann did not keep a full set of books during 2012 but estimates that the gross profit was 40% of sales and was able to supply the following information on 31/12/2012.

(i) Each week Jennifer Ann took from stock goods to the value of €144 and cash of €216 for household expenses.
(ii) On 1/10/2012 Jennifer Ann borrowed €450,000, part which was used to purchase an adjoining business premises costing €306,000. It was agreed that she would pay interest on the last day of the month at the rate of 8% per annum. The capital sum was to be repaid in one lump sum in the year 2020 and, to provide for this, the bank was instructed to transfer €3,600 on the last day of every month from Jennifer Ann's business account into an investment fund.
(iii) During the year, Jennifer Ann lodged income on 9% investments of €4,500 to the business bank account and made the following payments: equipment €41,400, light and heat €13,680, interest €6,300, wages and general expenses €172,800, rates for 12 months €17,280 and college fees €8,100.
(iv) Jennifer Ann estimated that 20% of the following: light and heat **used** and interest **payable** should be attributed to the private section of the premises, also that €8,280 of the equipment should be allocated for private use. She further estimated that 60% of the college fees should be attributed to a family member and the remainder to an employee.
(v) Included in the assets and liabilities of the firm on 31/12/2012 were Stock €33,480, Debtors €70,200, Trade Creditors €33,300, Cash at bank €177,620, Electricity due €1,008 and €162 Interest earned by the investment fund to date.

You are required to show, with workings:

(a) Statement/Balance Sheet showing Jennifer Ann's profit or loss for the year ended 31/12/2012.
(b) Trading Profit and Loss account for the year ended 31/12/2012.
(c) What advice would you give to Jennifer Ann in relation to the management of funds?

11 ANN O'LOUGHLIN

Ann O'Loughlin invested €218,000 in a new business on 1/1/2012. She supplied the following information relating to the business on 31/12/2012:

Current ratio	3 : 1
Acid test	2 : 1
Credit to debtors	1.5 months
Stock turnover	12 times
Mark-up on cost	25%
Drawings for the year	€15,000
Depreciation on fixed assets	€30,000
Creditors	€14,000
Cash sales	€27,000
Total expenses (excluding depreciation)	€24,000

Current liabilities consist of **creditors** and **bank** €7,000.

Current assets comprise **stock**, **debtors** and **cash**.

Depreciation is calculated at 15% of cost for a full year.

Drawings include drawings of stock €2,500.

You are required to prepare in as much detail as possible:

(a) The Balance Sheet on 31/12/2012.

(b) The Trading Profit and Loss account for the year ended 31/12/2012.

(c) Ann O'Loughlin has applied for a bank loan of €50,000 at a 10% interest rate. Would you, as lending manager of the bank, recommend the granting of this loan? Use ratios, figures, and any other information to support your view.

12 Breda Connolly

On 1/1/2012 Breda Connolly purchased a business for €300,000 which included the following assets and liabilities: Premises €150,000, Wages due €900, Stock €20,000, Debtors €18,000, Trade Creditors €27,500, 3 months Insurance prepaid €340, 4% Investments €30,000 and Equipment €15,000.

During the year, Connolly did not keep a full set of books but estimates that the gross profit was 20% of sales and was able to supply the following information on 31/12/2012.

(i) Each week B. Connolly took from stock goods to the value of €60 and cash €140 per week for private use.
(ii) On 01/08/2012 B. Connolly borrowed €90,000, which, together with €25,000, of Connolly's personal funds, was used to purchase an adjoining business premises. It was agreed that the sum borrowed would be repaid in 20 equal half-yearly installments. The first installment becomes due on March 1st of next year. Interest was to be charged at the rate of 5% per annum to be paid monthly at the end of each month.
(iii) During the year, B. Connolly lodged to the business bank account, an IDA grant of €5,000 and Investment Interest €800.
(iv) B. Connolly made the following payments from the business bank account during the year: Light and Heat €6,000, Interest €1,500, Equipment (purchased on 01/07/2012) €12,000, Delivery vans (purchased on the 01/09/2012) €24,000, Wages and General Expenses €60,000, Annual insurance all risks policy €5,000. The payment for wages and general expenses includes €2,200 for repairs to a private house.
(v) B. Connolly estimated that 10% of insurance *payable* for the year, 20% of light and heat *used* and 20% of interest *payable* should be attributed to the private use.
(vi) Connolly has also decided to set up a Provision for Bad Debts amounting to 5% of debtors on 31/12/2012 and for depreciation 20% per annum on delivery vans and 10% on equipment held on 31/12/2012.
(vii) Included in the assets and liabilities of the firm on 31/12/2012 were Stock €16,200 which includes Stock of heating oil €200, Debtors €29,000, Bank overdraft €3,400, Electricity due €310 and Trade Creditors €31,200.

You are required to show, with workings, the:

(a) Statement/Balance Sheet showing Breda Connolly's profit or loss for the year ended 31/12/2012.
(b) Trading, Profit and Loss Account, for the year ended 31/12/2012.
(c) Provide a summary of the advice you would give to Breda Connolly after her first year of trading.

TOPIC

14

Cash Budgeting

Revenue is vanity, margin is sanity but cash is king.

Unknown

1 Slaney – Sample Exam Question

Slaney is preparing to set up business on 1/7/2004 and has made the following forecast for the first six months of trading.

	July	August	September	October	November	December	Total
Sales	525,000	588,000	616,000	630,000	658,000	672,000	3,689,000
Purchases	300,000	336,000	352,000	360,000	376,000	384,000	2,108,000

The expected selling price is €70 per unit.

The cash collection pattern from debtors is expected to be:

Cash customers – 30% of sales revenue will be for immediate cash and cash discount of 5% be received.
Credit customers – 70% of sales revenue will be from credit customers. These customers will pay their bills 50% in the month after the sale and the remainder in the second month after the sale.

The purchases will be paid for 50% in the month after purchase when a 2% cash discount will be received. The remaining purchases will be paid for in the second month after purchase.

Expected costs – Wages of €45,000 per month payable as incurred.
Variable overheads €10 per unit payable as incurred.
Fixed overheads (including depreciation) €52,000 per month payable as incurred.

Equipment will be purchased in July costing €48,000 which will have a useful life of 5 years.
To finance this purchase a loan of €50,000 will be secured at 10% interest per annum.
Interest is paid monthly but capital repayments will not commence until January 2005.

Interest to be paid monthly but capital repayment will not commence until January 2005.

You are required to:
(a) Prepare a cash budget for six months from July to December 2004.
(b) Prepare a budgeted Profit and Loss account for the six months ended 31/12/2004.

Solution Slaney

Receipts	July	August	September	October	November	December
Sales – Cash (30% less 5% discount)	149,625	167,580	175,560	179,550	187,530	191,520
Credit 1 month (35%)		183,750	205,800	215,600	220,500	230,300
Credit 2 months (35%)			183,750	205,800	215,600	220,500
Total receipts	149,625	351,330	565,110	600,950	623,630	642,320
Payments						
Purchases – 1 month (50% less 2% discount)		147,000	164,640	172,480	176,400	184,240
2 months (50%)			150,000	168,000	176,000	180,000
Wages	45,000	45,000	45,000	45,000	45,000	45,000
Equipment	48,000					
Variable overheads	75,000	84,000	88,000	90,000	94,000	96,000
Fixed overheads	51,200	51,200	51,200	51,200	51,200	51,200
Interest	417	417	417	417	417	417
Total payments	219,617	327,617	499,257	527,097	543,017	556,857
Net cash	(69,992)	23,713	65,853	73,853	80,613	85,463
Opening cash		(19,992)	3,721	69,574	143,427	224,040
Borrowing	50,000					
Closing cash	(19,992)	3,721	69,574	143,427	224,040	309,503

Budgeted Profit and Loss account

Sales			3,689,000
Less purchases			2,108,000
Gross profit			1,581,000
Less expenses			
Wages		270,000	
Variable overherads		527,000	
Fixed overheads		307,200	
Interest		2,500	
Depreciation		4,800	
Discount allowed	W	**55,335**	(1,166,835)
Discount received	W		**17,240**
Net Profit			431,405

Workings:

Discount allowed	3,689,000 at 30% at 5% = **55,335**
Discount received	1,724,000 at 50% at 2% = **17,240**

❷ LAGAN

Lagan is preparing to set up business on 1/7/2012 and has made the following forecast for the first six months of trading.

	Total	July	August	September	October	November	December
Sales	5,164,600	735,000	823,200	862,400	882,000	921,200	940,800
Purchases	2,951,200	420,000	470,400	492,800	504,000	526,400	537,600

The expected selling price is €70 per unit.

The cash collection pattern from debtors is expected to be:

Cash customers – 30% of sales revenue will be for immediate cash and cash discount of 5% will be received.
Credit customers – 70% of sales revenue will be from credit customers. These customers will pay their bills 50% in the month after the sale and the remainder in the second month after the sale.

The purchases will be paid for 50% in the month after purchase when a 2% cash discount will be received. The remaining purchases will be paid for in the second month after purchase.

Expected costs – Wages of €63,000 per month payable as incurred.
Variable overheads €10 per unit payable as incurred.
Fixed overheads (including depreciation) €72,800 per month payable as incurred.

Equipment will be purchased in July costing €67,200 which will have a useful life of 5 years. To finance this purchase a loan of €70,000 will be secured at 10% interest per annum. €584 interest to be paid monthly but capital repayments will not commence until January 2013.

You are required to:

(a) Prepare a cash budget for six months from July to December 2012.

(b) Prepare a budgeted Profit and Loss account for the 6 months ended 31/12/2012.

3 CORRIB

Corrib is preparing to set up business on 1/7/2012 and has made the following forecast for first six months:

	July	August	September	October	November	December	Total
Sales	615,000	645,000	840,000	870,000	915,000	945,000	4,830,000
Purchases	285,000	315,000	360,000	375,000	495,000	576,000	2,406,000

The expected selling price is €60 per unit.

The cash collection pattern from debtors is expected to be:

Cash customers	30% of sales revenue will be for immediate cash – cash discount of 5% will be received.
Credit customers	70% of sales revenue will be from credit customers. These customers will pay their bills 60% in the month after the sale. The remainder to be paid in the second month after the sale.

The purchases will be paid for 50% in the month after the purchase – a 2% cash discount will be received. The remaining purchases will be paid for in the second month after the purchase.

Expected costs	Wages €60,000 per month payable as incurred.
	Variable overheads €15 per unit payable as incurred.
	Fixed overheads (including depreciation) at €67,500 per month payable as incurred.

Equipment will be purchased in July costing €72,000. This will have a useful life of 5 years. To finance this purchase a loan of €66,000 will be secured at 9% interest per annum. Interest to be paid monthly, but capital repayments will not commence until January 2013.

You are required to:

(a) Prepare a cash budget for six months from July to December 2012.

(b) Prepare a budgeted Profit and Loss account for the six months ended 31/12/2012.

4 LIFFEY

Cash Budgeting

Liffey had the following assets and liabilities on 1 July 2012.

Assets		
Stock	56,800	
Debtors	19,500	
Bank	11,250	
Insurance prepaid	1,400	89,950
Liabilities		
Capital		89,950

Kenny expects the sales for the next 7 months will be as follows:

	July	August	September	October	November	December	January
Sales in €	96,000	101,000	103,000	99,000	95,000	91,000	90,000

(i) 70% of sales are for cash, with 30% on credit collected one month after the sale
(ii) Gross profit as a percentage of sales is 20%.
(iii) Liffey wishes to keep a minimum cash balance of €3,000 at the end of each month.
(iv) All borrowings are in multiples of €1,000 and interest is at the rate of 8% p.a.
(v) Purchases each month should be sufficient to cover the following month's sales.
(vi) Purchases are to be paid for by the end of the month.
(vii) A machine was purchased on 1 July for €20,000 (depreciation 20% p.a. on cost).
(viii) Liffey rents the premises for €114,000 p.a. payable monthly.
(ix) The total wage bill for the 6 months is €15,600 paid in equal monthly payments.
(x) A delivery van will be purchased for cash on 1 September for €40,000 (depreciation 15% p.a. on cost).
(xi) Insurance to be paid for 9 months from 1 November will be €3,420 (payable in November).
(xii) One-third of the money borrowed on 31 July is to be repaid at the end of December together with interest to date on the repaid amount.

You are required to prepare:

(a) Cash budget for the six months from July to December.
(b) Budgeted Profit and Loss account for the six months ended 30/12/2012.
(c) What are the objectives of **budgeting**?

5 SILVER

Cash Budgeting

Silver had the following assets and liabilities on 1 July 2012.

Assets		
Stock	40,000	
Debtors	32,400	
Cash	200	
Rent prepaid (3 months)	900	73,500
Liabilities		
Capital	70,400	
Wages due	3,100	73,500

Silver expects the sales for the next 7 months will be as follows:

	July	August	September	October	November	December	January
Sales in €	58,000	69,000	89,000	80,000	98,000	90,000	73,000

(i) 40% of sales are for cash and a discount of 5% will be allowed on these sales. 60% are on credit collected one month after the sale.
(ii) Gross profit as a percentage of sales is 25%.
(iii) Silver wishes to keep a minimum cash balance of €4,000 at the end of each month.
(iv) All borrowings are in multiples of a €1,000 and interest is at the rate of 12% p.a.
(v) Purchases each month should be sufficient to cover the following month's sales.
(vi) Purchases are to be paid for in the month of purchase.
(vii) A machine was purchased on 1 August for €20,000 (depreciation 12% p.a. on cost).
(viii) Silver rents the premises for €4,800 p.a. payable in advance on 1 October.
(ix) Wages are paid one month in arrears. The wages are:

July	August	September	October	November	December
€6,500	€6,000	€6,700	€5,400	€6,500	€6,300

(x) Equipment will be purchased for cash on 1 September for €20,000.
(xi) One-quarter of the money borrowed on 31 January is to be repaid at the end of June together with interest to date on the repaid amount.

You are required to prepare:

(a) Cash budget for the six months from July to December 2012.
(b) Budgeted Profit and Loss account for the six months ended 31/12/2012.
(c) 1. Define a cash budget.
2. Describe its advantages.

6 SUIR

Suir Plc is preparing its budget for the first six months of 2012 and has produced the following:

	Nov.	Dec.	Jan.	Feb.	Mar.	Apr.	May	June	July
Sales €	15,000	20,000	25,000	30,000	30,000	25,000	30,000	25,000	10,000

You are given the following information.

Debtors are expected to settle their accounts as follows:
(i) 10% of sales will be settled in cash in the month of sale on which a discount of 5% will be granted.
(ii) Of the credit sales, 50% of customers will settle their accounts the month following sale.
(iii) The remainder will be collected in the second month following sale.

The gross profit is expected to be 50% of sales.

The stock of goods at the beginning of the month will be 25% of the sales requirement for that month.

Creditors are paid in the month following delivery.

New equipment costing €22,000 will be purchased in January.

General administration expenses (which includes €1,800 depreciation) are paid monthly as incurred. They are:

January	February	March	April	May	June
€11,800	€8,800	€8,800	€8,800	€8,800	€8,800

You are required to prepare:
(a) A Schedule of monthly receipts from **debtors** for the period January to June 2012.
(b) A Schedule of monthly payments to **creditors** for the same period.
(c) A Cash **budget** for the same period.
(d) Explain what is meant by the **Principal budgeting factor**.

7 NORE

Nore Ltd is preparing its budget for the first six months of 2012 and has produced the following:

Sales Forecast

	€
January	170,000
February	150,000
March	140,000
April	160,000
May	180,000
June	170,000
July	190,000

You are given the following information.

Debtors are expected to settle their accounts as follows:

(i) 20% of sales will be settled in cash in the month of sale at a discount of 5%.

(ii) Of the credit sales, 50% of customers will settle their accounts the month following the sale. The remainder will be collected in the second month following the sale.

The gross profit is expected to be 40% of sales.

The stock of goods at the beginning of the month will be 20% of the sales requirement for that month.

Creditors are paid in the month following delivery.

Monthly expenses, to be paid within the month, are expected to be 15% of sales each month.

You are required to prepare:

(a) A Schedule of monthly receipts from **debtors** for the 4-month budget period March to June 2012.

(b) A Schedule of monthly payments to **creditors** for the same period.

(c) A Cash Budget for the 4 months March to June 2012, given that the opening cash balance on 1 March is €24,000.

(d) Why do firms prepare budgets?

(i) What are the objectives of budgeting?

(ii) What are the advantages of budgeting?

8 BROSNA

Cash Budgeting

Brosna had the following assets and liabilities on 1 January 2012.

Assets			
Fixed Assets			100,000
Current Assets			
Stock	7,120		
Debtors	30,000		
Cash	9,625		
Insurance prepaid (3 months)	1,500	48,245	
Creditors Falling Due Within the Year			
Liabilities			
Accruals	8,688		
Creditors	22,313		
Wages due	5,620	36,621	11,624
			111,624
Financed by			
Capital			100,000
P&L account			11,624
			111,624

You are given the following information:

		Jan.	Feb.	Mar.	Apr.	May	June	July	(Dec. 2011)
(i)	Sales in €	38,000	50,000	54,000	48,000	56,000	72,000	76,000	50,000

(ii) 40% of sales will be settled in cash in the month of sale at a discount of 5%, the balance in full in the following month.

(iii) The Gross profit is expected to be 25% of sales.

(iv) The stock of goods at the beginning of each month will be 20% of the cost of the sales requirement for that month, except for January as the Opening stock of €7,120 is given.

(v) 50% of Purchases are paid for immediately after a 5% discount has been offered. The remaining purchases will be paid in the month following purchase.

(vi) Vehicle was purchased on 1 January, costing €37,500. Depreciation is charged at 20% p.a.

(vii) Insurance paid in April for 6 months is €2,500.

(viii) Wages are paid in arrears and are as follows:

Jan.	Feb.	Mar.	Apr.	May	June
5,000	7,600	8,400	7,800	8,000	9,000

(ix) Brosna Ltd is to make up any projected cash shortfalls by borrowing from the bank at 12% at **the start of the month**. At the end of June, 20% of borrowings will be repaid along with any interest due in that period. All borrowings will be in multiples of € thousands.

You are required to prepare:

(a) Schedule of monthly cash receipts from **debtors** for 6 months from January to June 2012.

(b) Schedule of payments for purchases for the same period.

(c) Cash budget for the same period.

(d) Budgeted Profit and Loss account for 6 months ended 30/06/2012.

9 CAMCOR

Camcor Ltd had the following assets and liabilities on 1 Jan 2012.

Assets			
Fixed Assets (including equipment 60,000)			120,000
Current Assets			
Stock	8,550		
Debtors	45,000		
Cash	11,550		
Rent prepaid (3 months)	1,800	66,900	
Creditors falling due within the year			
Liabilities			
Accruals	10,425		
Creditors	26,775		
Wages due	6,750	43,950	22,950
			142,950
Financed by			
Capital			120,000
P&L account			22,950
			142,950

You are given the following information:

		Jan.	Feb.	Mar.	Apr.	May	June	July	(Dec. 2011)
(i)	Sales in €	57,000	90,000	90,000	72,000	84,000	108,000	114,000	75,000

(ii) 40% of sales will be settled in cash in the month of the sale at a discount of 5%. The balance of sales will be settled in the following month.
(iii) The gross profit is expected to be 25% of sales.
(iv) The stock of goods at the beginning of each month after Jan. will be 20% of the sales requirement for that month.
(v) 50% of purchases are paid for immediately after a 5% discount has been offered. The remaining purchases will be paid in the month following the purchase.
(vi) Equipment was purchased on 1 Jan costing €45,000. Depreciation is charged at 20% p.a.
(vii) Rent paid in April for 6 months is €3,000.
(viii) Wages are paid in arrears and are:

Jan.	Feb.	Mar.	Apr.	May	June
9,750	10,500	11,700	10,050	10,800	12,750

(ix) Camcor Ltd is to make up any projected cash shortfalls by borrowing from the bank at 12% on **the first day of the month**.
At the end of June 2012 any borrowings will be fully repaid along with interest due on loans in that period.
All borrowings are in multiples of €1,000 with a minimum of €1,000 to be held at the end of each month.

You are required to prepare:

(a) Schedule of monthly cash receipts from **debtors** for 6 months from January to June 2012.
(b) Schedule of payments to **creditors** for the same period.
(c) Cash budget for the same period.
(d) Budgeted Profit and Loss account for the 6 months ended 30/06/2012.
(e) Explain what is meant by the **accruals principle** in accounting.

TOPIC 15

Production Budget

When man speaks of the future, the Gods laugh.
Unknown

1 Roche – Sample Exam Question

Roche Production

Roche Ltd has recently completed its annual sales forecast to December 2009.
It expects to sell two products – Super at €220 and Supreme at €260.

All stocks are reduced by 20% from their opening levels by the end of 2009 and are valued using the FIFO method.

	Super	**Supreme**
Sales are expected to be	10,000 units	4,200 units

Stocks of finished goods on 1/1/2009 are expected to be:

Super	600 units	@	€120 each
Supreme	450 units	@	€140 each

Both products use the same raw material and skilled labour in different quantities as follows:

	Super	**Supreme**
Material X	7 kg	5 kg
Material Y	6 kg	8 kg
Skilled labour	7 hours	8 hours

Stocks of raw materials on 1/1/2009 are expected to be:

Material X	5,000 kg	@	€2.5 per kg
Material Y	3,000 kg	@	€4.5 per kg

The expected price of raw materials during 2009 are:

Material X	€3 per kg
Material Y	€5 per kg

The skilled labour rate is expected to be €13 per labour hour.

Production overhead costs are expected to be:

Variable	€4 per hour
Fixed	€204,080 p.a.

You are required to prepare:

(a) **Production budget** in units.

(b) **Raw materials purchases budget** in units and value.

(c) **Production cost/manufacturing budget.**

(d) **Budgeted trading** account.
(Budgeted cost of a unit of Super and Supreme are €180 and €210 respectively.)

(e) 1. Explain what is meant by a **capital budget**.
2. The **Principle budgeting** factor is sales demand in most organisations.
State 2 other items that could be considered to be **principle budgeting** factors.

Solution Roche

Production Budget

	Super Units	Supreme Units
Required by sales	10,000	4,200
Closing stock (80% of opening)	480	360
Less opening stock	(600)	(450)
Budgeted production in units	9,880	4,110

Raw Materials Purchases Budget

	Material X in kg	Material Y in kg
Super (9,800 × 7)(9,880 × 6)	69,160	59,280
Supreme (4,110 × 5)(4,110 × 8)	20,550	32,880
	89,710	92,160
Add closing stock	4,000	2,400
Less opening stock	(5,000)	(3,000)
Required purchases in kg	88,710	91,560
Purchase price	€3	€5
Purchase cost	€266,130	€457,800

Production Cost Budget

			€	€
Opening stock of raw materials				
	Super	(5,000 @ 2.50)	12,500	
	Supreme	(3,000 @ 4.50)	13,500	26,000
Purchases		(266,130 + 457,800)		723,930
				749,930
Closing stock of raw materials				
	Super	(4,000 @ 3)	12,000	
	Supreme	(2,400 @ 5)	12,000	(24,000)
				725,930
Labour	Super	(9,880 × 7 × 13)	899,080	
	Supreme	(4,110 × 8 × 13)	427,440	1,326,520
Variable overheads	Super	(9,880 × 7 × 4)	276,640	
	Supreme	(4,110 × 8 × 4)	131,520	408,160
Fixed overheads				204,080
Cost of manufacture				2,664,690

Budgeting Trading Account

				€
Sales of finished goods	(10,000 × €220)	+	(4,200 × €260)	3,292,000
Opening stock of finished goods				
Super (600 × 120)	72,000			
Supreme (450 × 140)	63,000		135,000	
Cost of manufacture			2,664,690	
Less closing stock of finished goods				
Super (480 × 180)	86,400			
Supreme (360 × 210)	75,600		(162,000)	2,637,690
Gross profit				654,310

Capital Budget

This budget deals with any planned capital expenditure, e.g. purchase of fixed assets and planned capital receipts such as the sale of fixed assets. Decisions relating to these items would be the responsibility of the directors, while the implementation of the capital budget is the responsibility of the financial controller.

Principal Budgeting Factor

Other than sales demand the principal budget factor could also be:

- Supply of raw materials.
- Availability of labour.
- Capacity of the plant.
- Available of capital.

2 MORRIS

Morris Plc has recently completed its annual sales forecast to Dec. 2012.
It expects to sell two products – Basic at €220 and Luxury at €260.

All stocks are reduced by 20% from their opening levels by the end of 2012 and are valued using the FIFO method.

	Basic	**Luxury**
Sales are expected to be	15,000	6,300

Stock of finished goods on 1/1/2012 are expected to be:

Basic	900 units	at	€180 each
Luxury	675 units	at	€210 each

Both products use the same raw material and skilled labour in different quantities as follows:

	Basic	**Luxury**
Material X	7 kg	5 kg
Material Y	6 kg	8 kg
Skilled labour	7 hours	8 hours

Stock of raw materials on 1/1/2012 is expected to be:

Material X	7,500 kg	@	€2.50 per kg
Material Y	4,500 kg	@	€4.50 per kg

The expected price of raw materials during 2012 are:

Material X	€3.0 per kg
Material Y	€5.0 per kg

The skilled labour rate is expected to be €13 per labour hour.

Production overhead costs are expected to be:

Variable	€4 per hour
Fixed	€306,120

You are required to prepare:

(a) Production budget in units.
(b) Raw Materials Purchases Budget in units and value.
(c) Production Cost/Manufacturing Budget.
(d) Budgeted Trading Profit and Loss account.
(Budgeted cost of a unit of **basic** and **luxury** are €200 and €250 respectively.)
(e) What factors are taken into account in arriving at the expected sales of 15,000 **basic** and 6,300 **luxury** for 2012?

3 WILKINSON

Wilkinson Plc has recently completed its annual sales forecast to Dec. 2012.
It expects to sell two products – Satin at €200 and Silk at €290.

All stocks are reduced by 20% from their opening levels by the end of 2012 and are valued using the FIFO method.

	Satin	Silk
Sales are expected to be	6,000 units	7,500 units

Stocks of finished goods on 1/1/2012 are expected to be:

Satin	450 units	at	€180
Silk	250 units	at	€210

Both products use the same raw material and skilled labour in different quantities as follows:

	Satin	Silk
Material A	7 kg	5 kg
Material B	5 kg	6 kg
Skilled labour	7 hours	8 hours

Stock of raw materials on 1/1/2012 is expected to be:

Material A	6,500 kg	at	€3.0 per kg
Material B	5,000 kg	at	€4.5 per kg

The expected price of raw materials during 2012 is:

Material A	€4.0 per kg
Material B	€5.0 per kg

The skilled labour rate is expected to be €12 per labour hour.

Production overhead costs are expected to be:

Variable	€4.00 per hour
Fixed	€201,940

You are required to prepare:

(a) Production Budget in units.
(b) Raw Materials Purchases Budget in units and value.
(c) Production Cost/Manufacturing Budget.
(d) Budgeted Profit and Loss account. (Closing stock valuation not given.)

4 PEZULA

Pezula Plc has recently completed its annual sales forecast to Dec. 2012.
It expects to sell two products – Silver at €200 and Gold at €400.

All stocks are reduced by 20% from their opening levels by the end of 2012 and are valued using the FIFO method.

	Silver	Gold
Sales are expected to be	10,000 units	7,500 units

Stock of finished goods on 1/1/2012 are expected to be:

Silver	800 units	at	€200 each
Gold	600 units	at	€250 each

Both products use the same raw material and skilled labour in different quantities as follows:

	Silver	Gold
Material I	5 kg	7 kg
Material II	6 kg	8 kg
Skilled labour	8 hours	10 hours

Stock of raw materials on 1/1/2012 is expected to be:

Material I	6,000 kg	at	€3 per kg
Material II	4,000 kg	at	€4 per kg

The expected price of raw materials during 2012 is:

Material I	€4.00 per kg
Material II	€5.00 per kg

The skilled labour rate is expected to be €12 per labour hour:

Production overhead costs are expected to be:

Variable	€5.50 per labour hour
Fixed	€457,560

You are required to prepare:

(a) Production Budget in units.
(b) Raw Materials Purchases Budget in units and value.
(c) Production Cost/Manufacturing Budget.
(d) Budgeted Profit and Loss account. (Closing stock valuation not given.)
(e) What factors do companies look for when deciding their budgeted sales for the year?

5 Jess Kelliher

Jess Kelliher Plc has recently completed its annual sales forecast to December 2012.
It expects to sell two products – Regular at €180 and Superior at €220.

All stocks are reduced by 20% from their opening levels by the end of 2012 and are valued using the FIFO method.

	Regular	Superior
Sales are expected to be	5,000 units	4,000 units

Stock of finished goods on 1/1/2012 are expected to be:

Regular	400 units	at	€140 each
Superior	300 units	at	€160 each

Both products use the same raw material and skilled labour in different quantities as follows:

	Regular	Superior
Material A	5 kg	4 kg
Material B	6 kg	7 kg
Skilled labour	8 hours	9 hours

Stock of raw materials on 1/1/2012 is expected to be:

Material A	6,000 kg	at	€2.50 per kg
Material B	5,000 kg	at	€3.50 per kg

The expected price of raw materials during 2012 are:

Material A	€3 per kg
Material B	€4 per kg

The skilled labour rate is expected to be €10 per labour hour.

Production overhead costs are expected to be:

Variable	€4 per hr
Fixed	€187,050 p.a.

You are required to prepare:

(a) A **Production budget** in units.

(b) A **Raw materials purchases budget** in units and value.

(c) A **Production cost/manufacturing budget**.

(d) A **Budgeted trading** account. (You are required to calculate the budgeted cost of a unit of Regular and Superior on 31/12/2012.)

(e) 1. Explain what is meant by a **Capital budget**.
2. What is the difference between **controllable** and **non-controllable costs**?

6 KATE O'BRIEN

Kate O'Brien Plc has recently completed its annual sales forecast to Dec. 2012.
It expects to sell two furniture products – Ruby at €270 and Diamond at €330.

All stocks are **increased by 10%** from their opening levels by the end of 2012 and are valued using the FIFO method.

	Ruby	**Diamond**
Sales are expected to be	7,500 units	6,000 units

Stock of finished goods on 1/1/2012 are expected to be:

Ruby	600 units	@	€140 each
Diamond	450 units	@	€160 each

Both products use the same raw material and skilled labour in different quantities as follows:

	Ruby	**Diamond**
Timber	5 kg	4 kg
Metal	6 kg	7 kg
Skilled labour	8 hours	9 hours

Stocks of raw materials on 1/1/2012 are expected to be:

Timber	9,000 kg	@	€2.00 per kg
Metal	7,500 kg	@	€3.00 per kg

The expected prices of raw materials during 2012 are:

Timber	€3.00 per kg
Metal	€4.00 per kg

The skilled labour rate is expected to be €12.00 per labour hour.

Production overhead costs are expected to be:

Variable	€5.00 per hour
Fixed	€229,770 p.a.

Selling costs are €2.00 per unit sold.
General Administration expenses are €30,000 per annum.

You are required to prepare:

(a) A **Production budget** in units.
(b) A **Raw materials purchases budget** in units and value.
(c) A **Production cost/manufacturing budget**.
(d) A **Budgeted trading** account and a Profit and Loss account. (You are required to calculate the budgeted cost of a unit of Ruby and Diamond on 31/12/2012.)

7 PAT TYMON

Pat Tymon is preparing to set up a business on 1/7/2012. Below is the sales budget for its first 6 months.

Sales Revenue	July	Aug.	Sept.	Oct.	Nov.	Dec.
Sales in units	12,000	12,750	15,000	16,500	17,250	15,750
Sales revenue in €	360,000	382,500	450,000	495,000	517,500	472,500

(i) The collection pattern from sales is expected to be:
Cash customers 30% of the sales revenue will be for immediate cash.
Credit customers 70% of sales revenue will be from credit customers. These debtors will pay their bills 50% in the month after sale and the remainder in the second month after sale.

(ii) The product requires 6 kg of Material A which costs €1.50 per kg.

(iii) Stocks of finished goods are maintained at 60% of the following month's sales requirements.

(iv) Stocks of raw materials sufficient for 10% of the following month's requirements (in kg) are held at the end of the month.

(v) One month's credit is received from suppliers.

(vi) Expenses of the business will be settled as follows:
Expected costs Wages €30,000 per month payable as incurred.
Variable overheads €5.00 per unit payable as incurred.
Fixed overheads (incl. depreciation) €43,500 per month payable as incurred.
Capital costs Equipment will be purchased in July for €45,000 and has a useful life of 5 years.
To finance this a loan of €36,000 will be secured at 10% p.a.
Interest to be paid monthly, loan repayments will not commence until Jan. 2013.

You are required to:

(a) Prepare a **Production budget** for 4 months from July to October 2012.

(b) Prepare a **Materials purchases budget** for the 4 months from July to October 2012.

(c) Prepare a **Cash budget** for the same time period.

(d) Prepare a **Budgeted Trading Profit and Loss** account for the same time period if the budgeted cost of a unit of finished goods is €30.

(e) What is an **adverse variance**? Identify 3 causes of adverse variances.

8 SWIFT

Swift has the following balances on 1/7/2012.

Stock of finished goods	7,200 units
Stock of raw materials	1,800 kg
Debtors	€117,000
Creditors	€100,500
Bank	€8,700

Sales Forecast	July	Aug.	Sept.	Oct.	Nov.	Dec.
Sales in units	13,500	14,250	16,500	18,000	18,750	17,250

The following information is also available:

(i) The product requires 6 kg of Material SR4 which costs €1.80 per kg.
(ii) The selling price of the product is €18 per unit.
(iii) 40% of sales are for cash with 60% on credit collected one month after the sale.
(iv) Stocks of finished goods are maintained at 60% of the following month's sales requirements.
(v) Stocks of raw materials sufficient for 10% of the following month's requirements in kg are held at the end of each month.
(vi) One month's credit is received from suppliers.
(vii) Wages are €18,000 per month payable as incurred.
(viii) Variable overheads are €3 per unit produced per month payable as incurred.

You are required to:

(a) Prepare a **Production budget** for 4 months from July to October 2012.
(b) Prepare a **Materials purchases budget** for the 4 months from July to October 2012.
(c) Prepare a **Cash budget** for the same time period.
(d) Prepare a **Budgeted Profit and Loss account** for the same time period if the budgeted cost of a unit of finished goods is €15.
(e) Explain the term **Budgetary control**.

9 MULDOON

Muldoon had the following balances on 1/7/2012.

Stock of finished goods	3,800 units
Stock of raw materials	19,100 kg
Debtors	€221,760
Creditors	€98,000
Cash 1/1	€42,000

Sales Forecast	May	June	July	Aug.	Sept.	Oct.	Nov.	Dec.
Sales in units	8,000	10,000	12,000	14,500	15,500	17,000	19,500	20,000

The following information is also available:

(i) The product requires 7 kg of Material A which costs €3.50 per kg.
(ii) The selling price of the product is €28 per unit.
(iii) 40% of sales are for cash with 60% of credit sales collected one month after the sale, the remainder one month later.
(iv) Stocks of finished goods are maintained at 30% of the following month's sales requirements.
(v) Stocks of raw materials sufficient for 20% of the following month's requirements in kg are held at end of each month.
(vi) One month's credit is received from suppliers on which a 5% discount is given.
(vii) Wages are €12,000 per month, payable as incurred.
(viii) Variable overheads are €3 per unit sold per month, payable as incurred.

You are required to:

(a) Prepare a **Production budget** for 4 months from July to October 2012.
(b) Prepare a **Materials purchases budget** for the 4 months July to October 2012.
(c) Prepare a **Cash budget** for the same time period.
(d) Would you grant overdraft facilities to Muldoon based on her budgets?
(e) Explain the term **Master budget**.

TOPIC

16

Product Costing

You don't drown by falling in the water. You drown by staying there.

Edwin Louis Cole

1 McCormack – Sample Exam Question

McCormack Ltd has three departments: Processing, Assembly and Finishing.

The following costs relate to 2008.

	Total	Processing	Assembly	Finishing
Indirect materials	360,000	170,000	100,000	90,000
Indirect labour	500,000	300,000	120,000	80,000
Machine maintenance	28,000			
Plant depreciation	80,000			
Light and heat	70,000			
Rent and rates	64,000			
Factory canteen	50,000			

The following information relates to the three departments.

	Total	Processing	Assembly	Finishing
Floor space in square metres	16,000	8,000	5,000	3,000
Volume in cubic metres	42,000	24,000	12,000	6,000
Plant valuation at book value in €	500,000	300,000	150,000	50,000
Machine hours	80,000	40,000	30,000	10,000
Number of employees	100	60	30	10
Labour hours	140,000	80,000	35,000	25,000

Job No. 510 has just been completed. The details are:

	Direct Materials	Direct Labour	Machine Hours	Labour Hours
Processing	10,000	2,000	60	50
Assembly	2,400	4,600	30	90
Finishing	—	800	6	12

The company budgets for a profit margin of 25%.

You are required to:

(a) Calculate the overhead to be absorbed by each department stating clearly the basis of apportionment used.

(b) Calculate a suitable overhead absorption rate for each department.

(c) Compute the selling price of Job No. 510.

(d) 1. Explain what is meant by a **step fixed cost** and give an example.

2. Outline 2 differences between **management** and **financial** accounting.

Solution

(i) Overhead Analysis

	Total	Processing	Assembly	Finishing	Basis
Indirect materials	360,000	170,000	100,000	90,000	Actual
Indirect labour	500,000	300,000	120,000	80,000	Actual
Machine maintenance	28,000	14,000	10,500	3,500	Machine hours
Plant depreciation	80,000	48,000	24,000	8,000	Plant value
Light and heat	70,000	40,000	20,000	10,000	Volume
Rent and rates	64,000	32,000	20,000	12,000	Floor space
Factory canteen	50,000	30,000	15,000	5,000	Employees
	1,152,000	634,000	309,500	208,500	

(ii) Overhead Absorption Rate

	Processing Machine hours	Assembly Labour hours	Finishing Labour hours
Budgeted overheads / Budgeted hours	634,000 / 40,000	309,500 / 35,000	208,500 / 25,000
Overhead rate per machine hour	15.85		
Absorption rate per labour hour		8.84	8.34

(iii) Selling price of Job No. 510

							€
Materials	10,000	+	2,400			=	12,400
Labour	2,000	+	4,600	+	800	=	7,400
Overheads							
Processing	60	×			15.85	=	951
Assembly	90	×			8.84	=	795.6
Finishing	12	×			8.34	=	100.08
Production cost	75%					=	21,646.68
Profit	25%					=	7,215.56
Selling price	100%					=	28,862.24

(iv) Step Fixed Cost

Step fixed costs are costs that are fixed within a certain range of activity but changes outside that range. For example, rent could be fixed up to a certain level of production. However, if production increases and results in the rental of more factory space, then the rent would increase to a new level. Thus the fixed costs would increase in steps.

Management Accounting

1. It is concerned with planning for the future and providing information for planning/budgeting.
2. Has an internal focus giving information to aid planning and decision-making.
3. It is not governed or restricted by legislation or legal requirements.
4. Reports are prepared as often as the managers require.
5. Reports are prepared for cost centres/departments.

Financial Accounting

1. It is concerned with recording past events – Profit & Loss, Balance Sheet and Cash Flow Statements.
2. Mainly an external focus with information for shareholders, managers and creditors.
3. It is governed and regulated by legislation and accounting standards such as the FRS.
4. Reports are usually prepared once a year.
5. Reports are prepared for the business as a unit.

2 FOODIES

The following are the specifications for a job quotation received from **Foodies Plc**. Materials costs €10 per kg and there are 80 kgs required for the job.

	Hours
Preparation Department	50
Cooking Department	20
Finishing Department	16

The monthly budgeted overheads are as follows:

	€ Fixed	€ Wages	€ Variable
Preparation Department	1,500	6,000	2,200
Cooking Department	3,000	13,750	3,500
Finishing Department	2,200	7,200	1,320

Budgeted hours for the month are:

Preparation Department	1,000
Cooking Department	2,500
Finishing Department	800

General administration overheads are expected to be €34,400 for the month.

You are required to:

(a) Calculate the fixed and variable overhead absorption rates for each department in direct labour hours.
(b) Calculate the administration overhead absorption rate in direct labour hours.
(c) Calculate the selling price of the job if the profit is set at 20% of the selling price.
(d) Give two reasons for product costing and explain each one.
(e) Outline the difference between **marginal** and **absorption** costing. Indicate which method should be used for accounting purposes and why.

3 Lockie

Lockie Ltd has three departments – Manufacturing, Packaging and Polishing.

The following costs relate to 2012:

	Total	Manufacturing	Packaging	Polishing
Indirect materials	288,000	136,000	80,000	72,000
Indirect labour	400,000	240,000	96,000	64,000
Machine maintenance	22,400			
Plant depreciation	64,000			
Light and heat	56,000			
Rent and rates	51,200			
Factory canteen	40,000			

The following information relates to the three departments.

	Total	Manufacturing	Packaging	Polishing
Floor space in square metres	12,800	6,400	4,000	2,400
Volume in cubic metres	33,600	19,200	9,600	4,800
Plant valuation at book value in €	400,000	240,000	120,000	40,000
Machine hours	64,000	32,000	24,000	8,000
Number of employees	80	48	24	8
Labour hours	112,000	64,000	28,000	20,000

Job No. 45A has just been completed. The details are:

	Direct Materials	Direct Labour	Machine Hours	Labour Hours
Manufacturing	8,000	1,600	48	40
Packaging	1,920	3,680	24	72
Polishing	—	640	5	10

The company budgets for a profit margin of 25%.

You are required to:

(a) Calculate the overhead to be absorbed by each department stating clearly the basis of apportionment used.

(b) Calculate a suitable overhead absorption rate for each department.

(c) Compute the selling price of Job No. 45A.

(d) 1. Explain the difference between **direct** and **indirect** costs.

2. What is a **cost centre**?

4 Ben and Nevis

1. **Ben Plc** has 2 production departments, namely A and B. It also has 2 ancilliary service departments, namely P and Q.

The expected overhead costs for the next period are as follows:

Overhead	**Total**
Factory heating	14,400
Factory cleaning	3,000
Factory canteen	16,200
Depreciation of equipment	24,000
Depreciation of factory buildings	30,000

The following information relates to the **production** and **service** departments of the factory:

	Production		**Service**	
	Dept. A	**Dept. B**	**Dept. P**	**Dept. Q**
Volume in cubic metres	2,250	4,500	1,500	750
Floor area in square metres	900	1,200	600	300
Number of employees	90	90	45	45
Book value of equipment	22,500	15,000	7,500	15,000
Machine hours	4,500	1,500	—	—

You are required to:

(a) Calculate the overhead to be absorbed by each **department** stating the basis of apportionment used.

(b) Transfer the **service departments'** costs to the **production departments** A and B on the basis of machine hours.

(c) Calculate **machine hour overhead absorption rates** for departments A and B.

(d) Explain what is meant by **re-apportionment of overheads**.

2. **Overabsorption and Underabsorption of Overheads**

Nevis Plc estimates fixed overheads next year to be €18,000. It intends to produce 3,000 units, incurring 4,000 labour hours and 800 machine hours.

(a) Calculate the overhead absorption rate using all **three different methods**.

(b) Show the **over/under absorption** if the actual overheads incurred work out to be €16,200 and units produced were:

(i) 2,800 units

(ii) 3,000 units

(iii) 3,400 units

(iv) 1,900 units

5 MIAH

Miah Plc, a manufacturing company, provides the following information in relation to two departments: Cutting and Fitting, along with information in relation to Job No. 789B.

	Direct Labour	Labour Hours	Machine Hours	Manufacturing Overheads
Budget	**€**			**€**
Cutting	45,000	18,000	67,500	270,000
Fitting	135,000	60,000	22,500	69,000
Actual				
Cutting	60,000	22,500	75,000	210,000
Fitting	112,500	52,500	25,500	69,000

During this period, Job 789B incurred the actual costs and actual times in departments as follows:

	Direct Materials	Direct Wages	Labour Hours	Machine Hours
Cutting	€110	€100	15 hours	30 hours
Fitting	€50	€70	25 hours	10 hours

You are required to:

(a) Calculate a suitable departmental overhead absorption rate for the **cutting** and **fitting** departments. (Use the **dominant activity principle**.)

(b) Show the **over/under absorption** by department, and in total for the period, as well as stating the overall effect on profit.

(c) Calculate the **production cost of Job No. 789B** and the selling price if profit is 20% of the selling price.

(d) Explain with examples: **controllable** and **uncontrollable** costs.

6 Troy and Nathan

(i) Valuation of Closing Stock

The following information relates to the purchases and sales of **Troy Ltd** for the year 2012.

Period	Details	Quantity and Price
1/1 to 31/3/2012	Purchases on credit	2,300 at €14
	Credit sales	1,300 at €19
	Cash Sales	600 at €21
1/4 to 31/6/2012	Purchases on credit	2,500 at €17
	Credit sales	1,150 at €22
	Cash sales	1,200 at €22
1/7 to 30/9/2012	Purchases in credit	2,950 at €17
	Credit sales	1,250 at €19
	Cash sales	1,600 at €21
1/10 to 31/12/2012	Purchases on credit	3,100 at €19
	Credit sales	1,700 at €22
	Cash sales	660 at €19

On 1/1/2012 there was an opening stock of 6,580 units at €12 each.

You are required to:

(a) Calculate the value of the closing stock using FIFO method.

(b) Prepare a trading account for the year ended 31/12/2012.

(ii) Product Costing

Nathan Ltd has three departments with budgeted costs for next year.

Department	Wage Rate	Fixed Costs	Variable Costs
Alpha	€17 per hour	€3.50 per hour	€5 per hour
Beta	€22 per hour	€6.00 per hour	€12 per hour
Gamma	€19 per hour	€11.50 per hour	€7 per hour

General administration overhead absorption rate per hour is budgeted to be €4.50.
The following are the specifications for a quotation for Job No. 2345.
Materials 4,000 units at €3.70 per unit.
Labour hours in each department are:

Alpha	35 hours
Beta	25 hours
Gamma	60 hours

You are required to:

(a) Calculate the selling price of Job 2345 if the profit margin is set at 20%.

(iii) Absorption Rates and Over/Under Absorption

Enda May budgets overheads to be €32,000, while producing 4,000 units using 5,000 labour hours and 1,000 machine hours.

You are required to:

(a) Calculate overhead absorption rates using the **three different methods** of overhead absorption.

(b) Calculate the **over/under absorption** if:

1. Enda May actually produces 4,500 units.
2. Enda May actually uses 5,500 labour hours.
3. Enda May actually incurs 900 machine hours.

(c) Explain the difference between **allocation** and **apportionment** of costs.

7 WYNNIE

(i) Valuation of Closing Stock

The following information relates to the purchases and sales of **Wynnie Ltd** for year 2012.

Period	Details	Quantity and Price
1/1 to 31/03/2012	Purchases on credit	6,300 at €8 each
	Credit sales	2,800 at €11 each
	Cash sales	2,900 at €12 each
1/4 to 30/06/2012	Purchases on credit	5,800 at €9 each
	Credit sales	2,650 at €13 each
	Cash sales	2,700 at €13 each
1/7 to 30/9/2012	Purchases on credit	5,750 at €9 each
	Credit sales	2,750 at €12 each
	Cash sales	2,900 at €11 each
1/10 to 31/12/2012	Purchases on credit	6,200 at €11 each
	Credit sales	2,900 at €13 each
	Cash sales	3,500 at €12 each

On 1/1/2012 there was an opening stock of 6,700 units at €8 each.

You are required to:

(a) Calculate the value of the closing stock using the FIFO method.

(b) Prepare a trading account for the year ended 31/12/2012.

(ii) Absorption Rates and Pricing of Job

The following are the job specifications for Job 65A.
Material costs are 25 rolls at €50 per roll.

Cutting Department 75 Hours **Welding Department** 150 Hours **Finishing Department** 24 Hours

The monthly budgeted overheads are as follows:

Department	Fixed €	Variable €
Cutting	3,300	9,600
Welding	2,100	12,600
Finishing	900	4,400

Budgeted hours for the month are:

Cutting Department 600 **Welding Department** 1,400 **Finishing Department** 400

The wage rate for the factory is: Cutting Dept. €9 per hour, Welding Dept. €8 per hour, Finishing Dept. €10 per hour. General administration overheads are expected to be €6,000 for the month.

You are required to:

(a) Calculate the fixed overhead absorption rate for each department in direct labour hours.

(b) Calculate the administration overhead absorption rate in direct labour hours.

(c) Calculate the selling price of the job if the profit is set at 20% of selling price.

(iii) Over and Under Absorption

The following information refers to the budgeted and actual costs of **Curley Meats Plc.**

Budgeted	**Direct Labour Hours**	**Machine Hours**	**Total Overheads**
Cutting Dept.	2,880	12,600	50,400
Weighing Dept.	16,200	3,600	12,960
Packaging Dept.	7,200		14,400

Actual	**Direct Labour Hours**	**Machine Hours**	**Total Overheads**
Cutting Dept.	3,600	14,400	55,800
Weighing Dept.	13,320	5,400	10,800
Packing Dept.	9,000		16,200

You are required to:

(a) Calculate departmental overhead absorption rates for each department.

(b) Show the over/under absorption by each department in total for the period.

(c) State the overall effect on profit.

8 GARY JOHN

Gary John, a manufacturing company, has the following budgeted overheads for its Production Departments 1 and 2, and its Service Departments A and B, for year ended 31/12/2012.

Overheads	
Factory light and heat	16,000
Machinery insurance	19,000
Material handling	10,000
Canteen costs	54,000
Supervisor's salary	45,000
General repairs	15,000
Cleaning	9,000

The following information is also available:

	Total	**Production Dept. 1**	**Production Dept. 2**	**Service Dept. A**	**Service Dept. B**
Direct materials	160,000	96,000	64,000	—	—
Machine hours	120,000	80,000	40,000	—	—
No. of employees	72	24	18	16	14
Floor space in square metres	30,000	18,000	6,000	4,000	2,000
Machinery valuation	380,000	200,000	180,000	—	—
Volume in cubic metres	80,000	50,000	15,000	10,000	5,000

Job No. 72B has the following direct costs:

Materials	€5.4 per unit
Direct labour	€4.8 per unit

Budgeted production involves 6 hours in Dept. 1 and 7 hours in Dept. 2.

You are required to:

(a) Show an overhead analysis sheet to apportion overheads and re-apportion service department overheads on a machine/hour basis.

(b) Calculate a machine/hour overhead absorption rate for each department correct to two decimal places.

(c) Calculate selling price per unit of Job No. 72B if the profit is set at 20% of selling price per unit.

(d) Calculate the over/under absorption of overheads if the actual production overheads were €142,400, and the actual hours were 70,000 in Production Department 1 and 41,400 in Production Department 2. Show the effect on net profit.

(e) What are main differences between **direct** and **indirect** costs?

9 CONOR DANIEL

(i) Valuation of Closing Stock

The following information relates to the purchases and sales of **Conor Daniel Plc** for the year 2012.

Period	**Details**	**Quantity and Price**
1/1 to 30/4/2012	Purchases on credit	6,000 at €8 each
	Credit sales	1,800 at €18 each
	Cash sales	2,400 at €22 each
1/5 to 31/8/2012	Purchases on credit	4,400 at €12 each
	Credit sales	2,200 at €20 each
	Cash sales	2,600 at €24 each
1/9 to 31/12/2012	Purchases on credit	3,000 at €14 each
	Credit sales	2,400 at €20 each
	Cash sales	2,400 at €26 each

On 1/1/2012 there was an opening stock of 8,000 units at €8 each.

You are required to:

(a) Calculate the value of the closing stock using the FIFO method.

(b) Prepare a trading account for the year ended 31/12/2012.

(ii) Absorption Rates and Pricing of Job

The following are the job specifications for Job TR78:
Materials costs are €2,350.

	Hours
Dept. 1	40
Dept. 2	70
Dept. 3	30

The monthly budgeted overheads are as follows:

	Fixed €	**Wage Rates**	**Variable €**
Dept. 1	6,900	€17 per hour	7,200
Dept. 2	13,000	€21 per hour	15,000
Dept. 3	2,500	€19 per hour	4,500

Budgeted hours for the month are:

Dept. 1	600
Dept. 2	1,000
Dept. 3	500

General administration overheads are expected to be €18,900 for the month.

You are required to:

(a) Calculate the fixed and variable overhead absorption rate for each department in direct labour hours.

(b) Calculate the administration overhead absorption rate in direct labour hours.

(c) Calculate the selling price of the job if the profit is set at 20% of the selling price.

(iii) Over and Under Absorption

The following information refers to the budgeted and actual costs of **Perfect Pork Products Plc.**

Budgeted	**Direct Labour Hours**	**Machine Hours**	**Total Overheads €**
Cutting Dept.	16,000	70,000	280,000
Boning Dept.	9,000	2,000	72,000
Dispatch Dept.	40,000	—	80,000

Actual	**Direct Labour Hours**	**Machine Hours**	**Total Overheads**
Cutting Dept.	20,000	80,000	310,000
Boning Dept.	7,400	3,000	60,000
Dispatch Dept.	50,000	—	90,000

You are required to:

(a) Calculate a **suitable** departmental overhead absorption rate for each department.

(b) Show the over/under absorption by each department in total for the period.

TOPIC

17

Marginal Costing (with Flexible Budgeting)

You cannot discover new oceans unless you have the courage to lose sight of the shore.

Unknown

1 Doyle and Max – Sample Exam Question

(i) Doyle

Doyle Ltd produces a single product. The company's Profit and Loss account for the year ended 31/12/07 during which 14,000 units were produced and sold was as shown below. The company operated at 70% capacity.

	€	€
Sales (14,000 units)		560,000
Materials	120,000	
Direct labour	140,000	
Factory overheads	90,000	
Administration expenses	112,000	462,000
Net profit		98,000

The materials, direct labour, and a third of the factory overheads are variable costs. €62,500 of the administration expenses are fixed.

You are required to prepare:

(a) The company's break-even point and margin of safety.

(b) The profit the company would make in 2008 if it reduced the selling price by 5%, increased advertising by €10,000, and thereby increased sales to 20,000 units with all other cost levels unchanged.

(c) The number of units that must be sold at €36 per unit to provide a profit of 20% of the sales revenue received from the sale of these same units.

(d) The profit the company would make if a commission of 5% of sales was given to sales personnel and an extra €1 per unit is spent on enhanced packaging, thereby increasing the sales to 19,000 units at €42 per unit.

(e) For what purpose is the **contribution sales ratio** regularly used? When is the use of this ratio essential?

Max

Mixed costs can be separated into fixed and variable elements by using records of costs from previous periods. Max Plc manufactures a single component. The following production costs and output levels have been recorded during March, April and May.

Output levels	50%	75%	90%
Units	10,000	15,000	18,000
Costs	€	€	€
Direct materials	140,000	210,000	252,000
Direct labour	80,000	120,000	144,000
Production overheads	66,000	96,000	114,000
Other overhead costs	57,000	83,250	99,000
Administration expenses	25,000	25,000	25,000
	368,000	534,250	634,000

Profit is budgeted to be 15% of sales.

You are required to:

(a) Separate production overheads into fixed and variable elements.

(b) Separate other overhead costs into fixed and variable elements.

(c) Prepare a **flexible budget** for a 95% **activity** level using **marginal costing principles** and show the contribution.

Doyle Solution

		Total €	Per unit €
Sales		560,000	40
Less variable costs			
Direct materials	120,000		
Direct labour	140,000		
Factory overheads	30,000		
Administration	49,500	(339,500)	24.25
Contribution		220,500	15.75
Less fixed costs			
Factory overheads	60,000		
Administration expenses	62,500	(122,500)	
Net Profit		98,000	

(i) **Break-even point**	Fixed costs / CPU	122,500 / 15.75	= **7,778 units**
Margin of safety	Sales − Break-even	14,000 − 7,778	= **6,222 units**

(ii) Profit from reduced selling price

Sales	(20,000 @ 38)	760,000	
Less variable costs	(20,000 @ 24.25)	(485,000)	
Contribution		275,000	
Less fixed costs		(132,500)	
Profit		142,500	= **€142,500**

(iii) No. of units	Fixed costs / CPU − 20% of SP	122,500 / 11.75 − 7.2	= **26,924 units**

(CPU = 36 − 24.25 = 11.75)

(iv) New Profit		**Per unit**	**Total**	
Sales (19,000 units)		42.00		
Less variable costs	(24.25 + 1 + 2.1)	(27.35)		
Contribution	19,000 units at	14.65	= 278,350	
Less fixed costs			(122,500)	
Profit				**€155,850**

(v) 1. To calculate the break-even point.
2. When necessary figures are not available such as variable costs or selling price or units.

Max Solution

(i) Production overheads

		Units		Cost
				€
High		18,000		114,000
Low		(10,000)		(66,000)
Difference		8,000		48,000
Variable cost per unit 48,000/ 8,000			=	€6
Fixed cost element (10,000 × 6)	66,000	(60,000)	=	€6,000

(ii) Other overheads

		Units		Cost
High		18,000		99,000
Low		10,000		57,000
Difference		8,000		42,000
Variable cost per unit 42,000/8,000			=	€5.25
Fixed cost element (10,000 × 5.25)	57,000	(52,500)	=	€4,500

(iii) Flexible Budget (marginal costing format)

	€	€
Sales		785,000
Less variable costs		
Direct materials (19,000 × 14)	266,000	
Direct labour (19,000 × 8)	152,000	
Production (19,000 × 6)	114,000	
Other overhead (19,000 × 5.25)	99,750	631,750
Contribution		153,250
Less **fixed costs**		
Production overheads	6,000	
Other overheads	4,500	
Administration	25,000	35,500
Profit		117,750

Workings

Total cost is 85% of sales		
Total cost = 631,750 + 35,500	=	667,250
85% of sales	=	667,250
100%, i.e. sales	=	785,000

2 McCANNEY

Mary McCanney produces a single product. The company's Profit and Loss account for year 2012, during which 60,000 units were produced and sold, is as follows:

	€	€
Sales (60,000 units)		900,000
Materials	160,000	
Direct labour	98,000	
Factory overheads	80,000	
Administration expenses	140,000	
Selling expenses	150,000	628,000
Net Profit		272,000

The materials, direct labour and 60% of the factory overheads are variable costs. Apart from sales commission of 5%, the sales selling and administration expenses are fixed.

You are required to calculate:

(a) The company's break-even point and margin of safety in units.

(b) The number of units that must be sold in 2013 if the company is to increase its net profit by 15% over the 2012 figure, assuming the selling price and cost levels remain unchanged.

(c) The profit the company would make in 2013 if it reduced its selling price to €13, increased fixed costs by €50,000 and thereby increased the number of units sold to 75,000. All other cost levels and percentages remaining unchanged.

(d) The selling price the company must charge per unit in 2013 if fixed costs are increased by 15%, but the volume of sales and profit remain the same.

(e) The number of units that must be sold at €17 per unit to provide a profit of 10% of the sales revenue received from these same units.

(f) Prepare a break-even chart based on the original figures.

3 ZALON

The **Zalon** produces hair products. The company's Profit and Loss account for the year ended 31/12/2012 during which 65,000 units were produced and sold was as follows:

	€	€
Sales (65,000 units)		910,000
Materials	312,250	
Direct labour	152,500	
Factory overheads	143,000	
Administration expenses	100,000	
Selling Expenses	80,000	787,750
Net Profit		122,250

The materials, direct labour and 30% of the factory overheads are all variable costs. Apart from commission of 5% of sales, the selling and administration expenses are fixed.

You are required to calculate:

(a) The company's break-even point and margin of safety in units. Draw the break-even chart.

(b) The number of units that must be sold in 2013 if the company is to increase its net profit by 20% over the 2012 figure, assuming that the selling price and cost levels remain unchanged.

(c) The number of units that must be sold at €12 to provide a profit of 20% of the sales revenue from these units.

(d) The profit the company would make if it reduced its selling price by €2, increased fixed costs by €30,000 and thereby increased the number of units sold by 20%. All other cost levels remaining unchanged.

(e) The selling price the company must charge per unit in 2013 if fixed costs are reduced by 5%. The volume of sales and profit remain the same.

(f) Explain what is meant by **sensitivity analysis**?

4 ORION

Orion Plc produces a single product. The Profit and Loss account for the year ended 31/12/12 during which 96,000 units were produced and sold was as follows:

	€	€
Sales (96,000 units)		1,152,000
Materials	492,000	
Direct labour	222,720	
Factory overheads	86,400	
Administration expenses	124,800	
Selling expenses	106,800	1,032,720
Net Profit		119,280

The materials, direct labour and 45% of the factory overheads are variable costs. Apart from a sales commission of 5% of sales, the selling and administration expenses are fixed.

You are required to calculate:

(a) The company's break-even point and margin of safety in units.

(b) The number of units that must be sold in 2013 if the company is to increase its net profit by 20% over the 2012 figure, assuming the selling price and cost levels remain unchanged.

(c) The profit the company would make in 2013 if it reduced its selling price to €11, increased fixed costs by €18,000 and thereby increased the number of units sold to 110,400, with all other cost levels and percentages remaining unchanged.

(d) The selling price the company must charge per unit in 2013 if fixed costs are increased by 14%, but the volume of sales and profit remain the same.

(e) The number of units that must be sold at €13 per unit to provide a profit of 10% of the sales revenue received from these same units.

(f) Prepare a break-even chart based on the original figures.

5 GAZZA AND JEN

Gazza Plc produces a single product and its Profit and Loss account for year 2012 during which they produced and sold 20,000 units was as follows:

	€	€
Sales (20,000 units at 70% capacity)		1,120,000
Materials	240,000	
Direct labour	280,000	
Factory overheads	180,000	
Administration expenses	224,000	924,000
Net Profit		196,000

The materials, direct labour and a third of the factory overheads are variable costs. €125,000 of the administration costs are fixed.

You are required to:

(a) Calculate the break-even point and margin of safety.

(b) Draw a break-even chart based on the above figures.

(c) Calculate the profit the company would make if it reduced the selling price by 5%, increased advertising by €20,000, and thereby increased sales to 30,000 with all other cost levels unchanged.

(d) Find the number of units that must be sold at €50 to provide a profit of 20% of the sales revenue from these same units.

(e) Find the profit the company would make if a commission of 5% of sales is given to personnel, and an extra €1 per unit is spent on enhanced packaging, thereby increasing the sales to 25,000 units at €60 per unit.

Jen Plc manufactures a single product. The following flexible budgets are prepared:

Output level	60%	70%	90%
Units	4,800	5,600	7,200
	€	€	€
Materials	14,400	16,800	21,600
Wages	9,600	11,200	14,400
Production overheads	10,760	11,720	13,640
Other overheads	6,840	7,480	8,760
Administration expenses	5,000	5,000	5,000
Total	46,000	52,200	63,400

Profit is budgeted to be 25% of sales.

You are required to:

(a) Separate production and other overheads into **fixed** and **variable** elements.

(b) Prepare a flexible budget for an 85% activity level using **marginal costing** principles.

6 Remus

Remus Plc produces 200,000 units and the company's Profit and Loss account for the year ended 31/12/2012 was as follows:

	€	€
Sales (200,000 units at €6 each)		1,200,000
Less cost of sales		
Manufacturing costs	480,000	
Production overheads	180,000	
Other overheads	60,000	
Selling and distribution costs	244,500	964,500
Net Profit		235,500

It has been established that 60% of manufacturing costs and 50% of other overhead costs are variable. Apart from a sales commission of 15% of sales, the price, selling and distribution costs are fixed. Production costs are mixed and have behaved in the past as follows:

Year Ended	Output	Production Overheads
31/12/2010	90,000	€114,000
31/12/2011	108,000	€124,800
31/12/2012	120,000	€132,000

You are required to:

(a) Calculate the variable and fixed elements of production overheads.

(b) Calculate the break-even point in units and value.

(c) How many units have to be produced to achieve a profit of 25% of sales?

(d) Find the profit the company would make if it decreases its selling price by 60c per unit, thereby increasing sales to 250,000.

(e) Calculate the number of units that must be sold to attain a profit of €330,000, if selling price per unit decreases by 5% and fixed costs fall by €90,000.

(f) Explain what is meant by a **step fixed cost**.

Show the graph of the following step fixed costs:

Rent	€6,000	€15,000	€20,000	€30,000
Output	25,000	35,000	45,000	55,000

7 TOM AND JONES

Tom Ltd produces a single product. The company's Profit and Loss account for 2012 is as follows:

	€	€
Sales (60,000 units)		288,000
Materials	115,200	
Direct labour	57,600	
Factory overheads	20,400	
Administration expenses	38,400	
Selling expenses	27,200	258,800
Net Profit		29,200

The materials, direct labour and 40% of the factory overheads are variable costs. Apart from sales commission of 5% of sales, the selling and administration expenses are fixed.

You are required to calculate:

(a) The company's break-even point and margin of safety.

(b) The number of units that must be sold at €5.20 to provide a profit of 10% of the sales revenue received from these same units.

(c) The profit the company would make if it reduced its selling price to €4.40, increased fixed costs by €4,000 and thereby increased the number of units sold to 82,000. All other cost levels and percentages unchanged.

Jones Ltd produces 15,000 units for year 2012. 12,000 of these units were sold at €8 per unit.

The production costs were as follows:

Direct materials	50c	per unit
Direct labour	80c	per unit
Variable overhead	90c	per unit
Fixed overheads for year	€17,500	

You are required to:

(a) Prepare Profit and Loss statements under **marginal** and **absorption** costing principles.

(b) Outline the differences between **marginal** and **absorption** costing. Indicate which method should be used for financial accounting purposes and why.

8 MARGE AND BART

Marge

Marge Ltd produces a single product. The company's Profit and Loss account for 2012 is as follows:

	€	€
Sales (70,000 units)		1,960,000
Materials	650,000	
Direct labour	560,000	
Factory overheads	150,000	
Administration expenses	192,000	
Selling expenses	188,000	1,740,000
Net Profit		220,000

The materials, direct labour and 40% of the factory overheads are variable costs.
Apart from a sales commission of 5% of sales, the selling and administration expenses are fixed.

You are required to calculate:

(a) The company's break-even point and margin of safety.

(b) The selling price the company must charge per unit if fixed costs increase by 10% but the volume of sales and the profit remain the same.

(c) The profit the company would make if it reduced its selling price to €24, increased fixed costs by €50,000, and thereby increased the number of units sold to 85,000 with all other cost levels and percentages unchanged.

(d) What is the **contribution to sales ratio**? Use it to check the general accuracy of the break-even point.

Bart

Bart Ltd produces 5,400, units for the year 2012. 4,800 of these units were sold at €4.80 per unit. The production costs were as follows:

Direct materials	36c	per unit
Direct labour	54c	per unit
Variable overhead	42c	per unit
Fixed overheads for year	€2,700	

You are required to:

(a) Prepare Profit and Loss statements under **marginal** and **absorption** costing principles.

(b) Explain the difference between:
- (i) Fixed cost and variable cost
- (ii) Direct cost and indirect cost
- (iii) Controllable cost and uncontrollable cost
- (iv) Cost allocation and cost absorption

9 RED AND BULL

Red

Mixed costs can be separated into fixed and variable elements by using records of costs from previous periods. Red Plc manufactures a single component. The following production costs and output levels have been recorded during March, April and May.

Output levels	40%	60%	80%
Units	4,000	6,000	8,000
Costs	**€**	**€**	**€**
Direct materials	44,000	66,000	88,000
Direct labour	32,000	48,000	64,000
Production overheads	37,000	45,000	53,000
Other overhead costs	22,000	22,000	22,000
Administration expenses	16,000	18,500	21,000
	151,000	199,500	248,000

Profit is budgeted to be 20% of sales.

You are required to:

(a) Classify the above into fixed, variable and mixed costs.

(b) Separate production and administration overhead costs into fixed and variable elements.

(c) Prepare a **flexible budget** for a 90% **activity** level using **marginal** costing principles. Show the contribution.

Bull

Bull's Profit and Loss account for 2012 was as follows:

	€	€
Sales (40,000 units)		480,000
Materials	140,000	
Direct labour	84,000	
Factory overheads	72,000	
Administration expenses	46,000	
Selling expenses	95,000	437,000
Net profit		43,000

The materials, direct labour and 20% of the factory overheads are variable costs. Apart from a sales commission of €1 per unit, the selling and administration expenses are fixed.

You are required to calculate:

(a) The company's break-even point and margin of safety. Prove the accuracy of the break-even point by using the contribution to sales ratio.

(b) The selling price it must charge if fixed costs are increased by 10% but the volume of sales and profit remain the same.

(c) The number of units that must be sold at €11 to provide a profit of 10% of the sales revenue from these units.

10 John, Paul and George

John

The company's profit and loss account for the year ended 31/12/12 was as follows:

	€	€
Sales (40,000 units at €5 each)		200,000
Less cost of sales		
Direct materials	30,000	
Direct labour	24,000	
Factory overheads	68,000	
Other overheads	39,000	
Selling and distribution costs	14,000	175,000
Net Profit		25,000

Apart from a sales commission of 5% of sales, the selling and distribution costs are fixed. Factory overheads and other overheads are mixed and have behaved as follows:

Year Ended	Output	Factory Overheads	Other Overheads
		€	€
31/12/2010	55,000	91,250	48,000
31/12/2011	30,000	52,500	33,000
31/12/2012	40,000	68,000	39,000

You are required to:

(a) Show the variable and fixed elements in all mixed costs.

(b) Calculate the break-even point. Prove your answer by using the **contribution to sales ratio**.

(c) Draw the break-even chart.

(d) Calculate the number of units that must be sold in order to attain a profit of 5% of sales.

(e) Find the net profit if the company spent €15,000 on modernising its plant, when it is estimated that the variable cost per unit would decrease by €1.50 as sales increase to 45,000 units.

(f) Find the selling price if fixed costs are increased by 10% while sales and profit stay the same.

Paul

Paul Plc produces 10,000 units for the year 2012. 8,000 of these units were sold at €8 per unit.

The production costs were as follows:

Materials	60c	per unit
Labour	90c	per unit
Variable overhead	70c	per unit
Fixed overhead	€5,000	

You are required to prepare:

(a) Profit and Loss statements under **marginal** and **absorption** costing principles.

George

The following is the budget of the production department for an activity level of 80%.

	Fixed	Variable	Total
	€	€	€
Wages	12,000	7,200	19,200
Salaries	9,000		9,000
Rent	3,500		3,500
Maintenance	4,000	1,280	5,280
Variable overhead		2,400	2,400
Other overhead	300	1,680	1,980

You are required to prepare:

(a) The budget (total figures) for an 85% activity level.